THE CRISIS OF ISLAM

THE CRISIS OF ISLAM

Dr Suhail Saheed

MD PUBLICATIONS PVT LTD
NEW DELHI
www.mdppl.com

Published by :

MD Publications Pvt Ltd
"MD House", 11, Darya Ganj,
New Delhi - 110 002
Phone : +91-11-41563325 (Customer Service)
+91-11-41562846 (Editorial)
E-mail (orders): order@mdppl.com
Website: www.mdppl.com

ISBN: 978-81-7533-242-3

Published and Printed by Mr. Pranav Gupta on behalf of MD Publications Pvt Ltd at Mohit Enterprises, New Delhi.

Preface

Islam as a religion is central to the lives of over a billion people, but its outer expression as a distinctive civilization has been undergoing a monumental crisis. Buffeted by powerful adverse currents, Islamic civilization today is a shadow of its former self. The most disturbing and possibly fatal of these currents – the imperial expansion of the West into Muslim lands and the blast of modernity that accompanied it – are now compounded by a third giant wave, globalization.

The Islamic world is locked in an internal struggle over how best to address and ultimately solve the problems endemic to many of its societies: namely, widespread poverty, extreme economic inequality, the prevalence of government by despotic rulers, and the inability to keep pace with emerging economies. The crisis concerns the choice the Islamic world faces between two diametrically opposed solutions. Nuclear Bombs throughout the Middle East is stressed as the biggest crisis. Islam is experiencing a crisis of credibility and authority that stems directly from the nature of Islam itself. This makes it difficult to come up with solutions of any sort because few Muslims will be willing to alter the structure of their religion.

The Crisis of Islam ranges widely through thirteen centuries of history, but in particular it charts the key events of the twentieth century leading up to the violent confrontations of today: the creation of the state of Israel, the Cold War, the Iranian Revolution, the Soviet defeat in

Afghanistan, the Gulf War, and the September 11th attacks on the United States. Today's crisis grows in part out of the structure of Islam itself – a faith without denominations, hierarchies, and centralized institutions. The absence of such structures has been a source of strength that has permitted the faith to adapt to local conditions and win converts around the world. But it is also a weakness that makes it difficult for Muslims to come together and speak with one voice on important issues – to say what is and what is not true Islam.

The crisis has three related historical causes: the marginalization of traditional Muslim authorities over the past century and a half; the rise of new authorities with inferior credentials but greater skill in using print and, more recently, electronic media; and the spread of mass literacy in the Muslim world, which made the challengers' writings accessible to vast new audiences.

I am very grateful to Mr Pranav Gupta, Director of MD Publications Pvt Ltd, New Delhi for his kind cooperation and support for this book.

Dr Suhail Saheed

Contents

1

Defining Islam

There was disagreement among the Muslim participants and panelists as to whether Islam is a faith to be defined by the individual according to his reading of the sacred texts, or whether Islam is rather a way of life that cannot be separated from government. A consensus was established that there is a difference between who should speak for Islam and who does speak for Islam. Osama Bin Laden, for example, does not have the support of most Muslims, and yet he tries to claim the authority to speak for the Muslim world, which he is sometimes granted—at least in the mind of the other. The discussion of Western perceptions restated that Islam is not a monolith and that the West should develop a more complex understanding of the Islamic world. There was no such agreement, however, when it came to whether the West is indeed "hated" by the Muslim world and, if so, why.

Likewise, conflicting opinions emerged as to whether the West's perceptions of Islam constitute discrimination and vilification, or whether these attitudes and fears are driven (or justified) by a recent history of Americans being killed by people claiming Islam as their motivation. Omayma Abdel-Latif, political correspondent for *Al-Ahram*, Egypt, was the first panelist to address "Who Speaks for Islam?" She took issue with the question itself, pointing out that by asking this, we imply that there should be one person or entity who speaks for the whole Islamic world, which would be an oversimplification given the diversity of Islamic voices. Therefore, no one should speak for Islam as a whole, though certainly there is an established, government-backed religious establishment that does try to do so.

However, Islamic religious texts say there should be no mediation between the individual and God, so the position of this establishment has no actual legitimacy. In fact, the alliance between the religious authorities and the state is an issue of increasing debate in the Muslim world. Abdel-Latif maintained, though, that it would take at least a generation to break this unfortunate alliance. She concluded by asking why we would want an institution to be able to speak for Islam and if its purpose would be to achieve reconciliation with extremists. The second speaker on this question was Mohamed Talbi, professor emeritus of history at the University of Tunis, Tunisia. His answer was clear: the only one who can speak for Islam is God. Although there are many Muslims, there is one Islam, articulated by the Qur'an.

According to Talbi, the elite today are largely de-Islamized and cannot speak for the average Muslim. The *'ulama* 11 are reading scripture with "the eyes of the salaf." 12 But what is required is for the Qur'an to be read with "the eyes of the living." Furthermore, the mixture of currents within the Muslim world—which mirrors the differences that exist within other religions—also shows that there can be no unified voice but the Qur'an itself. Muslims must read this text rather than base their religious identity on interpretations, which are tainted by human intervention and political agendas. The Qur'an must serve as the only reference for the West, as well, if it wishes to speak about Islam. Following this analysis, Haji Mahfuz Haji Omar, chief of youth of the Islamic Party of Malaysia, defended his party's view of Islam as a political religion.

He argued that, in addition to being a bond between an individual and God, as Professor Talbi claimed, Islam is a way of life, as is prescribed by the divine teachings. Thus

Islamic law must bear upon the system of government in a Muslim country. Indeed, the flourishing of Islamic civilization during the period of al-Andalus, for instance, coincided with the practice of Islam as a political religion. On the other hand, the fall of the Ottoman Empire, which signaled the separation of church and state in much of the Islamic world, initiated the period of turmoil that has led to the current critical situation. Haji Mahfuz continued by explaining that secularism itself has actually caused the suffering of many Muslims (e.g., Afghanistan under the Soviets) and it is in reaction to secularism that extremist "reform" movements have gained momentum.

In contrast to Haji Mahfuz's argument against the separation of church and state, James Phillips, Middle East policy expert at the Heritage Foundation in Washington, D.C., began his statement on "Islam from the Perspective of the Other" by praising America's long-standing commitment to this very separation as the foundation of religious tolerance. Phillips maintained that since power corrupts, religious leaders must stay out of politics in order to avoid abuses of power such as the Spanish Inquisition—a manipulation of religion into a strategy to eliminate the Jewish creditors who had financed the king's war debt. Indeed, the combination of religion and state is a "lethal experiment."

With regard to the perceptions of Islam in the Western world, Phillips admitted that many Americans do equate the Islamic faith with extremist Islamist movements; this conflation is not the fault of the media, but has resulted from decades of experiences in which Americans have been murdered by people claiming Islam as their motivation. Phillips insisted, however, that the Bush administration (despite the typically a historical American misstep in using the term "crusade") does not share this perspective and has made clear that the target of American foreign policy is not Islam, but terrorism. We are now engaged, Phillips said, in a struggle against a radical ideology, a quasi-totalitarian political force that would like to impose its will on Muslims as well as Westerners. In fact, Muslims should be extremely wary of movements like Al-Qaeda, which tend to use violence against their own people in order to export their revolutions within the Islamic world.

In conclusion, Phillips stressed that the battle against terrorism is ideological rather than religious or civilizational, and that Osama Bin Laden, power-hungry though he may be, speaks for a cult movement and not for Islam. Hoda Badran, Egyptian chairperson of the Alliance for Arab Women, presented the commentator's remarks for this session. She highlighted the theoretical versus practical dimensions of the question, "Who speaks for Islam?" In other words, although many Muslims may agree with Professor Talbi that only God should speak for Islam, the reality is much more complex. Not only do governments and other movements claim the authority of Islam, but the relationship between the individual and God cannot be entirely free from human intervention, since the Qur'an itself is situated in history, having been written down by men or passed along by word of mouth. In addition, there are a large number of Muslims who cannot read and must access their religion through the interpretation of a religious leader.

Therefore, while limiting Islamic authority to the Qur'an may be the ideal, the reality is that Islam is written into the constitutions of many Muslim countries whose officials purport to be its guardian. With regards to James Phillips' comments, Hoda Badran said that his question, "Why do they murder us?" cannot be answered without addressing the Islamic world's grievances against American policy. The general floor discussion then began with one speaker considering the problem of Islamic authority as an issue of foundations as well as a question of how to adapt to new circumstances. In terms of foundations, he argued that Islam always had a clergy, even if it was an informally hierarchical one, and that this clergy was traditionally independent from the government and derived its authority from the vox populi.

As for adapting this tradition to new circumstances, the speaker emphasized that it is all right to develop various new institutions—just as the early Islamic world saw a plurality of schools of law—as long as the individual is free to choose among these authorities for himself. The problem we now face, then, is the existence of government-backed councils that dictate how individuals should interpret their faith. The issue of historicity was brought up by several other participants who echoed concerns that the Qur'an itself has undergone human intervention. Also underlined was the point that although God's message is one, its expression has been different in different periods of history. Talbi responded to these concerns by agreeing that the Qur'an must certainly be adapted to our own time. We must act in accordance with the book's prescriptions, whereas traditions, no matter how established, must be discarded if they contradict the Qur'an. With respect to the problem of authority, Talbi dismissed the issue by stating that this is not a religious problem but a political one—and "who has the force, has the authority."

The discussion also raised the problem of the treatment of women in the Muslim world. One female participant told the story of how she was not even allowed to pray at her husband's funeral. She insisted that women have the same right to talk to God and should not be segregated. Talbi answered this comment by quoting from the Qur'an, which says that man and woman are the same soul divided into two and each part has the same name. He maintained that, therefore, segregation—while it may be a historical fact beginning with men feeling crowded out of the mosques by women—is not dictated by the Islamic religion and it is women's duty to become theologians and read the Qur'an for them.

Media prejudice in the Western and Muslim worlds was also reconsidered during this session. A Western speaker asked whether it was true that the theory that September 11 was a Jewish conspiracy had been widely accepted by Muslim public opinion in the Middle East. A

Muslim participant answered that no, this theory was spread by the Internet and did not hold water for most Muslims, especially intellectuals. In terms of the perceptions of the Other, several participants not only discussed the vilification of the Muslim in American movies and television, but also raised the problem of the West considering itself a "yardstick" by which to measure the Islamic world. This sort of one-way analysis makes Muslims feel frustrated and objectified. These feelings are compounded by the fact that America lends financial and military support to countries including Israel by which Muslims consider themselves oppressed.

Phillips opposed this argument, explaining that even if Palestinian grievances are used as a justification for the September 11 attacks, this was counterproductive since the attacks have actually garnered greater support for Israel and its use of force. Phillips again warned that Al-Qaeda's co-opting of issues like Palestine signifies its desire to seize power in that region as well. The discussion ended on the topic of Muslim minorities in the West. One speaker suggested that Western governments are trying to bureaucratize the Islamic faith in an attempt to exercise greater control over the religion and its adherents. For example, governments turn Islamic studies into an educational discipline, they create official-sounding organizations like the "Muslim Council," and they sometimes go so far as to look for a Muslim "pope" within the particular society.

However, these efforts by the state to structure Islam most often backfire by fueling resentment and rebellion in the younger generation of Muslims. Another Western participant added that indeed 3–5 percent of the European population is now Muslim and that the protection of this minority against discrimination must be a top priority for the European Union. In fact, with the EU considering Turkey's application for membership, the West must resist Islamophobia and instead must continue, as Talbi has helped us do, to distinguish the Islamic faith from unacceptable forms of Islamic extremism. The concluding speaker summarized two important points made during this fourth plenary session. First, there must be more widespread dialogue within the Islamic world itself to prevent various Muslim schools of thought from forming coalitions and trying to speak for Islam as a whole.

Second, both Western and Islamic states co-opt Islam for their own end, and often use government money or force to spread their understanding of the faith; yet, even when states think they can control Islam, they most often fail. While these ideas were well received by most participants, the session left many questions unresolved, for instance: Why does humanity respond so poorly to other religions in moments of crisis? If people cannot read the Qur'an for themselves, who can they trust to interpret the sacred text? If Islam is thought of by many as a way of life, will secular Islamic societies continue to experience fundamentalist revolutions? How can we stop the media from allowing certain individuals and groups to speak for Islam when these groups arex unrepresentative of the Muslim world overall? Defining Islam, with all these implicit questions about Islamic authority and Western perceptions, thus remains an extremely complicated task on which no real consensus could be reached.

What is a civilization? Is there a "Clash of Civilizations" as Samuel Huntington claims? If there is not, is there a clash of ideologies, a clash of fundamentalisms, and a clash of perceptions? Is the clash political, cultural, or religious? What role does the medium play in creating or solving this clash? Is the clash inevitable or solvable, and if solvable, how? The plenary session on Debating Civilizations considered these difficult questions and concluded that there is no Clash of Civilizations per se. Despite rejecting Huntington's thesis, however, there was a consensus that some sort of clash is taking place. Malise Ruthven, author and former lecturer at the University of Aberdeen, United Kingdom, spoke on "Islam Clashing with the West."

Focusing on iconography as a locus of civilizational difference, he explained the conflicting Islamic and Christian traditions in how divinity is portrayed. Whereas Islamic art depicts God through geometric patterns that suggest the experience of infinity or of "the ultimate," a sort of paganism has been built into the Western iconic tradition, which, from early Christian tombs to Caravaggio to Michelangelo, shows Christ and Mary (and sometimes God himself) as human figures. Clearly, religiously based identities have a cultural component. Despite the opposing artistic traditions, Ruthven expressed hope that the problems between the West and the Islamic world would be resolved within the media, as our cultural differences are mediated and mutual understanding is promoted through audiovisual technologies and Internet chartrooms.

Mohamed Sid-Ahmed, Egyptian author and columnist for Al-Ahram, offered the perspective on "Islam Coexisting with the West." He expressed the view that despite our civilizations becoming more interdependent through globalization, there is now a political clash between the West and terrorism, which has taken the place of Communism since the fall of the Berlin Wall signaled the end of a bipolar system. But while the West "agreed to disagree" with the Soviet Union, there is no such agreement to tolerate the terrorist threat. This threat can be eliminated, however; while the shift of political oppositions was inevitable, a Clash of Civilizations is not. Yet for terrorism to be conquered, the twenty-first century must witness a closing of the gap between the developed countries and the rest of the world, which widened during the twentieth century. It is only, Sid-Ahmed claimed, when underdevelopment is corrected that people will no longer be willing to kill themselves to harm their enemies.

And since this suicide tactic multiplies terrorists' power by making them unafraid of consequences, a resolution of this issue may be the only way to avoid a third world war.

Rather than argue for or against a certain type of clash, Karl Meyer, editor of the World Policy Journal, United States, spoke on "The Media and Civilizational Understanding." Through the example of the West's bleak forecasts for Spain after Franco, he illustrated how press clichés do not determine history. Meyer also discussed the media as "an equal-opportunity offender"; in other words, though they may present Islam in generalized and distorted terms, this is the way in which the media treat almost all of their subjects. Furthermore, the media are not alone responsible for their misperceptions and misdiagnoses. "Experts" and historians are just as fallible, as they proved by failing to predict the rise of the ayatollahs in Iran and by insisting on (a now pacifist) Germany's essentially angry and aggressive character.

Nevertheless, Meyer admitted, the media can play a role in fomenting violence, and we now face a critical test of the media's power to influence events for better or for worse. In her commentator's remarks, Baroness Nicholson of Winterbourne, first vice chairman, Committee on Foreign Affairs, Human Rights, Common Security, and Defense Policy, European Parliament, suggested that Meyer's reference to the youth in post-Franco Spain wanting to "be free of all orthodoxies" may indeed summarize the fears of religiously motivated fundamentalist movements. Perhaps, then, the clash is not between civilizations or religions, but between the secular and the faithful? Islam, Christianity, and Judaism have more similarities than they do differences, she noted, pointing in particular to the oppression of women that she believes is common to all organized religions. Baroness Nicholson also asked that participants try to distinguish between civilization and culture.

For instance, does "civilization" require or imply a common language, a common body of literature or law or beliefs? Does civilization require physical mingling or can it exist, as Malise Ruthven proposed, over the Internet? In response to the question of the meaning of civilization, the discussion then turned to the fact that Osama Bin Laden does not use the term "civilization," and so perhaps our dialogue is collapsing political mythology and current events. Does an intellectual debate that involves issues relating to democracy, treatment of women, iconic traditions, and so on, have relevance to a terrorist movement that—rather than responding to this debate—is fighting back violently against what it perceives as anti-Muslim oppression? Building on this idea, another participant asked, if there is not a Clash of Civilizations, what is the meaning of our discourse?

Are we really discussing something else that lies behind this problem, and if so, what? One answer is that today we live in a global civilization in which we share science and technology, a common economy, and a worldwide system of communications. In order to differentiate ourselves from others within this universal society, we must look toward religion and/or history—the areas where our identities diverge. But with the United States as a unipolar power, how will these differences be confronted? In order to maintain peace and security, the United States must offer other cultures equal recognition and must cease acting as the "producer and teacher" despite its military and economic strength. Returning to the debate over the clash, participants backed a variety of concepts deriving, and yet diverging, from Hungtington's argument. One American participant stated that if Islam is considered a substitute for the "Red Menace," then the religion is indeed being treated as an ideology and thus the clash is still a clash of ideologies.

Others countered this idea, maintaining that the Cold War is over and the age of ideologies and of state supremacy has passed; we now face a supra-state conflict between liberty and totalitarianism, and the only solution is to offer hope through programs that bring more prosperity to regions where fanatic militants find support. Yet others held that the clash is between fundamentalisms, which are growing in popularity in the United States (Jerry Fallwell, Franklin

Graham, and the Radical Right) as well as in the Islamic world. In this sense, the Islamic world is no different from any other civilization or region or society, in that frustrations lead naturally to extremism and the system itself must be improved in order to provide stability and overcome grievances. In conclusion, the session on Debating Civilizations revealed that some sort of clash is certainly occurring and that, for the moment, this clash is inspiring more questions than answers.

It could not be resolved whether the clash is between religions, ideologies, fundamentalisms, or perceptions; nor whether this clash is insurmountable; nor whether the key to solving it is media or democracy or something else entirely. Participants did seem to agree that the world has suffered from the earthquake like collapse of Communism, which has inevitably led to a shift of "blocs." Many also agreed that to avoid further escalation of conflicts, and especially to avoid a third world war, widespread poverty and inequality must be addressed in order to stop interventions by those who use the miseries of the poor as a weapon against the rest of the world. What does history tell us? Who controls historical memory and how is it used? The fifth plenary session discussed these questions and the various ways in which history is important to the Muslim-Western encounter.

Panelists agreed that control over history is widely sought and, once obtained, is often used by social and political elites to maintain the status quo. On the other hand, memory is fleeting and history is continuously redefined as new events occur. It is a fallacy, for instance, to view Muslim history as frozen in a specific, earlier period, whether the Baghdad of the Abbasids or the Granada of the Nasrids. History is also important in showing that, in both the Islamic and Western worlds, there has been, throughout the ages, more cultural and religious diversity than is usually recognized. Although the panelists cautioned against overgeneralizing, some participants thought that the continuities in Muslim history needed to be noted; as opposed to the widespread vision of the Islamic past as long periods of warfare and instability punctuated by dynastic rule, history shows stable social and political patterns and consistent advances in knowledge.

The session also put forward the view that there is a continuous and common historical process from which none can disengage and to which everyone contributes. This concept is significant, it was suggested, since it may help undermine the combative implications of the Clash of Civilizations approach and perhaps help lay the groundwork for greater understanding. Richard Bulliet, professor of history at Columbia University in New York City, discussed the political uses of history. He made the important points that neither can we know what will be remembered in the future nor can we determine who will decide what is historically significant. He illustrated this idea by recalling an event that occurred on September 11, 1901—the assassination of the American president, William McKinley. *The New York Times* published an article the day after his assassination remarking on the effect his death would have on later generations.

The fact that very few people today are aware of this event shows how immediate perceptions do not always reflect the way things are remembered later on. Bulliet argued that although it would be inappropriate to say that lessons can be drawn from history, there are broad ideas that emerge from historical narratives. Perhaps most important, historical memory is fleeting and can be easily manipulated. Bulliett also suggested that schoolbooks are crucial to this process because they shape the attitudes of students and one might even say indoctrinate the young. The Western perspective on Muslim societies could be improved by integrating them into the "master narrative" of world history. Students would benefit from revised history books taking a more integrative approach. Modern Western textbooks ignore, for instance, the enormous cultural and economic exchange between the southern and northern Mediterranean in the twelfth and thirteenth centuries.

Instead, this period is portrayed as a time of great warfare between Muslims and Christians. The academy's presentation of the Islamic and Christian worlds as enemies has thus been so deeply ingrained in our consciousness that we are unable to recognize it as the foundation of our modern conception of Islam as dangerous, hostile, and unmodern. Abdesselam Cheddadi, professor of history at the University of Rabat, Morocco, next discussed the question of historical memory and asked how it should be approached at both local and global levels in Western and Muslim societies. Historical memory is an essential element of each culture and draws on a canon of texts that apply to the past, present, and future. Moreover, it is expressed through theology, mythology, philosophy, and history. Cheddadi argued that historical memory operates on several levels; it functions, in part, as an ideology or way of organizing thinking and reality. History is used to construct a version of events that is accepted as true and immutable but, in fact, freezes what should be a fluid social process.

History, therefore, becomes naturally and inherently conservative. Historical memory is also vital for the formation of societal identity, but risks imposing a literalist interpretation of the past. Ibn Khaldun, the great fourteenth century historian of Muslim societies, for example, sought to uncover society's laws and to understand the internal rhythms of a community. Yet even as he is celebrated as a great historian of the Muslim world, contemporary historians have distorted his approach. First, in trying to follow an Islamic vision, Islamist historians do not take social realities into account. Second, it must be recognized that Islamist history is inevitably exclusionist, emphasizing "Islamic" tradition, with the broader social milieu ignored. Ibn Khaldun reminds us that histories that derive their authority from revelation and "truth" are problematic. The challenge for the future, then, is how to create a just, nuanced scholarship to overcome these regressive tendencies. Hassan Hanafi, professor of philosophy, University of Cairo, Egypt, the session's third panelist, discussed the difference between using history and reading history. He argued that one of the major problems with history is that it is often misused and falsified, and he cautioned against overstating the influence of the West.

One of the problems of Western scholarship, according to Hanafi, is that it fails to understand that modernism too, comes out of tradition. Therefore, easy dichotomies like "Islam and the West" or "modernity and tradition" must be imploded. Hanafi claimed that there exists a universal code of ethics, a set of normative guidelines that apply on both shores of the Mediterranean. Nevertheless, individuals and societies around the world suffer the consequences of impersonal, globalizing forces. Likewise, "unhelpful" Western ideologies have posited the West's ultimate victory and the resultant End of History. The reality, however, is more complex. Muslims perceive the West as acting on double standards. In Muslim societies, many people experience feelings of inferiority and it remains unclear what role minority groups can play and whether civil society will evolve as an alternative to the current state structure. Hanafi went on to discuss the obsession with economics underlying current rhetoric and political models.

Minority and human rights, gender issues, and social fragmentation are all masked by the world's focus on profit. Ideas such as the End of History and the Clash of Civilizations hide the possibility that we could be witnessing the beginning of a new civilizational upheaval, comparable in its effect on global affairs to World War II. As Hanafi sees it, in our current economics-oriented mode, power is granted to the International Monetary Fund and the World Bank, organizations that divide the world into center and periphery to dismantle weaker nations in the name of "prosperity." This division taints our perception of the other in both the Islamic and Western worlds. Westerners view those souths of the Mediterranean as backward, poor, ignorant, and supportive of terrorists. Similarly, many Muslims have appropriated notions of Westerners as materialistic, secular, egoist, hypercritical, and nihilistic.

How can we, Hanafi asked, erase these DIAimages, which shape our views and limit our communication? We must, above all, remember that history is cyclical and that justice, not power, should be the global norm. As commentator, James Piscatori extrapolated from these presentations several functions of history. First, history can be seen as the filter through which one's place in the world is defined. History contributes to the mythology of a society, such as the Pilgrims' place in the American imagination or Andalusia in the Spanish national consciousness. Second, history legitimizes the interests of groups and governments and mobilizes support. These same interests, however, are framed and at times defined by cultural parameters. While this is not to suggest that there are ingrained civilizational differences, it is clear those Muslim political positions on Palestine and Kashmir, for example, have much to do with solidarity with other Muslim nations.

Third, history can be conceived in terms of the search for authenticity, which carries the connotation of taking control of one's own cultural destiny. Perhaps this quest is inevitably exclusionary, however. Women, for example, tend to be written out of history for a variety of reasons. The result is that what was meant to be an empowering interpretation of history might end up reaffirming traditional social and political hierarchies. Finally, history is important as a source of perspective; history informs our understanding of daily life and often connects people across societies. While this may seem a neutral process, time and culture influence even the "facts" of history and histories themselves often have hidden agendas. In the ensuing discussion, one participant made the point that the general understanding of Islam depends on what is emphasized in histories. If, for example, greater attention were given to Sufism or the millet system of the Ottoman Empire or Jadidism, different perspectives would result and Islam would appear more moderate.

Other participants argued that Islam emerges from a wide variety of specific situations and contacts, which, if better understood, would help avoid the reductionist view that Islam is inevitably "this" or "that." Modernism, as well, is a specific way of seeing history. One speaker asked that modernity be defined. Another suggested that due to the current power structure, the writing of grand narratives could end up encouraging hegemonic thinking. On the other hand, a rethinking of history might generate the possibility that Islam and the West are actually two parts of the same civilization. Others suggested that we may instead need more focused topical histories, concentrating on themes like poverty, gender, and minority status rather than on religions. In summary, participants appreciated that while history can be easily manipulated and controlled, it can also be defining. The challenge is how to recognize this fact without being trapped into essentialized readings of one another's traditions.

Political Islam

While it was deemed necessary to move on from considering the broad intellectual framework of the discussion toward a more disciplined focus on particular issues, there was no overall consensus among the participants in this working group about the subject of discussion, namely political Islam and its relations with the West. As one speaker put it: "There remain the problems of conceptualizing in the fields of research, exchange and action which requires contributing." Relations between Islam and the West, and the question of "who speaks for Islam," the subject of the previous days' debate, should be discussed not only between Muslims, but also in the wider community of historians, anthropologists, and others. According to this view, it was religion itself, rather than Islam, that needed to be explored.

Not only must the whole issue of Islam be rethought; an entirely new approach to the study of religious phenomena must be adopted to take into account Western monotheism and the history of theological systems as they developed in the Mediterranean basin. *Dialogues* must unlearn and abandon the idea of speaking about "political Islam" as a category distinct from the broader role that religions play in nurturing modern radicalisms. Echoing views previously aired during the plenary sessions, several speakers felt that the very choice of headings involved an absence of balance necessary to a conversation between equal parties, with Islam and Islamist movements being the objects of concern or improvement. Western policies had been imposed unilater-ally, without consultation. How can Muslims influence change?

According to this view the bipolar vision implied by such phrases as "Islam and the West" and "North and South" needs to be transcended. While perceiving things in terms of such crude categories might have been acceptable in 1967 or even after the Iranian revolution in 1979, later events have taken the world beyond such polarities. In several Muslim countries, Islamist parties are already participating in parliamentary institutions. *Dialogues* needs a comparative framework in which religiously affiliated movements, including Jewish and Christian fundamentalisms, can be measured against the rise of right-wing parties in Europe. Why must all Islamist parties be tarred with the label of anti-Westernism, while many are in fact engaged in constructive dialogue with Western governments?

One speaker felt that the idea of dialogues could be taken forward by an exploration of common cultural ground or mutualities. Another insisted that in any future engagements between the West and Islamist movements—an engagement considered inevitable by many speakers—priority should be given to democratic principles: there could be no discussion with parties holding to fascist ideologies, which the speaker defined as giving priority to restoring the shari'ah, the Muslim code of religious law. Other speakers, however, saw no conflict between the agenda of Islamist parties and democracy—elections in several Muslim countries had been conducted fairly. Excessive concern about the "Islamic menace" was itself undemocratic. The danger posed by political Islam has been exaggerated.

Another speaker addressed the issue of the practicalities of democracy, pointing out that in some Western countries, electoral procedures were far from flawless. A workshop should be held with participants from various Islamist tendencies invited to discuss electoral issues like the mechanics of voting, the role of political parties involved in the process, and controls over the nomination of candidates. Wider political concerns, including the fear that winners would derail the electoral system when in power, should also be addressed. It is *jumhuriyyah* (republic) rather than *imarah* (Islamic leadership) that needs encouragement. In his concluding remarks, the chair of the first working group argued against the Clash of Civilizations thesis, maintaining that the broader aims of Islam and democracy are fully compatible. Speaking of the Arab world in particular, he observed that in none of twenty-two Arab countries, however, could political sovereignty be said to belong to the people in line with Islamic teachings. Few nations hold truly free elections where the people exercise freedom of choice.

Marxist rule and political pluralism have been tried with mixed results. Why could a further effort not be made to develop Muslim societies in line with their own traditions? The existing national state has been over dependent on foreign powers. Islamic discourse has proved a good tool for mediating social contests. The legitimization of Islamic movements is another imperative; many are currently forced underground and in some countries, even moderate groups are subject to police repression. In some cases, Islamists who "repented" and renounced violence were still harassed by police after being released from prison. The chair concluded, "It is time to go beyond what we have inherited during the past four decades. We must look towards a new world system."

Governance and Accountability

In the second working group, the issues of political accountability and good governance were addressed. What are the dangers and limitations inherent in promoting democracy? Is it even the business of the West to promote democracy in the Muslim world? What are the "rules of the game"? How do we overcome anxieties that one party would manipulate the system to its advantage? How do we establish political order on an equitable basis, ensuring a system that is "interactive" and "open to all"? One theme to emerge clearly in the discussion was that responsive governance must be permitted to develop locally, that recipes or prescriptions imposed by the West would fail. Attention should rather focus on examples of full citizen participation and pluralism. Outside intervention should be avoided, with local people making their own decisions. Rulers sustained by and accountable to foreign governments generally fail to gain support among their own people. The same logic applies to projects funded from abroad.

A second theme to emerge was that governance could not be considered without taking account of gender. To whom are rulers accountable if not to at least the female half of their populations? New thinking is needed about gender, and theories that pit women against men should be avoided. Moreover, it was noted that increasing the representation of women in parliaments would not automatically rectify gender imbalances. Several speakers drew attention to how unequal control of media and communications has led to mutual misperceptions between the Islamic and Western worlds. On the other hand, as one participant pointed out, Western television networks are not so much deliberately hostile to Islam and Muslims as glaringly and generally superficial.

There should be a follow-up workshop to address the DIAimages and clichés responsible for many of the current misperceptions between the Islamic and Western worlds. Another practical suggestion was to explore the idea of a "Global C-Span"-type channel, on which the best material from different parts of the world, including (for example) soap operas from Muslim countries, would be shown. One speaker pointed to the "dismal" quality of Arab television, while mentioning the recent United Nations report on Human Development in the Arab World, which drew attention to the paucity of foreign books being translated into Arabic as compared to Greek and Spanish. One response was that the cultural situation in Arab lands has been disadvantaged by the suppression of the medieval Arab legacy of free thought and intelligent debate. Efforts should be made to distribute books about classical Arab civilization.

A further suggestion was for a follow-up workshop on media representation, which would not only examine the way in which Islam and Muslims are represented in the Western media, and vice versa, but look more broadly at the ways in which politics and culture in Islamic societies are transformed by media DIAimages. The atrocity of 9/11, broadcast all over the world, was a media event par excellence, while for suicide bombers, the videotaping of valedictory statements provides an incentive to death and martyrdom. Three categories of media would need to be investigated: news, entertainment, and education. The issue of corruption was addressed somewhat briefly, with one speaker pointing out that the responsibility lay with Western governments and businesses, since arms commissions and other bribes have found their way into Western banks.

Another speaker pointed out, however, that in contrast to China where investment was being nurtured by funds from the Chinese Diaspora, Arabs and Iranians were liable to keep their funds abroad, exhibiting a lack of confidence in the economies of their own societies. In her concluding statement, the chair of the second working group argued that *Dialogues* must attempt to bring in new partners. Participation should be open to all those willing to attend, without exclusion. The program should foster an interactive process, encouraging networking between individuals. Participants should share their positive experiences, with the emphasis placed on options rather than dictums, and avoiding prescriptive solutions. Guidance, not intervention, should be the watchword.

The issue of women and gender must be addressed, but with sensitivity. Women should be empowered within the context of their respective cultures. The empowerment of women is closely bound up with the question of accountability. Women "occupy half the planet," but many still do not possess identity cards enabling them to vote, and where they have been allowed to participate in elections, they have sometimes shown where to put their fingers on the voting sheets. The matter of gender should be viewed without "cosmetics." The deliberations reached several conclusions.

Civilizational Clash

Many pointed to defined historical and doctrinal differences between Western and Muslim societies, but the overwhelming view of the conference was that these antipathies are neither insurmountable nor ingrained. This is in part because civilizations do not operate as monoliths, and in part because there is no longer (if there ever was) a neat divide between them. Moreover, participants pointed to overlapping interests and areas of mutually beneficial interaction. Whatever "clash" exists is mainly a clash of perceptions, and this can be shaped and ameliorated, to a considerable extent, by honest and good willed interaction.

Challenges of Democratization

The conference concluded that Western efforts to instill greater political participation and pluralism in the Muslim world appeared heavy-handed and hypocritical. There was an overwhelming consensus that Western democracy is not the only model and that Muslim societies need to work out their own arrangements. Western nations should set a good example and provide assistance when sought, but the presumption that the West can teach democracy, and that Muslim societies need to learn from them, was specifically rejected.

Media Responsibilities

Participants voiced considerable criticism of media depictions of Muslims and Islam, and many believe that these were even more biased in the aftermath of September 11, when the immediate demands for coverage of historically and politically complex topics led to less than satisfactory accounts. The role of the media is, however, vitally important to promoting accurate DIAimages of the Other and connecting widespread communities through shared information.

Islamic Authority

Participants vigorously discussed the nature of authority and legitimacy in the contemporary Muslim world. Although there was considerable disagreement over who, if anyone, should speak for Islam, there was broad agreement that, while there is only one Qur'an, there are many Islams in terms of historical interpretation and social manifestation. Muslims belong to a global community based on shared belief in a number of principles, but modern improvements in education and communications, among other factors, have encouraged many people outside the traditional religious class to interpret doctrine and revelation. The implications of this ongoing reexamination of the nature of Islamic authority and authenticity are potentially momentous for the development of both modern Islamic thought and relations between Islam and the West.

Muslims in the West

The conference unanimously acknowledged not only that Islam now constitutes an integral part of the West, but also that the future of the Muslim-Western encounter depends to a great degree on how Western Muslims influence developments in the majority-Muslim world. Millions of Muslims have migrated to the West for political and economic reasons, and a second generation of native-born European and North American Muslims has now acquired citizenship in multicultural, liberal democracies. This shift is inducing change in Western societies at the same time as it encourages new thinking in Muslim circles. Western states face the challenge of meeting Muslim claims to better treatment and equal opportunity, etc., without attempting to impose cultural or political uniformity on them. Muslims, for their part, face the challenge of being loyal and committed citizens without abandoning their Islamic beliefs and practices or cutting themselves off from developments in the larger Muslim world.

In the early 2000s Ja'far Umar Thalib was the man to watch, the flame-eater and flame-thrower of the moment. Following the economic and financial crises that rocked Southeast Asia in 1998, Indonesia was thrown into turmoil. Overnight the collapse of the value of the Thai Baht led to the subsequent collapse of the Indonesian Rupiah, Filipino Peso and Malaysian Ringgit. President Suharto was ultimately overthrown by angry demonstrators led by students who stormed the Parliament in Jakarta. While the country was reeling from the effects of the economic meltdown, racial and religious tempers flared. The unfortunate Chinese minorities were singled out as economic traitors and the Chinese quarter of Glodok in central Jakarta was set to the torch by angry mobs looking for scapegoats.

In the outer island provices of Moluccas, Muslim-Christian antipathy flowed into the streets and led to mass killings on both sides. It was during this time that Ja'far Umar Thalib, one of the lesser-known firebrands of Indonesia, came to the fore. Based at his *pesantren* in Kaliurang, Jogjakarta, Ja'far rallied his students and followers and created the notorious *Laskar Jihad* (Army of Jihad), a semi-underground movement of militant volunteers who were then dispatched to the Moluccas to avenge the killing of Muslims by Christians.

The *Laskar* was but one of many right-wing conservative militant movements that flourished during the troubled months that followed the toppling of Suharto. The weak leadership of B. J. Habibie, Abdurrahman Wahid and Megawati Sukarnoputri that followed did little to help, as it lent weight to the impression that nobody was running the country. Acting with impunity the *Laskar Jihad* opened training camps that gave paramilitary combat training to the hundreds of assorted unemployed *premans* (freemen, mercenaries) who swelled the ranks of the *Laskar*. Soon after they were sent to the Moluccas by boats where, needless to say their presence merely made things worse. While the *Laskar Jihad* did battle with Christian militias such as the *Laskar Kristen*, the Moluccas burned and the capital of Ambon looked like a battleground. Since then the *Laskar* and its leader have been making the headlines in Indonesia.

Following the debacle in the Moluccas Ja'far Umar Thalib and the *Laskar Jihad* turned their attention to the cosmopolitan cities of Jakarta, Jogjakarta and Surakarta, where they became famous (or infamous) for their tough brand of moral policing: Attacking and destroying night-clubs, discos, cinemas, video stores, etc all became their hallmark. In time their commando-like members, dressed in soldiers outfits, even raided hotels to demand that Western tourists leave the country.

By 2002, however, the *Laskar* had become an embarrassment for the country and were told to disband in no uncertain terms. Local political observers argued that this pointed to intimate connections between the *Laskar* and the Indonesian security forces, something that Ja'far himself admitted in his press interviews several years ago. Having served their role as trouble-makers on the pay of the rich and powerful, they have had their strings cut and Ja'far Umar Thalib is now very much an isolated and discredited individual.

Not even the other Indonesian radical groups like the *Majlis Mujahidin Indonesia* (MMI), *Hizbut Tahrir Indonesia* (HTI) or *Fron Pembela* Islam (FPI) would care to talk to him. Left alone at his *pondok,* Ja'far has little to do but tend his flock. *"I have returned to my original struggle, my original Jihad, which is education"* the man admits. This chapter sets out to examine the rise and fall of men like Ja'far Umar Thalib and the discourses they advocate and bring to the fore. In particular it sets out to locate these men in the context of Indonesia's relatively open public discursive space, and it tries to examine how the struggle for dominance and prominence in that space is determined by the subject-positions of the individual speakers themselves and their links to various educational, political and ideological streams in the country. While analysing the ideas and discourses of the men in question we will try to locate them in the context of the respective educational institutions they belong to – in this case the respective *pesantrens* they helped to found and develop – as well as the political movements they have come to be affiliated with.

Our working thesis here is that in the case of both Abu Bakar Bashir and Ja'far Umar Thalib, their public standing and credibility depends as much on the educational institutions they have been identified with as on their respective educational, family and political backgrounds as well. Neither individual can be understood out of this broader context of overlapping educational (specifically *pesantren*) networks that happen to overlap with political networks as well. The analysis is based upon fieldwork data collected in the months of May and June 2007, while in Central Java conducting research on the modernisation and reform process of Indonesia's Islamic universities and *pesantrens*. It features interviews with two of the most famous spokesmen for what in Indonesia is often referred to as the *garis keras* (hardline) of the Islamist movement, Ustaz Abu Bakar Bashir and Ustaz Ja'far Umar Thalib; both of whom were (and remain) household names in the country for a number of reasons.

While the interviews demonstrate that neither individual has changed the tone, tenor and content of their rhetoric or the political stands they assume in private and public, what is important and interesting to note is how both men have become relatively silent in the domestic political context of late. This relative silencing of Abu Bakar Bashir and Ja'far Umar Thalib raises obvious questions that we need to ask, such as: What does this say about the domestic discursive terrain of Indonesian Muslim politics, and where does this place men like Bashir and Ja'far? What are the factors that determine the rise (and subsequent decline) of men like them? Does this signify that Indonesian Islam has and will maintain its predominantly moderate character and that marginal – albeit vocal – radical groups have not been able to shift the discursive centre of Indonesian Muslim politics to a more radical, exclusive, communitarian or even militant register? In order to answer some of these questions we now turn to the profile of the two men in question, before locating their respective subject-positions on the wider landscape of Indonesian Muslim politics and Islamist discourse.

Ustaz Abu Bakar Bashir and Ustaz Ja'far Umar Thalib

It would be a mistake to assume that all of the outspoken Islamist leaders of Indonesia share a similar background and are in complete agreement over their long-term goals and objectives. While some outstanding similarities and parallels can be detected, it is nonetheless important to emphasise the particularity and specificity of each individual profile and biography, for the variable factors that have affected the personal development of each of these individuals may hold some of the answers that explain their outlook on life, Islam, politics and political affiliations. The two men who are of interest to us here hail from very different backgrounds and have had very different career paths, each with a trajectory of its own. Their sudden rise to public prominence after 2001 and the

Bali bombings of 2002 have more to do with the vagaries of the media and media representation; though it has to be stated from the outset that their commonality of views and the subject-positions they have assumed in public have more to do with their place within the constellation of Indonesia's complex plural politics. We offer here a brief summary of the life and times of both of them, beginning with Ustaz Abu Bakar Bashir.

Ustaz Abu Bakar Bashir

Abu Bakar Bashir was born in Jombang, East Java, on 17 August 1938 and his family were originally of Arab (Yemeni, Hadramaut) origin. During his childhood Bashir received most of his basic religious education from his father and household, and was brought up according to the traditional conservative values of his Arab-Javanese parents. He was sent by his father to the Pesantren Gontor in Ponorogo, East Java; and upon his graduation from the Pasentren proceeded to further his studies at the Al-Irsyad Islamic University in Surakarta. During his university years he took part in the activities of the Muslim students of Solo and joined the *Himpunan Mahasiswa* Islam (HMI, Union of Muslim Students) and was ultimately popular among some of the followers of the HMI and GPII, which was also being propagated by the various Islamic agencies in Indonesia that were currently being supported and funded by Arab-Sunni states such as Saudi Arabia.

Bashir, Abdullah Sungkar and their friends were also influenced by the ideas of the Indonesian Islamist-nationalist intellectual Muhammad Natsir, who was then seen as the figurehead of the Masjumi movement as well as the Darul Islam movement; the latter of which had been engaged in a rebellion against the central government of Indonesia and determined to set up an Islamic state in Indonesia (*Negara* Islam *Indonesia,* NII) by any means necessary. The banning of Masjumi in 1960 (by Sukarno), the persecution of Islamists like Muhammad Natsir and the virtual eradication of the Darul Islam movement forced many

Islamists to take to underground activities and attracted more followers to their cause. Bashir was by then an active supporter of the Darul Islam movement, as was Abdullah Sungkar. Thanks to their involvement and public support of the *Darul* Islam movement, Bashir and Abdullah Sungkar were imprisoned in the late 1970s, for anti-state activities. It was in prison that Bashir and Sungkar grew even more radical in their thinking and ambitions. They condemned and rejected the secular *Pancasila* ideology of the Indonesian state and rejected values and concepts such as universal suffrage, pluralism and democracy on the grounds that these were modern, Western secular concepts that were un-Islamic.

In 1985 Bashir fled into exile in Malaysia. Between 1985-1998 Bashir was based in the Southern state of Johor in Malaysia and there he set up his own religious school. While teaching at his religious school at Sungai Manggis in Johor, Bashir attracted a number of Indonesian students and ex-*Mujahideen* who joined him there. Ustaz Bashir taught his students that they should reject all forms of secularism, abide only Islamic (*shariah*) law and not the secular laws of the country and prepare for a *jihad* for an Islamic state. Bashir and Abdullah Sungkar were finally able to return to Indonesia following the downfall of President Suharto in 1998. Once in Indonesia he returned to his *Pesantren* in Ngruki, Solo and resumed his teaching activities there. Analysts suggest that by then Bashir was also the head of the shadowy *Jamaah Islamiyah* movement which he was accused of setting up during his exile in Malaysia.

Notwithstanding such allegations of clandestine underground activities, Bashir was prominently involved in the setting up of the *Majlis Mujahidin Indonesia* (MMI). At the founding congress of the MMI in Jogjakarta in August 2000, he was elected as its first *Amir* (leader). It should be noted, however, that although Bashir and some of his followers from the *pesantren* al- Mukim joined and helped to develop the MMI, the latter was an entity entirely distinct and separate from the *pesantren* that Bashir had also helped to form decades earlier. Following the Bali bombings in October 2002, Indonesian and international security and intelligence agencies accused Abu Bakar Bashir of being the head of the *Jamaah Islamiyah* (JI).

He was also, by then, the official head of the highly vocal and visible right-wing conservative organisation the *Majlis Mujahidin Indonesia* (MMI). From 2002 the MMI and other right-wing Solo-based organisations such as the *Fron Pembela* Islam (FPI) and *Fron Pemuda* Islam *Solo* (FPIS) have been at the forefront of numerous protests and demonstrations against the Indonesian government as well as foreign powers. They publicly supported the *Taliban* during the American- led invasion of Afghanistan in 2002 and have opposed the US-led invasion and occupation of Iraq. In March 2005 Bashir was found guilty of masterminding the bombing attacks on Bali in 2002, and sent to Cipinang jail in Jakarta. However he was released in June 2006, much to the dismay of other Western governments including the United States of America and Australia.

Ustaz Ja'far Umar Thalib

Of Arab (Hadrami) and Malay ancestry, Ja'far Umar Thalib was born in Malang, East Java on 29 December 1961. His grandfather, Abdullah Amir ibn Thalib, originated from Hadramaut and migrated to Southeast Asia at the end of the 19th century, first settling in British Malaya, then the colony of Singapore and finally ending up in Banjarmasin, Kalimantan (Borneo). His father Umar ibn Thalib was the first to be born in the (then) Dutch East Indies and as a youth was brought up by his uncle after the death of his father. Umar was given a strict religious education and soon became an active member of the *al-Irshad* reformist movement formed by Arab-Muslims (including his own relatives) in Indonesia in 1913. The movement was a puritan organisation that strove to purify Indonesian Islam of pre-Islamic ideas and practices, as well as Western secular ideas and values. Umar ibn Thalib also delved into the world of politics and later became a leader of the Masjumi movement (that was banned by Sukarno in 1960) and later Muhamadiyah. In 1961 his seventh son Ja'far Umar Thalib was born.

In 1981 Ja'far involved himself in the activities of another neo-Salafi movement, Persis, when he enrolled in the Persis *Pesantren* of Bangil, near Surabaya. At the *pesantren* of Bangil Ja'far worked as one of the writers for the *pesantren's* periodical, *al-Muslimun*. Through this publication Ja'far made his own position clear to a wider public and he was soon known as one of the most conservative and orthodox neo-Salafi thinkers in the country, often engaging in polemics with other scholars and schools of thought that he regarded as being too 'soft' on the question of the Islamic state and Muslim politics in Indonesia. In 1985 he left the *pesantren* of Bangil and took up a scholarship from the Saudi-funded *Lembaga Ilmu Pengetahuan* Islam *dan Bahasa* (LIPIA) based in Jakarta. After securing a scholarship from LIPIA he was sent to Saudi Arabia to study. While in Saudi Arabia in 1986–87, Ja'far came under the influence of several Wahhabi teachers such as Muhammad Nasr al-Din al-Albani and Rabi' ibn Hadi Umar al-Madkhali, who taught him both Qur'anic and Hadith studies as well as Wahhabi *dakwah* methodology.

After his studies in Saudi Arabia, Ja'far then travelled to Pakistan where he enrolled at the Syed Maudoodi International Islamic Institute (SMII), an educational centre run by the *Jama'at-e Islami* party. Ja'far did not spend much time studying at the SMII. While in Pakistan he took part in militia training (along with other foreign volunteers from Southeast Asia and the Arab states) before fighting with the *mujahideen* against the Soviets in Afghanistan. In Pakistan, Ja'far made contact with the Islamist *Jama'at-e Islami* party and its *mujahideen* network. In Afghanistan, Ja'far chose to fight with the *Jama'at al-Da'wa ila al-Qur'an wa Ahl-I Hadith* faction under its Salafi- oriented leader Jamil al-Rahman. There he learned and accepted the doctrine of *takfir* which requires Muslims to excommunicate and revolt against their own leaders should they not live up to the standards of good Muslims. It was also in Pakistan and Afghanistan that Ja'far claims that he met with Abdul Rasul Sayaf and Osama ben Laden.

There is little to prove any of Ja'far's claims about his activities in the Afghan *mujahideen* campaign, although he and his followers maintain that he took active part in the fighting there. In 1989, Ja'far returned to Indonesia where he taught at the al-Irshad *pesantren* in Salatiga, Central Java, then in 1990 he travelled to Yemen to study under the Wahhabi teacher Muqbil ibn Hadi al-Wadi', a member of a Saudi-funded Islamist movement. In 1993, Ja'far finally returned to Indonesia and based himself at Jogjakarta. In 1994, he opened his own *pesantren* – the *Pesantren Ehya as-Sunnah* – at Kaliurang and helped to establish the *Jama'ah Ihya al-Sunnah* community. By then Ja'far had established himself as the foremost spokesman and leader of the Salafi community in Indonesia. From his *pesantren,* he published his own magazine called *Salafy* which was soon to be the most visible media arm of the neo-Salafi movement in the country. In his articles and commentaries, Ja'far condemned what he saw as the creeping secularisation of Indonesia, rejected the country's *Pancasila* ideology, opposed the democratic process and derided the values of democracy, pluralism and toleration of diversity.

Ja'far's writings lamented the loss of Muslim identity and ethics and criticised the West and pro- Western governments for what he called the 'grand design' to destroy Islam and Muslims the world over. He encouraged his followers to take up the struggle of Islamist politics, and while doing so condemned traditionalist organisations like the *Nahdatul Ulama* for what he regarded as their quietist approach to political problems and issues. Ja'far insisted that Muslim power was only achievable via *Jihad* – though his understanding of *Jihad* included both political as well as military struggles. Ja'far began to preach his Wahhabi ideas to his followers, and his movement called for the implementation of *shariah* law among the Muslims. The *Jama'ah Ihya al-Sunnah* quickly gained a following among Islamist student activists in local Javanese university campuses and the movement spread its ideas even further via the student and activist networks. On 14 February 1998, Ja'far helped to create the *Forum Komunikasi Ahlu Sunnah wal-Jamaah* (Communication Forum of the Followers of the Sunnah and the Community of the Prophet, FKAWL).

The FKAWL later served as the umbrella organisation for a number of militant Islamist groupings; one was *Laskar Jihad* (Jihad Army), led by Ja'far himself. Following the downfall of President Suharto in May 1998, Ja'far and his neo-Salafi followers campaigned and mobilised themselves again. In 1998 they demanded that Islamic law be made the only law of Indonesia and called for the setting up of an Indonesian Islamic state. President Suharto's successor B. J. Habibie was the first political figure to be attacked by Ja'far and his followers. Ja'far demanded that Habibie make way for the immediate Islamisation of the Indonesian state, for failure to do so would mean a betrayal of Islam. Cognisant of the fact that Habibie was trying his best to maintain the support of the country's Muslims and wanted to keep the Islamist movements within the ambit of the democratic process, groups like the Salafis sought to exploit the weaknesses and dependency of the Habibie administration.

Demonstrations by the Salafis were held in Jakarta and other major cities, and were further intensified when Habibie was forced to step down after the elections of 1999 that led to the appointment of the next President.Abdurrahman Wahid (Gus Dur). It was during the rule of Gus Dur that Ja'far and his supporters were at their most strident. Sidel (2006) notes that this was the period when the Islamist parties of the country had come together to form what was then known as the Central Axis (*Poros Tengah*) in Indonesian politics, in a desperate bid to ensure that the more secular forces behind the Democratic Party (PDIP) did not gain power in the country. But Gus Dur eventually alienated many of the more conservative Islamists who had supported his bid for power. The President's hesitant recognition of the state of Israel and the Jewish holocaust was compounded by his later decree to recognise the (then nonexistent) Indonesian Communist Party (PKI).

Fed up with what they saw as the wavering of the President on the issue of the Islamic state, the Salafis turned against the President and were among the most vocal groups calling for the early removal of Gus Dur from office. At the same time inter-religious conflict had broken out in the outer island provinces, most notably in the Moluccas. Through the *Forum Komunikasi Ahlu Sunnah wal-Jamaah* Ja'far and his followers launched the *Laskar Jihad* at the FKAWL's *Tabligh Akbar* in Jogjakarta in January 2000. (In the same year that Ustaz Abu Bakar Bashir created the *Majlis Mujahidin Indonesia*, MMI, in the same city.) Apart from Ja'far Umar Thalib the other notable founder-leaders of the *Laskar Jihad* were other prominent Salafis such as Muhammad Umar As-Sewed, Ayip Syafruddin and Ma'ruf Bahrun.

The *Laskar* was formed as a military-run outfit and ran as an adjunct of the FKAWL that was based in Jogjakarta. Then in April 2000 the *Laskar* held their first mass rally at the Senayan stadium of Jakarta, where they vowed to send thousands of *mujahidin* to the Moluccas to avenge the killings of Muslims and destruction of Muslim property by Christian groups and militias such as the *Laskar Kristen*. In time entire brigades of Laskar militia were sent to the Moluccas and the inter-religious conflict there intensified until the situation was finally brought to order by the belated intervention of the Indonesian armed forces.

During this period Ja'far and the *Laskar* continued in their polemics against the Indonesian government and vented their wrath on the new President, Megawati Sukarnoputri, who had come to power following the graceless exit of Gus Dur. Condemning her on the grounds that a woman could not lead a Muslim country, Ja'far and the Salafis of the

FKAWL also claimed that Megawati was a stooge who was being secretly manipulated by an invisible oligarchy of Christian, Chinese and secular generals of the armed forces. Ja'far alluded to the party of Megawati – the *Partai Demokrasi Indonesia* (PDI) – as a 'secular leftist front' dominated by Chinese and Communist sympathisers. By this point both Ja'far and the Salafi movement were seen as frontline political actors engaged in *realpolitik* in the country. Megawati's period of unstable leadership was made all the more tenuous with Ja'far's claim that the former was an unwitting accomplice to the Western-Christian-Zionist plot to undermine and weaken Islam in Indonesia and the world over.

During this time Ja'far's attacks on the Indonesian government reached their peak and the *Laskar Jihad* was seen as one of the most violent sectarian radical movements in the country. Despite the virulent attacks on Megawati's government however, Ja'far proved to be a less able military commander than his rhetoric suggested: The *Laskar's* forays into the Moluccas were cut short by the intervention of the Indonesian armed forces and by 2001 many of the *Laskar* militants had been neutralised by the elite forces of KOPASSUS (Special Forces Command). By May 2002 Ja'far himself was arrested by Indonesian authorities for ordering the execution of one of the *Laskar* members who was accused of rape and murder; and by October Ja'far was forced to disband the *Laskar Jihad*. Following his arrest, detention and subsequent release from prison, Ja'far made several revelations in the Indonesian print media about his links and co-operation with the country's armed forces and intelligence services. This only helped to alienate him further and eventually made him a marginalised figure in the world of Indonesian radical Islamist politics.

Positions and Visibility

A cursory overview of the very different biographies and genealogies of Abu Bakar Bashir and Ja'far Umar Thalib would show that the two men – while sharing somewhat similar views of Islam based on a common appreciation of Wahabi and neo-Salafi doctrines inculcated since childhood – are very different personalities indeed. Abu Bakar Bashir's denunciation of politics and the political process as inherently corrupt and corrupting contrasts to the position of Ja'far Umar Thalib who sees politics and engagement with politics as a necessary evils at times. In the case of the latter, the conscious decision to enter the political fray marks a radical departure from the more apolitical, quietist stand assumed by generations of Salafis and neo-Salafis in Indonesia, many of whom have preferred the more indirect method of Islamisation from below.

And while Abu Bakar Bashir has condemned the political process itself as un-Islamic and denounced democratic politics as being diametrically opposed to what he calls *'Allah-cracy'*, Ja'far Umar Thalib's more florid political path has shown that he is prepared and able to play the game of politics – shifting his support from one administration or politician to another – as long as it serves his own agenda and political interests. Both men have opted for the use of the media to disseminate their messages to the wider Indonesian and international public, and Bashir in particular has demonstrated a keen awareness of how the media works and how the demonisation of his own image can be turned around to suit his own interests. Rhetorical pyrotechnics and political symbolism have served the interests of these new leaders who have managed, within a relatively short space of time, to place themselves at the centre of Indonesian politics and debates on Islam in Indonesia. However it should also be noted that both men have adopted very different public styles of discourse, opting to send out different messages to different audiences and political constituencies at different stages of their own political development and the development of the organisations they have founded and led.

One factor that determines the extent to which they are taken seriously is the platforms from which they speak. Both

Bashir and Ja'far are identified as Muslim scholars operating from their respective *pesantrens;* and it is thanks in part to their status as Muslim scholars that they have managed to secure for themselves the vital cultural capital and scholarly credibility that gives their voices the authority it purports to have. We now turn to the respective institutions and movements linked to both men and will try to examine how their own subject-positioning has been done with reference to the larger bodies they are attached to, both institutional and organisational.

Abu Bakar Bashir, Pesantren al-Mukmin and the Majlis Mujahidin Indonesia (MMI)

Both Abu Bakar Bashir and Ja'far Umar Thalib share a similar background in terms of their respective subject-positions in Indonesia: Both are highly qualified and experienced *Ulama* (scholars) who are linked to Islamic educational institutions of their own and who have their own bases of popular political support outside the sphere of their educational institutions. It is this double-basis of academic and political support that gives them the aura of charisma and credibility that many other public figures in Indonesia lack today. Bashir's stronger (and older) claim to be a scholar of repute rests in part on his family history and background (linked to the *al- Irshad, Persis* and *Darul* Islam movements) and his association with the religious school he helped to found, the *Pondok Pesantren al-Mukmin* of Ngruki, Surakarta.

The *Pondok Pesantren al-Mukmin* is located in the middle of Desa Ngruki, in the Kebupaten Sukoharjo, in the centre of Surakarta, Central Java. Visitors to the Desa Ngruki will note that it is a culturally and religiously plural area with as many mosques as there are churches, and in the vicinity of the *pondok pesantren* are thirteen churches (both Catholic and Protestant) that are still in use by the local Christian community. It is also important to note that during the peak of inter-religious conflict that swept across the outer island provinces of Indonesia in the early 2000s, none of the Churches in Ngruki were attacked or threatened in any way.

This reflects Surakarta's complex plural society which has always accommodated religious and cultural differences and apart from the Christian minority there has always been a strong presence of Chinese, India and Arab merchants who also play a visible role in the city's *batik* and gold trade. Surakarta (Solo) has also been the base for the Central Javanese *abangan* ('nominal' Muslim) culture and was historically one of the bases for the now-extinct *Communist Party of Indonesia* (PKI) that was banned after 1965.

Today it happens to be one of the most important support centres for the *Partai Demokrasi Indonesia-Perjuangan* (PDIP) party of Megawati Sukarnoputri, former President of Indonesia and daughter of the country's founder- leader Sukarno. Since 2002 the *pesantren* Ngruki has been stigmatised by its association with the scholar Ustaz Abu Bakar Bashir, who also happens to be the *Amir* (leader) of the radical *Majlis Mujahidin Indonesia* (MMI) movement that was formed in Surakarta in 2000. But it has to be noted that Bashir is only one of the original eight founders of the *pesantren* and that today he has little, if any, influence in the running of the school itself. From the outset the *pesantren* was run by its own foundation (Yayasan Ngruki) that was put together by the contributions of the founders.

The *Yayasan Pendidikan* Islam *al-Mukmin Ngruki* (YPIA) is the foundation that oversees the management of the *pesantren al-Mukmin* and the other institutions under its care. Most of the educational institutes under the YPIA are not run according to the *pondok* (boarding school) system and the students do not actually live on the premises. The sole exception is the *pondok pesantren al-Mukmin* which offers boarding (*pondok*) services as well. The schools run by the YPIA are open to students from all family backgrounds and are non- political in the sense that they accept students from families linked to other groups such as the Muhamadiyah and Nahdatul Ulama (NU). The YPIA is run by its board of directors, most of whom are drawn from the alumni of the various schools and colleges run by the YPIA itself.

The board of directors of the YPIA in turn determines the allocation of funds, management, development and appointment of directors and assistant directors at the various institutions under its management. The board does not, however, intervene or interfere directly in the running of the institutions under its care. Of all the educational institutions run by the YPIA, only the *Pondok Pesantren al-Mukmin* offers board and lodging to its students. Many of the students come from different parts of the country and as such do not have accommodation in the city of Surakarta, and are therefore compelled by circumstances to stay at the *pondok* themselves. The Pondok Pesantren is run by a Director (*Direktor*) who is appointed by the members of the board of the YPIA. The Direktor of the *pondok* is given room to administer the *pondok* according to his needs, and since 1969 several changes have been made by successive directors to the overall administrative structure of the *pondok* itself.

In general, the structure has remained relatively unchanged with one Director heading a committee made up of three Assistant Directors (Sometimes also referred to as Vice-Directors (*Wakil Direktor*). Within the closed compound of the *Pondok Pesantren* one finds the following institutions operating: One *Sekolah Tadika* (Kindergarten) for children between the ages of 4 to 6; The *Madrasah Sanawiyah* (Primary level madrasah) that is open to boys and girls (though located in separate compounds) for boys and girls between the ages of 12 to 15; The *Madrasah Aliyah* (Senior level madrasah), also for boys and girls (located in separate compounds) for boys and girls between the ages of 15 to 18; And the *Kulliyatul Muallimin/Muallimat* (teachers college) for male and female students aged between 15 to 19 years, that offer degrees equivalent to the SPG (*Sekolah Perguruan Guru Agama*, Religious Teachers Training College) degree offered by SPG equivalent institutions run by the *Departemen Agama* (Department of Religious Affairs) of the Indonesian state.

There is also a Logistics bureau (*Biro Logistik*) located within the *pondok pesantren* which manages the daily running of the school and whose activities include food production, distribution of books and uniforms, health care, emergency relief and communications within the *pondok* and the vicinity of the Desa Ngruki. All of these educational services are carried out within the enclosed confines of the *pondok pesantren* and cater to the students who are full-time residents of the *pondok* only. No external students are allowed to enter and participate in the activities within the *pondok* itself. Today (2007) the *pondok pesantren* of Ngruki has around 1,500 students, both boys and girls.

At full capacity the *pondok pesantren* can and has accommodated around 3,500 students, though following the Bali bombings and the media coverage on Abu Bakar Bashir the enrolment at the *pondok* has dropped considerably. The curriculum of the *pondok pesantren* is set by the Director of the *pondok* and the members of the YPIA, but also has to abide by the standards set by the *Departemen Agama* (Religious Affairs Department) of the Indonesian government. In terms of teaching standards and practice, the teaching at Ngruki is modelled on other famous modern pesantrens of Indonesia, such as the *Pondok Pesantren Darussalam Gontor*, in Ponorogo, East Java. For the teaching conducted at the *Kulliyatul Muallimin/Muallimat*, the standardised textbooks approved by the *Departmen Agama Indonesia* have been used, to ensure that the graduates are eligible for the SPG (*Sekolah Perguruan Guru Agama*, Religious Teachers Training College) degree offered by SPG equivalent institutions managed by the Indonesian Department of Religious Affairs.

Class sizes at the *pondok pesantren* are relatively fixed to around 50 per class, maximum. (In keeping with the standard class sizes of state schools and colleges.) The boys and girls at the *pondok* are houses in dormitories (*asrama*) for boys (*putra*) and girls (*putri*) respectively. The girls' compound, located at the original site of the first *pondok*, is entirely cut off and enclosed within a walled area. In both the boys and girls' compounds there are dormitories, classes, libraries, sports areas, kitchens, mosques and laundry areas. Food for the students is cooked on the premises and served three times a day at the different messes that are located on the grounds of the *pondok*. Record-keeping at the *Pondok Pesantren Ngruki* has been lax since the 1990s, and has depended mainly on the Directors of the institution. During the 1980s records were kept of all students, with information related to their family backgrounds and even the political affiliation of their families.

However since the mid-1990s records have been poorly kept and no comprehensive record of students' backgrounds exists today. The Directors of the *Pondok Pesantren al-Mukmin* insist that their institution is on par with the other state-run educational institutions in Indonesia and that it can match the standard of any secular (non-religious) school. In 2006, of the 93 graduates of the senior *Madrasah Aliyah* of *Pondok Pesantren Ngruki*, 72 graduated with the equivalent of a high school diploma and proceeded to enrol in the universities (including Islamic universities, UINs) of Indonesia.

Pondok Pesantren Ngruki, Abu Bakar Bashir and the Jama'ah Islamiyyah

Ustaz Abu Bakar Bashir was one of the original eight founders of the *Pondok Pesantren al- Mukmin Ngruki* and is the only living founder today. He served as the Director of the Pondok Pesantren for 4 years, during the early 1980s, but left the post after he was forced to flee into hiding in Malaysia in 1985. Since his return to Indonesia in 1998, Abu Bakar Bashir has resumed his teaching responsibilities at the *Pondok Pesantren*, though he has never been given any administrative power or authority ever since. At present (2007) Bashir serves as one of the many advisory consultants to the *Pondok's* board of directors, but has no power to implement any reform of the system. It is important to note that from the outset, even when the *pondok* was first founded, Bashir has not had any power to determine the *pondok's* curriculum or teaching methods.

While some of the alleged bombers linked to the bombing of Bali in 2002 were known to be alumni of Ngruki and students of Bashir himself, he was and remains only one of the many teachers employed by the *pondok*. Despite Abu Bakar Bashir's relatively marginal place and role in the daily running of the *pondok pesantren*, the *Pondok Ngruki* has received global attention by the media due to the alleged links to the *Jama'ah Islamiyah* network and the Bali Bombers. But it should be noted that from the day it was set up (in 1969) Ngruki has been one of the most monitored and studied religious institutions in Indonesia, due to its links to Abu Bakar Bashir and Abdullah Sungkar, both of whom were of *al-Irshad* and *Persis* backgrounds and who were both associated with the banned *Darul Islam revolt* of the 1950s-1960s. Thus Sidel (2006) has concluded that there has been 'a long history of intelligence surveillance and infiltration of the Ngruki network of Abu Bakar Bashir.

It was in the context of the close monitoring of the *Pesantren*, after all, that Bashir, and the school's co-founder Abdullah Sungkar, had been arrested and imprisoned in the late 1970s, and in the wake of their flight into exile to Malaysia in 1985, the caretakers of the *Pesantren* agreed to allow the security services and its agents an active role in the management of the school.' The *Pondok Pesantren al-Mukmin* of Ngruki therefore has become not only one of the most famous *pondoks* of Indonesia, but also one of the most monitored and controlled institutions of Islamic education in the country. This also accounts for how and why its curricula remains both modern and in keeping with the standards set by the religious departments and institutions of the state; and also accounts for why its students have been able to make the transition from the *pondok* to state-run and state-recognised institutions of higher learning all over the rest of Indonesia.

Bashir therefore has become a somewhat marginalised and isolated figure in the *pesantren* he helped to create himself in 1969. Cognisant of the fact that he is now only one of the many figures of the *pesantren*, Bashir has tried to gain further leverage in public by working with other groupings in the country who support his own view and interpretation of political Islam. The most publicly visible group linked to Bashir today happens to be the *Majlis Mujahidin Indonesia* (MMI). Since it was formed in 2000 the *Majlis Mujahidin* has grown to be one of the more visible actors and players on the increasingly complex scene of political Islam in Indonesia. Following the Tsunami catastrophe and the Jogjakarta earthquake of 2005, the MMI were among the first on the scene to give relief aid and to help in the process of reconstruction.

At the same time the MMI has been unrelenting in its struggle to disseminate its own brand of anti-Western, anti-Zionist and anti-democratic vision of society. This has led some to label the group as an adjunct to a wider pan-Islamic anti-Western movement, with its links to other radical Islamist groups abroad. However it would be over-stretching the facts to claim that the formation of the *Majlis Mujahidin Indonesia* was part of a wider global network of Islamist militancy tracing its links and origins to movements like *al-Qaeda*. The domestic variables all point to the fact that the MMI was very much a result of a long historical process of local Islamist activism dating back to movements like Persis and *al-Irshad*, and the *Darul Islam* revolt of the 1950s.

Indeed, as Sidel (2006) notes, the founding Congress of the MMI in Jogjakarta between 5-7 August 2000 was timed to coincide with the anniversary of the proclamation of the Islamic State of Indonesia (*Negara Islam Indonesia*) by Selkarmadji Maridjan Kartosoewirjo, the leader of the *Darul Islam* movement, that took place on 7 August 1949. Since 2005, however, the MMI and its leader Bashir have been relatively quiet on the Indonesian scene due to a host of local and external variable factors that we shall discuss below. What is clear, however, is that the marginalised Bashir has been forced to seek support and a platform outside the *Pondok Pesantren al-Mukmin* due to the fact that he was silenced by the other teaching staff of the institution itself; proof that even a firebrand like Bashir does not have the power to determine the fate and profile of such institutions entirely according to his will or on the basis of his forceful personality.

Ja'far Umar Thalib, Pesantren Ehya as-Sunnah and the Laskar Jihad (LJ)

Compared to the more well-known and older *Pondok Pesantren al-Mukmin* of Ngruki, Surakarta, the *pesantren* founded and run by Ja'Far Umar Thalib is a pale counterpart. Hasan (2006) has noted that the *Pondok Pesantren Ehya as-Sunnah* hardly compares to the more well-known and better-organised and funded *pesantren* of Abu Bakar Bashir. In his words: 'It (the *pesantren* of Ja'far Umar Thalib) appeared unadorned and poor. It was built on no more than three hundred square meters rented for a period of ten years and centred around a modest mosque initially named *Jamil al-Rahman* but later changed to *Uthman ibn Affan*. Approximately a hundred meters from this mosque there were two crammed dormitories each about a hundred meters square, with walls made of bamboo and dirt floors covered with mats and plastic.

The *pesantren* had some seventy students whose ages ranged from seven to seventeen. They were taught by the four teachers who rented houses in the nearby area. Some of them were day students who had lodgings in the nearby areas. The students were divided to three groups according to their age categories.' There was no significant student activity (in fact no classes were being held at all from what we could observe), and the only remarkable features were the few women (who may or may not have been students or relatives of the students and teachers) who walked about fully covered from head to foot in black *jilbabs* (robes). In terms of its organisational structure and administration, the *Pondok Pesantren Ehya as-Sunnah* does not have the financial support and institutional cohesion of Bashir's *pesantren al-Mukmin* of Ngruki.

Indeed, there is little evidence of any local support from the local community of Kaliurang and the small community of students and teachers resident in the *pondok* are an isolated community that seems to have little, if any, contact with the locals. Nor is the *Pesantren Ehya as-Sunnah* given much weight by other Islamists as a major centre of Islamic teaching, as none of its students have graduated with the same standardised qualifications that would afford them with the means of moving on to other higher institutions of learning. It is not clear whether the *ijazahs* (diplomas) offered by Ja'far's *pesantren* are even recognised by the Indonesian civil service or educational institutions, and apart from the propaganda-laced journals and magazines published by the *pesantren* the place has produced no scholars or students of note.

Perhaps for these reasons Ja'far Umar Thalib's reputation has been built more on the reputation of the *Laskar Jihad* which he formed in 2000 and the media attention paid to the activities of the *Laskar,* both in the Moluccas (when they made international headlines) and during their *razzias* that were conducted in the cities of Central and East Java in the early 2000s. Here again, it has to be noted that the *Laskar Jihad* was very much a product of Indonesia's convoluted domestic inter-racial and inter-religious politics. The movement, as Sidel (2006) has noted, was, from the outset, very much a local Indonesian phenomenon that could not be identified as part of the global Islamist movement.

Allegations that the *pesantren* of Ja'far or the *Laskar Jihad* were working in co-ordination with other international Islamist groups (that were prevalent in the media until a while ago) strike one as hollow when we take into account the fact that Ja'far himself has never identified himself or his movement and followers as part of a wider pan-Muslim *Jihadist* movement. In fact Ja'far Umar Thalib himself was well known in Indonesian Islamist circles as one of the most vocal critics of *al-Qaeda* and Osama ben Laden. Furthermore Sidel (2006) and others have alluded to the massive amount of data and anecdotal evidence to support the claim that during the initial stages of its development the *Laskar* was even supported (indirectly) by elements of the Indonesian armed forces that were on the side of the Muslims. In his landmark study of the movement, Noorhaidi Hasan (2006) has argued that the development and rise of the *Laskar* was in many ways an expression of an orchestrated mass panic or anxiety among Indonesian Muslims following the turbulent months and years that came after the end of the Sukarto Presidency.

Seen in this light: 'The case of *Laskar Jihad* demonstrates that the activism espoused by a militant groups is very much determined by the political opportunities and constraints at work at a particular time and place. The group's decision to resort to violence was associated with the state's inability to carry out its primary role as the guardian of social order and enforcer of the law. Indonesia's transition from an authoritarian state to a fledgling democracy disturbed the nation's equilibrium; consequently proponents of the status quo tried hard to involve new political allies in their negotiations with the opposition. This problem was made exacerbated by the fact that the emerging Indonesian democracy was still fragile, because of, among other causes, a serious lack of functional democratic traditions and the narrow political interests of the parties involved.

Needless to say, the newly liberated public sphere which enabled all sections of Indonesian society to express their opinions and interests, contributed a great deal to this phenomenon.' Thus structural factors that opened up new political opportunity structures within the Indonesian body politics accounted in part for the meteoric rise of groups like *Laskar Jihad* and elevated its leader to a position of consi-derable public prominence. It has been noted by many observers (and reported in the Indonesian media) that Ja'far and his *Laskar* lent themselves to numerous political parties and movements and took active part in the political maneu-verings that took place in the capital of Jakarta between 2000 to 2002 as well.

The most notorious instances of the *Laskar's* political maneuvering were the demonstrations – always timed and planned strategically to maximise its mediatic effect – against the governments of Gus Dur and Megawati Sukarnoputri.

These moves were not undetected in Indonesian political and Islamist circles, and soon enough earned both Ja'far and the *Laskar* the reputation of being a 'mob for hire' outfit, ready to be deployed for politically strategic ends (in this case, agitating for the early dismissal of Gus Dur and blocking Megawati's rise to power and the Presidency of Indonesia). Also during the Moluccas debacle, it has been noted by media observers and scholars alike that the deployment of the *Laskar* in strife-torn areas where Muslim- Christian violence had peaked was aided and abetted by both Indonesian military personnel and politicians based in Jakarta who hoped to deflect attention from the economic and political crises that had rocked the centre of power in Jakarta as well.

Proof of the hollow pretensions and inflated claims of Ja'far and the *Laskar* was evident during the latter stages of the Presidency of Megawati Sukarnoputri, when efforts were made to garner a consensus among the political and military elite in Jakarta; after which groups like the *Laskar* were of no further use. Following Megawati's promotion of former high-ranking officers like Lieutenant-General (rtd.) A. M. Hendropriyono to the post of head of the National Intelligence Agency (BIN, *Badan Intelijens Negara*), efforts were made to monitor, infiltrate, disarm and eventually shut down all the radical movements in the country, including the *Laskar Jihad*. The *Laskar Jihad's* untimely departure from the stage of Indonesian politics and Ja'far's graceless exit from the public domain demonstrates the fact that he and such groups remain an aberration in the Indonesian context. If Ja'far is such a discredited man in Indonesian Islamist circles today, it is partly due to the result of the impression that he had been a witting pawn in the country's politics and that he had allowed the *Laskar* to be 'bought' by patrons and pay-masters based in the capital.

Notwithstanding the spectacular mediatic effects of hordes of armed religiously-inspired militants burning and killing their way across the Moluccas, the equally spectacular defeat of the *Laskar* at the hands of the better-trained and armed soldiers of the Indonesian army later in 2002 demonstrated in no uncertain terms that the state was still in power and that the army was in charge. Ultimately, as Hasan (2006) has concluded, the tone and temper of Islam in Indonesia is determined not by the vocal pyrotechnics of men like Ja'afr Umar Thalib (or Abu Bakar Bashir), but rather by structural, economic, political and discursive constraints that are beyond their power to determine. In Hasan's words: 'The *Laskar Jihad's* mission to the Moluccas and other troubled spots in Indonesia by no means indicates that militant Islam has successfully taken over the Indonesian public sphere.

This action ultimately served to highlight the marginal position of militant Muslims and their unsuccessful efforts to popularise their discourse glorifying militancy and the use of violence. In other words it is more a sign of weakness than a harbinger of success for militant Muslims... Because such militants pursue their struggle through spectacular violence, Jihadi Islam remains on the political periphery and may never succeed the strategic landscape of the country. It certainly did not change the map of Indonesian Islam.' Ja'far Umar Thalib and Abu Bakar Bashir may retain their respective subject-positions and use whatever means at hand to gain leverage over the other enunciators and speakers on the domestic Indonesian Islamist scene, but their changing fortunes and public prominence and credibility depend as much on internal and external variable factors well beyond their control. The final question which we will now raise in our conclusion will be: What is the future for these two men and the schools of thought they represent?

There is no reason to believe that either Ustaz Abu Bakar Bashir or Ustaz Ja'far Umar Thalib will alter their views and public opinions for the sake of public relations or window-dressing. Indeed the most amazing thing about both men is how their views have been consistent from the very beginning, and how little they have wavered in their views on Islam, the Islamic state, Hudood punishments, Shariah law, relations with the West and non-Muslims in general. One of the factors that undoubtedly accounted for their sudden rise to public notoriety in the early 2000s was the consistency of their respective discourses: Coming at a time of great political turmoil, when the sphere of undecidability had expanded to cover all areas of social life from politics to economics, culture to education, theirs was a voice that was at least fixed, coherent and stable.

At a period when Indonesian society desperately needed clear, decisive leadership men like Abu Bakar Bashir and Ja'far Umar Thalib stood out among the rest, thanks to their fixed and albeit narrow views on Islam, Muslim politics and the future of Muslims in Indonesia. Furthermore their standing as scholars with educational institutions behind them further supported their claims to speak as *ulama* with authority and credibility before the wider public. With the race-riots of 1998 a close memory and inter-religious violence flaring in the Moluccas then, their narrow prescriptions for Muslim unity and *Jihad* against the West met with stronger acclaim and support then, from an Indonesian public tired of the wavering and dithering of successive Presidential administrations, from Habibie to Gus Dur.

Not surprising then, if Abu Bakar Bashir and Ja'far Umar Thalib managed to capture the imagination of so many and the fascination of the media as well. By the mid-2000s, however, Indonesia was beset by other problems that it had not anticipated: The Tsunami that devastated Aceh and many coastal regions of Sumatra was followed by the earthquake that wrecked Jogjakarta and laid waste to places like Bantul. Here again groups like the *Majlis Mujahidin Indonesia* found the opportunity to come to the fore, offering aid and rescue services to traumatised victims in both Aceh and Jogja when the machinery of the state was slow to react. It was the *Majlis Mujahidin* that first arrived at the scene in Aceh, clearing the airport and thus opening the way for aid relief to be flown in to the victims of the Tsunami. Like many Islamist movements, the MMI's members were known for their dedication to the task, and spent many gruelling weeks recovering the dead, burying bodies, rebuilding houses, erecting tent-cities and delivering aid – albeit with a heavy dose of their own propaganda as part of the delivery package.

Things, however, have changed visibly in Indonesia since the fall of President Megawati Sukarnoputri and the rise to power of former-General-turned-President Bambang Susilo Yudhiyono. President Yudhiyono's stated commitment to the restoration of law and order across the country has been bolstered by significant symbolic gestures such as the resumption of cordial talks with the government of Timor Leste, and a more hands-on approach to immediate economic and social problems across the country. This is hardly surprising as since he came to power Indonesia has been beset with a host of domestic problems that have little to do with external actors and agents, ranging from the Tsunami that wrecked Sumatra to the earthquake in Jogjakarta to the current problem of the disastrous mud flow in the region of Sidoarjo, East Java. It is important to note that these natural disasters, coupled with on-going domestic legal and political issues such as the legal imbroglio surrounding the financial scandals in BULOG (the country's rice-distribution agency) all point to the fact that Indonesia's problems have been of its own making of late.

This has not only focused the attention of Indonesians to the domestic affairs of the country, but has also meant that radical Islamist groups like the *Majlis Mujahidin Indonesia* have little to complaint about the so-called 'International Western-Zionist-Christian plot against Islam'. On the international scene Indonesians are also cognizant that with the failure of the American- led adventures in Iraq and Afghanistan, the Bush administration is facing the prospect of a humiliating retreat from power. The Indonesian press, which has been an ardent follower of

American domestic politics, reminds its readers and viewers that the days of George Bush are coming to an end, which has also had the effect of taking the steam out of the more radical Islamist groups in the country that have enjoyed a love-hate relationship with the Bush administration, that can be described as their best enemy.

With the prospect of an eventual American retreat from Iraq on the cards and widely discussed, the more radical spokesmen of Indonesia's *garis keras* Islamist front have little else to do but reiterate the same claims of the perennial 'global conspiracy' against Islam, but with little cause to celebrate the occasional demonstration and bout of frenzied flag-burning. In time, despite their explosive debut on the stage of Indonesia's Islamist politics, it would appear as if men like Ja'far Umar Thalib and Abu Bakar Bashir have been eclipsed once again by the mainstream Muslim groupings of the country: the *Nahdatul Ulama* and *Muhammadiyah*, who are once again occupying the centre stage of Indonesian Islam and Muslim discourse. This is not to suggest that Abu Bakar Bashir or Ja'far Umar Thalib are doomed to be yesterday's men with little to offer to the Indonesian public, but it does demonstrate the extent to which the rise and popularity of men like them depend as much on the failures of the Indonesian state and the blunders of Western foreign policy vis-à-vis the Muslim world as much as it does on their own social standing as Muslim scholar-activists and the reputation of their respective religious schools and networks.

2

Crusaders to Imperialists

Western men and women have wiped the reality of the crusades from their minds. They ignore the important part crusading played in Christian history and they have forgotten how recently it was respectable. Unable to face up to the past, they have reinvented it to suit their notions of what it ought to have been. The irony is that in Islamist *jihadi* propaganda they are all crusaders themselves.

There is hardly a statement of Osama bin Laden which does not include a reference to present-day crusades, which, he is convinced, have been launched by the West in a global war. *Jihadis* like him identify as one of their most potent enemies a force they call Crusaderism, which they believe to be much more ancient than Marxism, Zionism and Colonialism. It lurks behind and manipulates these surrogates, with the sole purpose of destroying Islam. We cannot reply to the Islamists, because we do not comprehend or even recognize the sources of the language they use, and we fail to see that, even though they do not recognize this themselves, their point of reference is not the middle ages but the nineteenth century.

Positive ideas and images of the crusades survived in Europe into the very recent past. The rise of imperialism after 1800 was enveloped in clouds of pseudo-crusading rhetoric, portraying adventures in Algeria, Morocco and even Indo-China in crusading terms, although these enterprises had nothing at all to do with the old reality. There were a few para-crusading projects, in which genuine but distorted elements from the old movement were selectively re-used, and there was at least one authentic expression of crusading, the foundation by Cardinal Lavigerie in 1890 of a true military order, *L'Institut Religieux et Militaire des Frères Armés du Sahara*. The *Institut* did not last long, but its existence demonstrated how powerful a hold the crusades still had on the European imagination.

Nineteenth-century language and imagery drew on two influential sources. Joseph-François Michaud's epic *Histoire des croisades*, published between 1812 and 1822, had been imbued with a passionate nationalism and with a vision of the crusades as instruments of western civilization. The enthusiasm it generated in France and elsewhere was expressed in the popular association of imperialist ventures with pseudo-crusading. On the other hand, Sir Walter Scott's four crusade novels, published between 1819 and 1831, had painted a less flattering picture of crusaders who were brave and glamorous, but also vainglorious, avaricious, childish and boorish, facing Muslims who were their cultural superiors. The romantic imperialistic tradition stemming from Michaud was obviously at odds with the critically romantic one adopted by Scott and his followers.

To the romantic imperialists the crusaders had brought enlightenment to a heathen world, whereas in Scott's critically romantic version, they were barbarous and destructive and compared poorly with civilized and modern-thinking Muslims. But with the decay of imperialism in the twentieth century these contradictory visions fused in the West into a historiographical tradition which still colors popular conceptions and a similar convergence occurred in the Muslim world, although it was expressed in different terms. In the 1890s the Ottoman Turkish sultan Abdulhamid II, whose empire was under severe pressure from the

Russians, Greeks, French and British, asserted that the west had revived the crusades. His announcement aroused the interest of Muslims who had previously been indifferent to crusade history; they believed, after all, that they had comprehensively defeated the medieval European invaders of the Levant.

And Abdulhamid's equation of imperialism with crusading, for which he could hardly be blamed, given all the rhetoric that had washed round Western Europe, struck a chord with Arab Nationalism, beginning to emerge in response to the British and French occupation of much of North Africa and the Levant and the settlement of Jews in Palestine. It was easy for the Nationalists to interpret the Michaudist vision of western forces returning to complete a work of enlightenment as evidence that Europe, having lost the first round in the crusades, had embarked on another. The idea of a continuing western assault on the Arab world by the heirs of morally and culturally inferior crusaders featured in Arab writings between the World Wars and was given additional edge in the 1940s by what was seen to be complicity in the creation of the state of Israel on the very ground occupied by the "crusader" kingdom of Jerusalem. Twenty years later the Islamists, who rejected much of the rest of Arab Nationalism, began to take over and globalize this package.

It is notable that the West has not tried to counter their historical vision, in spite of the fact that it is obviously a distortion of reality. As co-heirs of the traditions that originated in the writings of Michaud and Scott, most westerners seem to regard crusading in much the same light, with the difference that they are ashamed of it rather than defiant. And, suffering from collective amnesia with respect to crusading in general and its association with imperialism in particular, they do not know what the Islamist *jihadis* are talking about. According to George W Bush, one of the demands of the "war on terrorism" is that every nation has to "prove" its loyalty to the US, or suffer the consequences.

It is clear that one of the "results" which Bush is demanding from "moderate Arabs" is to show their ability to politicise the Islamic faith. This will "prove" they are not terrorists in return for which the administration of George W Bush will supposedly help them remain in power.

No sooner said, no sooner done. The brother of the former King of Jordan was showcased on *Larry King Live* to quote a verse from the *Qu'ran* that he and King declared proved that Islam is against terrorism and upholds the view of tolerance which is compatible with "western civilised values". Conversely, what the Western powers call Islamic fundamentalism is portrayed as uncivilised. Demonstrations in countries such as Nigeria or Pakistan against the US aggression against Afghanistan are called "fanaticism". Newspaper headlines said "religious riots" are taking place.

The Anglo-American politicised notion of tolerance is that minorities within a society and whole nations and countries within the world are to be tolerated so long as they accept the Anglo-American values and institutions and serve them. In this way they prove they are "fit to govern". It has nothing whatsoever to do with Islam, the Islamic development, traditions or conceptions they give rise to. Creating a demand worldwide where people of Islamic faith have to take a defensive posture by "proving" that Islam is compatible with the Anglo-American imperialist notion of tolerance will not do. Why should the 1.3 billion people who are said to espouse the Islamic faith have to "prove" their "loyalty" to these arrogant big powers?

Secularism and Tolerance

The necessity to oppose the Anglo-American definitions of "secularism" and "tolerance" cannot be overestimated given the manner in which the world is being taken to the brink of war over "values". They are used to justify imposing Anglo-American institutions onto the entire world. It was on this basis that the British used the policy of "divide and rule" on the Indian subcontinent and fomented devastating communal massacres, creating the modern states of India, Pakistan and others. The rights of nations, nationalities and tribal peoples were trampled underfoot by politicising language rights and religious affairs amongst other things. The states in the Middle East were created in a similar fashion. Terrible consequences have been the result which must be addressed today if further tragedies are to be averted. There is a blackmail not to oppose the Western conception of "secularism" and "tolerance" for fear of being accused of communalism or terrorism. But the Anglo-American notion of secularism *is* communalism just as the conception of "tolerance" is a form of racism.

Both sanction state-organised racist attacks and state-terror and must be opposed. Similarly, all suggestions that Islamic Republics are medieval because they do not recognise the separation of Church and State and which condemn them on the basis of Eurocentric prejudices and considerations are purely for purposes of intimidating progressive people and stopping them from participating in the anti-imperialist struggle on one hand, and in the struggle for the renewal of their own societies by affirming their own right to conscience and their right to their own way of life, on the other. Looking at the Islamic experience from the angle of European experience which mandated the separation of Church and State within concrete historical circumstances will not do.

Institutionalised Christianity has plagued humankind since the time of the Crusades and throughout the middle Ages. It was institutionalised Christianity which imposed church dogma on the peoples of Europe and kept them in ignorance, not Islam. It is institutionalised Christianity which has been the refuge of all reactionary ruling circles since the Crusades, not Islam. Furthermore, to even suggest that in the United States or Britain there is a separation of Church and State is to not listen to the manner in which this "war on terrorism" is being waged. The reactionary forces which have come to the forefront in the US are pushing a version of

Christian fundamentalism seen in the manner in which the "war on terrorism" is being portrayed in a messianic fashion against "the forces of evil". What purpose will it serve to take what Islam stands for completely out of context of the historical development which was and is completely different to the development of what is called Western civilisation?

Islam has given rise to very concrete beliefs, traditions and customs, many brought forth to solve very definite problems of the societies which gave rise to it or espoused it and others because of an inability to do so. Needless to say this human experience is very different to the one which arose in the European context. If Islam is to be discussed and its contributions appreciated and if it is to be helpful to the peoples of Islamic belief and of the entire world in providing today's problems with solutions, it must be on its own terms and on the terms of the experience and problems which the people from these countries and the world experience. Islam like everything else in the world needs renovation, but not on the basis of the western experience, let alone Anglo-American imperialist "Western values" given the status of "universal values". The pressure on people who espouse the Islamic faith is very great.

This is a period of reaction, of counter-revolution, of retrogression in which the US imperialists are fighting to impose their hegemony over the entire world. Their demand for adherence to Anglo-American imperialist values and institutions is reactionary. The Islamic world is retaliating against the pressure exercised by Christian fundamentalism or what are called Western values or the values of the civilised world and the Anglo-American economic and political agenda. Far from criminalising such attempts to work out their own way of life, these attempts should be supported and provided with the kind of guidance and theory they require. To defend Islam on its own terms is a necessary task today. All attempts to defend Islam on the basis of considerations which George W Bush and the like consider to be "civilised values" should be rejected with all the contempt they deserve. There is no need for human beings, no matter what their beliefs, to be apologetic. All human beings and their beliefs are valid and only Hitlerites will argue otherwise. When Osama bin Laden and his followers refer, as they often do, to crusades and crusaders, they are not using language loosely. They are expressing a historical vision, an article of faith that has helped to provide moral justification for the actions of both Arab nationalists and radical Islamists.

It originated over a century ago, when the Turkish sultan and Sunni caliph, Abdulhamid II, publicized his conviction that the European powers, who had seized much of his territory and had engineered the "liberation" of other parts of his empire, had embarked on a new "crusade." In using this term, he was echoing romantic nonsense that had been washing around Europe, where many writers compared contemporary colonialism to crusading. But his language was taken up by the pan-Islamic press; the first Muslim history of the crusading movement, published in 1899, drew attention to the fact that "our most glorious sultan, Abdulhamid II, has rightly remarked that Europe is now carrying out a crusade against us in the form of a political campaign." Up to this point, Muslims had looked back on the crusades with indifference and complacency. They felt that they had beaten the crusaders comprehensively, driving them from the Levant and occupying far more territory in the Balkans than the Westerners had ever held in Palestine and Syria. But as they began to take an interest in the historical parallels between contemporary and medieval Christian-Muslim interaction, they were confronted with Western rhetoric portraying contemporary empire builders as quasi-crusaders returning to complete the work their ancestors had begun.

It was easy to gloss this with the view that Europe, having lost the first round in the crusades, had embarked on another. This struck a chord in Arab nationalism, which was beginning to emerge in response to the British and French occupations of much of North Africa and the Levant, and the settlement of Jews in Palestine. Even before the First World War an Arab author, warning against the threat posed by Zionist settlement, had taken as a *nom de plume* the name of Saladin, who was being adopted as a model counter-crusader. A university named after Saladin was opened in Jerusalem in 1915, and as early as 1920 he was praised for thwarting the *first* European attempt to subdue the East. In 1934 a writer maintained that "the west is still waging crusading wars against Islam under the guise of political and economic imperialism." By the 1950s the creation of the state of Israel, established on the very ground occupied by the crusader kingdom of Jerusalem, was being portrayed as an act of vengeful malice. The Lebanese novelist Mahmoud Darwish, referring to the invasion of Lebanon by the Israelis in 1982, described them as "leftover crusaders" and their siege of Beirut as "revenge for all medieval history."

Since the 1970s Arab nationalism has been challenged by pan-Islamism, an ideology enshrining the unity of all Muslims dedicated to the worship of one God. Islamists anathematize the nationalists, but they have adopted their view of crusading, even though the Islamists recognize its ideological base, and have globalized it. Nationalists, on the other hand, see crusading as colonialist avarice masked by religion, and their vision underwrites an Arab struggle for freedom from colonial oppression. The Islamists maintain that the term "crusading" can be applied to any offensive — including a drive for economic or political hegemony — against Islam anywhere by Christians, and to any aggressive action by their surrogates, like Zionists (which is why the terms "European Crusading" and "Jewish Crusading" are interchangeable), or even Marxists. Indeed, "international Zionism" and "international Communism" are ideologies employed by the imperialism of the outside world to mask its "crusaderism." This explains why Mehmet Ali Agha, the

Turk who tried to assassinate the Pope in 1981, could refer to John Paul II as "the supreme commander of the crusades."

Osama bin Laden's militant wing of Islamism is also inspired by a theory of jihad that demands turning inwards to purge Islam of infidels and heretics, renewing individual spirituality and creating a united, triumphant society dedicated to God. This is why Osama appears to be so emotional about infidel penetration, which, he believes, defiles Islam and particularly its holy places:

> Our lord, the people of the cross had come with their horses (soldiers) and occupied the land of the two Holy Places (Mecca and Medina) and the Zionist Jews fiddle as they wish with the al-Aqsa mosque.
>
> The Arabian Peninsula has never — since Allah made it flat, created its desert, and encircled it with seas — been stormed by any forces like the crusader armies, spreading in it like locusts, eating its riches and wiping out its plantations.... For over seven years the United States has been occupying the lands of Islam in the holiest of places, the Arabian Peninsula, plundering its riches, dictating to its rulers, humiliating its people, terrorizing its neighbors, and turning its bases in the Peninsula into a spearhead through which to fight the neighboring Muslim peoples. To be found fighting under the sign of the cross are not only Christians, but also their surrogates, Jews, Marxists and secularists. And Afghanistan has been for decades a theatre of crusading warfare in a world-wide conflict.
>
> This is a battle of Muslims against the global crusaders....God, who provided us with his support and kept us steadfast until the Soviet Union was defeated, is able to provide us once more with his support to defeat America on the same land and with the same people. In a war of civilizations, our goal is for our nation to unite in the face of the Christian crusade...This is a recurring war. The original crusade brought Richard (Lionheart) from Britain,

Louis from France and Barbarossa from Germany. Today the crusading countries rushed as soon as Bush raised the cross. They accepted the rule of the cross. It is this radical vision of crusade history which has suddenly and spectacularly forced itself on the outside world. Although merely a fantasy to the West, it finds expression in many Muslim societies. It is said that in mosques in Egypt, the word "crusader" has become a synonym for "Christian." In Indonesia last year, local preachers were referring to the dead at Bali in the same terms.

We are therefore confronted by a dangerous view of the past and of the present, moral as well as historical, shared by both Arab nationalists and Islamists. It has been spreading for a century and nothing has been done to counter it. Indeed, over and over again, in words and deeds, Westerners have thoughtlessly reinforced many Muslims' belief in it. Christianity has been on the defensive against Islam almost from Islam's very beginning. From medieval Muslim aggression to present-day aggression in America, Sudan, Armenia, Malaysia, Indonesia, etc., *jihad* (in the sense of "holy war"; the word itself simply means "struggle") is an historical and extant Islamic reality. Samuel Huntington, in his flawed but interesting book "The Clash of Civilizations", says:

"Violence also occurs between Muslims, on the one hand, and Orthodox Serbs in the Balkans, Jews in Israel, Hindus in India, Buddhists in Burma and Catholics in the Philippines. Islam has bloody borders."

Paul Fregosi writes in "Jihad":

The story begins around 650 C.E. with the first, unsuccessful siege of Constantinople, and continues with the invasion and occupation, sometimes for hundreds of years, of many European countries. Italy, Sicily, Portugal, France, Spain, Austria, Bosnia, Serbia, Croatia, Hungary, Rumania, Wallachia, Albania, Moldavia, Bulgaria, Greece, Armenia, Georgia, Poland, the Ukraine, and eastern and southern Russia were all battlefields where Islam conquered or was conquered in violent conflicts marked by cruelty, bloodlust, and a fearful loss of life, spread over considerably more than a thousand years. For over a century and a half the world had forgotten this fact, since most Muslim countries were politically impotent and ruled mainly as the colonies or protectorates of European powers.

European history has remained transfixed on the Christian Crusades of the eleventh to the thirteenth century, it has largely ignored these Muslim attacks and invasions...When accusing the West of imperialism, and Muslims are obsessed with the crusades, but have forgotten their own longer and more gruesome Jihad. The Crusades were a series of *defensive* wars against Islamic aggression in the Middle Ages and attempts to recapture the Holy Land from Muslim conquerors in order to allow safe pilgrimage and to protect and maintain the Christian presence there.

Jerusalem had been Christian for hundreds of years when Caliph Omar seized it, and following that victory, Muslims warred their way into Egypt, other parts of Africa, Spain, Sicily, and Greece, leaving Christians dead and churches in ruins. They stole lands in the area now known as Turkey, destroying Catholic communities founded by St. Paul himself. They seized Constantinople — the "second Rome" — and threatened the Balkans. They warred their way as far north as Vienna, Austria and Tours, France.

Referring to a battle which took place in A.D. 1243, the Arabian manuscript entitled *Essulouk li Mariset il Muluk* ("The Road to Knowledge of the Return of Kings") had this to say:

When they [Muslims] had despoiled all the country near to Damascus, they advanced to Jerusalem, took it by storm, and put all the Christians to the sword. The women and girls, having suffered every insult from a brutal disorderly soldiery, were loaded with chains. They destroyed the church of the Holy Sepulcher; and when they found nothing among the living, to glut their rage, they opened the tombs of the Christians, took out the bodies, and burnt them.

Not too shocking considering the Qu'ran teaches:

Q.9: 29"Fight those who believe neither in Allah nor the Last Day, nor hold that forbidden which hath been forbidden by Allah and His Messenger, nor acknowledge the religion of Truth, even if they are of the People of the Book [Jews and Christians, until they pay the Jizya with willing submission, and feel themselves subdued."

And Surah 47:4: "When ye meet the unbelievers, smite at their necks" and Surah 4:74: "To him who fighteth in the cause of Allah" [whether he is slain or gets victory] "soon shall we give him a reward of great value."

In other words, Christians are to "convert, submit, or die". The Hadith (in Abu Huraira) tells us the "prophet" said, "I have been ordered to fight with the people till they say, 'None has the right to be worshipped but Allah,' and whoever says, 'None has the right to be worshipped but Allah,' his life and property will be saved by me except for Islamic law, and his accounts will be with Allah, (either to punish him or to forgive him.)" OK, so why does the typical Westerner shiver when thinking of the Crusades? Why are Catholics hated for *defending* Christendom? For the same reasons Christians of all kinds, Protestant or Catholic, are hated in our increasingly secularized world: "I have given them thy word; and the world hath hated them, because they are not of the world, even as I am not of the world." (John 17:14) Christianity and its virtues have been under attack since the time of Christ and even more so since the so-called "Enlightenment."

After centuries of attacks on the Catholic Church in "Reformation" circles and the later, consequent rise of secular humanism, moral and cultural relativism, and Marxist political correctness, the Crusades came to be seen and taught as an example of "Western Imperialism" or "Colonialism." Because members of the Church were doing the fighting, Christianity itself (and Catholicism in particular) was slandered as a cause of war. Note how the same people who scream about the Crusades tend to be those who scream about "religion" in general as being at the root of wars, ignoring the fact that atheistic communism and pagan Nazism killed *hundreds of millions* in the 20th century alone. All this understood, it must be said that the Popes' noble, reasonable purposes for the war, however, became entangled with the purposes of those with secular interests and more interested in dynastic feuds, economic concerns over Mediterranean trade, or destroying the Eastern Roman Empire.

Many "bad guys" jumped onto the Crusade bandwagon and evil *was* done by some of the Crusaders: the sacking of Constantinople (including the destruction of churches) and the murder of Jews along Crusade routes most definitely took place and are deeply lamentable. There is *no excuse* for such behaviors except human evil, but this evil was not sanctioned in any way by the Church, in no way reflects on Church teachings or her purposes for the Crusades, and resulted in the excommunication of many Crusaders responsible.

Timeline of the Islamic Crusades

Truth about Islamic Imperialism

Historical facts say that Islam has been imperialistic—and would still like to be, if only for religious reasons. Muslim propagandists, for example, would like to impose Islamic law around the world. Historical facts say that Islam, including Muhammad, launched their own Crusades against Christianity long before the European Crusades. Today, Muslim polemicists and missionaries, who believe that Islam is the best religion in the world, claim that the West has stolen Islamic lands and that the West (alone) is imperialistic; they seem to imply that these lands have existed in the hands of Muslims since time immemorial, perhaps all the way back to Adam and Eve.

One hardliner Muslim emailed to me said about the developed West and the undeveloped Islamic countries: "You stole our lands" and then he held his finger on the exclamation key to produce a long string of them. Thus, *imperialism*, a word that has reached metaphysical levels and that is supposed to stop all debates and answer all questions, explains why Islamic countries have not kept up with the West. The emailer did not look inwardly, as if his own culture and religion may play a role. Instead, it is always the West's fault. Westerners—even academics—accept the notion that the West alone was aggressive. It seems that Islam is always innocent and passive. It is difficult to uncover the source of this western self-loathing. It is, however, a pathology that seems to strike Westerners more than other people around the globe. This anti-West pathology shows up in Westerners' hatred for the European Crusades in the Medieval Age.

It must be admitted that there is much to dislike about the European Crusades. If it is contrasted with the mission and ministry of Jesus and the first generations of Christians, then the Crusades do not look so good. But did the Europeans launch the first Crusade in a mindless and bloodthirsty and irrational way, or were there more pressing reasons? Were they the only ones to be militant? The purpose of this chapter is not to justify or defend European Crusades, but to explain them, in part—though scholarship can go a long way to defend and justify them. The word "crusade" (derived from the Latin word for "cross") in an Islamic context means a holy war or jihad. It is used as a counterweight to the Muslim accusation that only the Europeans launched crusades.

Muslims seem to forget that they had their own, for several centuries before the Europeans launched theirs as a defense against the Islamic expansion. This partial timeline spans up to the first European response to Islamic imperialism, when Pope Urban II launches his own Crusade in 1095. The timeline mostly stays within the parameters of the Greater Middle East. The data in bold print are of special interest for revealing early Islamic atrocities, their belief in heroism in warfare, or politics today. The Islamic Crusades were very successful. The Byzantines and Persian Empires had worn themselves out with fighting, so they created a power vacuum.

Into this vacuum stormed Islam. After the timeline, two questions are posed, which are answered at length.

The Timeline

630 Two years before Muhammad's death of a fever, he launches the Tabuk Crusades, in which he led 30,000 jihadists against the Byzantine Christians. He had heard a report that a huge army had amassed to attack Arabia, but the report turned out to be a false rumor. The Byzantine army never materialized. He turned around and went home, but not before extracting "agreements" from northern tribes. They could enjoy the "privilege" of living under Islamic "protection" (read: not be attacked by Islam), if they paid a tax. This tax sets the stage for Muhammad's and the later Caliphs' policies. If the attacked city or region did not want to convert to Islam, then they paid a *jizya* tax. If they converted, then they paid a *zakat* tax. Either way, money flowed back to the Islamic treasury in Arabia or to the local Muslim governor.

632-634. Under the Caliphate of Abu Bakr the Muslim Crusaders reconquer and sometimes conquer for the first time the polytheists of Arabia. These Arab polytheists had to convert to Islam or die. They did not have the choice of remaining in their faith and paying a tax. Islam does not allow for religious freedom.

633. The Muslim Crusaders, led by Khalid al-Walid, a superior but bloodthirsty military commander, whom Muhammad nicknamed the Sword of Allah for his ferocity in battle (Tabari, 8:158 / 1616-17), conquer the city of Ullays along the Euphrates River (in today's Iraq). Khalid captures and beheads so many that a nearby canal, into which the blood flowed, was called Blood Canal (Tabari 11:24 / 2034-35).

634. At the Battle of Yarmuk in Syria the Muslim Crusaders defeat the Byzantines. Today Osama bin Laden draws inspiration from the defeat, and especially from an anecdote about Khalid al-Walid. In Khalid's day an unnamed Muslim remarks: "The Romans are so numerous

and the Muslims so few." To this Khalid retorts: "How few are the Romans, and how many the Muslims! Armies become numerous only with victory and few only with defeat, not by the number of men. By God, I would love it . . . if the enemy were twice as many" (Tabari, 11:94 / 2095). Osama bin Laden quotes Khalid and says that his fighters love death more than we in the West love life. This philosophy of death probably comes from a verse like Sura 2:96. Muhammad assesses the Jews: "[Prophet], you are sure to find them [the Jews] clinging to life more eagerly than any other people, even polytheists" (MAS Abdel Haleem, *The Qur'an*, Oxford UP, 2004; first insertion in brackets is Haleem's; the second mine).

634-644. The Caliphate of Umar ibn al-Khattab, who is regarded as particularly brutal.

635. Muslim Crusaders besiege and conquer of Damascus.

636. Muslim Crusaders defeat Byzantines decisively at Battle of Yarmuk.

637. Muslim Crusaders conquer Iraq at the Battle of al-Qadisiyyah (some date it in 635 or 636).

638. Muslim Crusaders conquer and annex Jerusalem, taking it from the Byzantines.

638-650. Muslim Crusaders conquer Iran, except along Caspian Sea.

639-642. Muslim Crusaders conquer Egypt.

641. Muslim Crusaders control Syria and Palestine.

643-707. Muslim Crusaders conquer North Africa.

644. Caliph Umar is assassinated by a Persian prisoner of war; Uthman ibn Affan is elected third Caliph, who is regarded by many Muslims as gentler than Umar.

644-650. Muslim Crusaders conquer Cyprus, Tripoli in North Africa, and establish Islamic rule in Iran, Afghanistan, and Sind.

656. Caliph Uthman is assassinated by disgruntled Muslim soldiers; Ali ibn Abi Talib, son-in-law and cousin to Muhammad, who married the prophet's daughter Fatima through his first wife Khadija, is set up as Caliph.

656. Battle of the Camel, in which Aisha, Muhammad's wife, leads a rebellion against Ali for not avenging Uthman's assassination. Ali's partisans win.

657. Battle of Siffin between Ali and Muslim governor of Jerusalem, arbitration goes against Ali

661. Murder of Ali by an extremist; Ali's supporters acclaim his son Hasan as next Caliph, but he comes to an agreement with Muawiyyah I and retires to Medina.

661-680. The Caliphate of Muawiyyah I. He founds Umayyid dynasty and moves capital from Medina to Damascus

673-678. Arabs besiege Constantinople, capital of Byzantine Empire

680. Massacre of Hussein (Muhammad's grandson), his family, and his supporters in Karbala, Iraq.

691. Dome of the Rock is completed in Jerusalem, only six decades after Muhammad's death.

705. Abd al-Malik restores Umayyad rule.

710-713. Muslim Crusaders conquer the lower Indus Valley.

711-713. Muslim Crusaders conquer Spain and impose the kingdom of Andalus. They seem to believe that the land belonged to them in the first place.

719. Cordova, Spain, becomes seat of Arab governorship.

732. The Muslim Crusaders are stopped at the Battle of Poitiers; that is, Franks (France) halt Arab advance.

749. The Abbasids conquer Kufah and overthrow Umayyids.

756. Foundation of Umayyid emirate in Cordova, Spain, setting up an independent kingdom from Abbasids.

762. Foundation of Baghdad

785. Foundation of the Great Mosque of Cordova

789. Rise of Idrisid emirs (Muslim Crusaders) in Morocco; foundation of Fez; Christoforos, a Muslim who converted to Christianity, is executed.

800. Autonomous Aghlabid dynasty (Muslim Crusaders) in Tunisia.

807. Caliph Harun al-Rashid orders the destruction of non-Muslim prayer houses and of the Church of Mary Magdalene in Jerusalem.

809. Aghlabids (Muslim Crusaders) conquer Sardinia, Italy.

813. Christians in Palestine are attacked; many flee the country.

831. Muslim Crusaders capture of Palermo, Italy; raids in Southern Italy.

850. Caliph al-Matawakkil orders the destruction of non-Muslim houses of prayer.

855. Revolts of the Christians of Hims (Syria)

837-901. Aghlabids (Muslim Crusaders) conquer Sicily; raid Corsica, Italy, France.

869-883. Revolt of black slaves in Iraq

909. Rise of the Fatimid Caliphate in Tunisia; these Muslim Crusaders occupy Sicily, Sardinia.

928-969. Byzantine military revival, they retake old territories, such as Cyprus (964) and Tarsus (969).

937. The Ikhshid, a particularly harsh Muslim ruler, writes to Emperor Romanus, boasting of his control over the holy places.

937. The Church of the Resurrection (known as Church of Holy Sepulcher in Latin West) is burned down by Muslims; more churches in Jerusalem are attacked.

960. Conversions of Qarakhanid Turks to Islam

966. Anti-Christian riots in Jerusalem

969. Fatimids (Muslim Crusaders) conquer Egypt and found Cairo.

c. 970. Seljuks enter conquered Islamic territories from the East.

973. Israel and southern Syria are again conquered by the Fatimids.

1003. First persecutions by al-Hakim; the Church of St. Mark in Fustat, Egypt, is destroyed.

1009. Destruction of the Church of the Resurrection by al-Hakim

1012. Beginning of al-Hakim's oppressive decrees against Jews and Christians

1015. Earthquake in Palestine; the dome of the Rock collapses.

1031. Collapse of Umayyid Caliphate and establishment of 15 minor independent dynasties throughout Muslim Andalus

1048. Reconstruction of the Church of the Resurrection completed

1050. Creation of Almoravid (Muslim Crusaders) movement in Mauretania; Almoravids (also known as Murabitun) are coalition of western Saharan Berbers; followers of Islam, focusing on the Quran, the hadith, and Maliki law.

1055. Seljuk Prince Tughrul enters Baghdad, consolidation of the Seljuk Sultanate.

1055. Confiscation of property of Church of the Resurrec-tion

1071. Battle of Manzikert, Seljuk Turks (Muslim Crusaders) defeat Byzantines and occupy much of Anatolia.

1071. Turks (Muslim Crusaders) invade Palestine.

1073. Conquest of Jerusalem by Turks (Muslim Crusaders)

1075. Seljuks (Muslim Crusaders) capture Nicea (Iznik) and make it their capital in Anatolia.

1076. Almoravids (Muslim Crusaders) conquer western Ghana.

1085. Toledo is taken back by Christian armies.

1086. Almoravids (Muslim Crusaders) send help to Andalus, Battle of Zallaca.

1090-1091. Almoravids (Muslim Crusaders) occupy all of Andalus except Saragossa and Balearic Islands.

1094. Byzantine Emperor Alexius Comnenus I ask western Christendom for help against Seljuk invasions of his territory; Seljuks are Muslim Turkish family of eastern origins.

1095. Pope Urban II preaches first Crusade; they capture Jerusalem in 1099

So it is only after all of the Islamic aggressive invasions that western Christendom launches its first Crusades. It could be argued that sometimes the Byzantine and western European leaders did not behave exemplarily, so a timeline on that subject could be developed. And sometimes the Muslims behaved exemplarily. Both are true. However, the goal of this timeline is to balance out the picture more clearly. Many people regard Islam as an innocent victim, and the Byzantines and Europeans as bullies. This hardly reflects historical reality as the multitude of aggressive Muslim military campaigns listed above show.

Moreover, we should take a step back and look at the big picture. If Islam had stayed in Arabia and had not waged wars of conquest, then no troubles would have erupted. But the truth is this: Islam moved aggressively during the

Caliphates of Abu Bakr and Umar in the seventh century, with other Caliphs continuing well beyond that; only then did the western Europeans react substantively. Finally, it must be noted that Islamic expansion continues until well into the seventeenth century. For example, the Muslims Crusaders conquer Constantinople in 1453 and unsuccessfully besiege Vienna for the second time in 1683 (earlier in 1529). By the seventeenth and eighteenth centuries, the Islamic Crusades receded, due to western resistance. Since that time until the present, Islamic civilization has not advanced very far. Two questions are posed and then answered at length.

Besides following Muhammad, why else did the Muslims launch their Crusades out of Arabia in the first place? It is only natural to ask why Islam launched its own Crusades long before Christendom did. In the complicated Muslim Crusades that lasted several centuries before the European Crusades, it is difficult to come up with a grand single theory as to what launched these Crusades. Because of this difficulty, we let three scholars and two eyewitness participants analyze the motives of the early Islamic Crusades.

World Religious Conquest

Muslim polemicists like Sayyid Qutb assert that Islam's mission is to correct the injustices of the world. What he has in mind is that if Islam does not control a society, then injustice dominates it, ipso facto. But if Islam dominates it, then justice rules it (*In the Shade of the Qur'an*, vol. 7, pp. 8-15). Islam is expansionist and must conquer the whole world to express Allah's perfect will on this planet, so Qutb and millions of other Muslims believe.

"Unruly" Energies in Arabia

Karen Armstrong, a former nun and well-spoken, prolific author and apologist for Islam, comes up short of a satisfactory justification for the Muslim Crusades:

Once [Abu Bakr] crushed the rebellion [against Islamic rule within Arabia], Abu Bakr may well have decided to alleviate internal tensions by employing the unruly energies within the ummah [Muslim community] against external foes. Whatever the case, in 633 Muslim armies began a new series of campaigns in Persia, Syria and Iraq.

Armstrong also notes that the "external foes" to Islam in Arabia in 633 are the Persians and the Byzantines, but they are too exhausted after years of fighting each other to pose a serious threat to Islam. Therefore, it moved into a "power vacuum," unprovoked (Armstrong, p. 227). She simply does not know with certainty why Muslims marched northward out of Arabia.

Religion, Economy, and Political Control

Fred M. Donner, the dean of historians specializing in the early Islamic conquests, cites three large factors for the Islamic Crusades. First, the ideological message of Islam itself triggered the Muslim ruling elite simply to follow Muhammad and his conquests; Islam had a divinely ordained mission to conquer in the name of Allah. The second factor is economic. The ruling elite "wanted to expand the political boundaries of the new state in order to secure even more fully than before the trans-Arab commerce they had plied for a century or more".

The final factor is political control. The rulers wanted to maintain their top place in the new political hierarchy by having aggressive Arab tribes migrate into newly conquered territories. This notion of "aggressive Arab tribes" supports Armstrong's observation. Thus, these reasons have nothing to do with just wars of self-defense. Early Islam was merely being aggressive without sufficient provocation from the surrounding Byzantine and Persian Empires.

Sheer Thrill of Conquest and Martyrdom

Khalid al-Walid, a bloodthirsty but superior commander of the Muslim armies at the time, also answers the question as to why the Muslims stormed out of Arabia, in his terms of surrender set down to the governor of al-Hirah, a city along the Euphrates River in Iraq. He is sent to call people to Islam or pay a "protection" tax for the "privilege" of living under Islamic rule (read: not to be attacked again) as dhimmis or second-class citizens. Says Khalid:

"I call you to God and to Islam. If you respond to the call, you are Muslims: You obtain the benefits they enjoy and take up the responsibilities they bear. If you refuse then, [you must pay] the jizyah. If you refuse the jizyah, I will bring against you tribes of people who are more eager for death than you are for life. We will fight you until God decides between us and you."

Thus, according to Khalid, religion is early Islam's primary motive (though not the only one) of conquering people.

In a short sermon, Abu Bakr says:

. . . Indeed, the reward in God's book for jihad in God's path is something for which a Muslim should love to be singled out, by which God saved [people] from humiliation, and through which He has bestowed nobility in this world and the next.

Thus, the Caliph repeats the Quran's trade of this life for the next, in an economic bargain and in the context of jihad (cf. Suras 4:74; 9:111 and 61:10-13). This offer of martyrdom, agreeing with Donner's first factor, religious motivation, is enough to get young Muslims to sign up for and to launch their Crusades out of Arabia in the seventh century.

Khalid also says that if some do not convert or pay the tax, then they must fight an army that loves death as other people love life.

Improvement of Life over that in Arabia

But improvement of life materially must be included in this not-so-holy call. When Khalid perceived that his Muslim

Crusaders desired to return to Arabia, he pointed out how luscious the land of the Persians was:

"Do you not regard [your] food like a dusty gulch? By God, if struggle for God's sake and calling [people] to God were not required of us, and there were no consideration except our livelihood, the wise opinion would [still] have been to strike this countryside until we possess it". . . . (Tabari 11:20 / 2031)

Khalid was from Mecca. At the time of this "motivational" speech, the Empire of Persia included Iraq, and this is where Khalid is warring. Besides his religious goal of Islamizing its inhabitants by warfare, Khalid's goal is to "possess" the land. Like Pope Urban II in 1095 exhorting the Medieval Crusaders to war against the Muslim "infidels" for the first time, in response to Muslim aggression that had been going on for centuries. Abu Bakr gives his own speech in 634, exhorting Muslims to war against the "infidels," though he is not as long-winded as the Pope. Muslim polemicists believe that Islam spread militarily by a miracle from Allah. However, these five earth-bound reasons explain things more clearly.

Historical facts demonstrate that most of the conquered cities and regions accepted the last of three options that were enforced by the later Muslim Crusaders: (1) fight and die, (2) convert and pay the zakat tax; (3) keep their Biblical faith and pay the jizya tax. Most preferred to remain in their own religion. However, people eventually converted. After all, Islamic lands are called such for a reason—or many reasons. Why? Four Muslim polemicists whitewash the reasons people converted, so their scholarship is suspect.

The Polemical Answer

First, Malise Ruthven and Azim Nanji use the Quran to explain later historical facts: "Islam expanded by conquest and conversion. Although it was sometimes said that the faith of Islam was spread by the sword, the two are not the same. The Qur'an states unequivocally, 'There is no compulsion in religion' (Sura 2:256)." (*Historical Atlas of Islam*, Cambridge, Mass: Harvard, 2004, 30). According to them, the Quran says there should be no compulsion, so the historical facts conform to a sacred text. This shaky reasoning is analyzed, below, under "historical facts." Next, David Dakake also references Sura 2:256, and defines compulsion very narrowly. Jihad has been misrepresented as forcing Jews, Christians, and other peoples of the Middle East, Asia and Africa to convert to Islam "on pain of death."

Finally, Qutb, also citing Sura 2:256, is even more categorical: "Never in its history did Islam compel a single human being to change his faith" (*In the Shade of the Qur'an*, vol. 8, p. 307). This is absurd on its face, and it only demonstrates the tendentiousness of Islamic scholarship, which must be challenged at every turn here in the West. It is a sad fact that this sort of "reasoning" and "critical thinking" permeates polemical Muslim "scholarship."

Historical Facts

But history does not follow Scriptures because people do not. Did the vast majority of conquered peoples make such fine distinctions, even if a general amnesty were granted to People of the Book? Maybe a few diehards did, but the majority? Most people at this time did not know how to read or could barely read, so when they saw a Muslim army outside their gates, why would they not convert, even if eventually? To Ruthven's and Nanji's credit, they come up with other reasons to convert besides the sword, such as people's fatigue with church squabbles, a few doctrinal similarities, simplicity of the conversion process, a desire to enter the ranks of the new ruling elite, and so on. But using the Quran to interpret later facts paints the history of Islam into a corner of an unrealistically high standard.

This misguided connection between Scripture and later historical facts does not hold together. Revelations or ideals should not run roughshod over later historical facts, as if all followers obey their Scriptures perfectly. To his credit, Ibn Khaldun (1332-1406), late medieval statesman, jurist, historian, and scholar, has enough integrity and candor to balance out these four Muslim apologists, writing a history that is still admired by historians today. He states the obvious:

> In the Muslim community, the holy war is a religious duty, because of the universalism of the Muslim mission and (the obligation to) convert everybody to Islam either by persuasion or by force.

When the Islamic Crusaders go out to conquer, carrying an Islamic banner inscribed in Arabic of the glory and the truth of their prophet, Ibn Khaldun would not deny that the army's mission, besides the material reasons of conquest, is to convert the inhabitants. Islam is a "universalizing" religion, and if its converts enter its fold either by persuasion or force, then that is the nature of Islam. Moreover, Ibn Khaldun explains why a dynasty rarely establishes itself firmly in lands of many different tribes and groups. But it can be done after a long time and employing the following tactics, as seen in the Maghrib (N and NW Africa) from the beginning of Islam to Ibn Khaldun's own time:

> The first (Muslim) victory over them and the European Christians (in the Maghrib) was of no avail. They continued to rebel and apostatized time after time. The Muslims massacred many of them. After the Muslim religion had been established among them, they went on revolting and seceding, and they adopted dissident religious opinions many times. They remained disobedient and unmanageable . . . . Therefore, it has taken the Arabs a long time to establish their dynasty in the . . . Maghrib.

Though European Crusaders may have been sincere, they wandered off from the origins of Christianity when they slashed and burned and forced conversions. Jesus never used violence; neither did he call his disciples to use it. Given this historical fact, it is only natural that the New Testament would never endorse violence to spread the word of the true God. Textual reality matches historical reality. In contrast, Muslims who slashed and burned and forced conversions did not wander off from the origins of Islam, but followed it closely. It is a plain and unpleasant historical fact that in the ten years that Muhammad lived in Medina (622-632), he either sent out or went out on seventy-four raids, expeditions, or full-scale wars, which range from small assassination hit squads to the Tabuk Crusade, described above.

Sometimes the expeditions did not result in violence, but a Muslim army always lurked in the background. Later on, Muhammad could exact a terrible vengeance on an individual or tribe that double-crossed him. These ten years did not know long stretches of peace. Therefore, it is only natural that the Quran would be filled with references to jihad and qital, the latter word meaning only fighting, killing, warring, and slaughtering. Textual reality matches historical reality. But this means that the Church had to fight back or be swallowed up by an aggressive religion over the centuries. Thus, the Church did not go out and conquer in a mindless, bloodthirsty, and irrational way—though the Christian Crusades were far from perfect. Islam was the aggressor in its own Crusades, long before the Europeans responded with their own.

3

Islam the House of War

The world is divided into the House of Islam and the House of War, the *Dar al-Islam* and the *Dar al-harb*. The *Dar al-Islam* is all those lands in which a Muslim government rules and the Holy Law of Islam prevails. Non-Muslims may live there on Muslim sufferance. The outside world, which has not yet been subjugated, is called the "House of War," and strictly speaking a perpetual state of *jihad*, of holy war, is imposed by the law. The law also provided that the *jihad* might be interrupted by truces as and when appropriate. In fact, the periods of peace and war were not vastly different from those which existed between the Christian states of Europe for most of European history. The law thus divides unbelievers theologically into those who have a book and profess what Islam recognizes as a divine religion and those who do not; politically into *dhimmis*, those who have accepted the supremacy of the Muslim state and the primacy of the Muslims, and *harbis*, the denizens of the *Dar al-harb*, the House of War, who remain outside the Islamic frontier, and with whom therefore there is in principle, a canonically obligatory perpetual state of war until the whole world is either converted or subjugated.

Down the many centuries, Muslims have seen themselves inhabiting the Dar al-Islam, and in this exclusive House of Islam they are to have their way in all matters great and small. Conquest delivered into their hands the unbelievers of many lands, and these were offered terms: death for the recalcitrant, and for the rest either conversion to Islam, or the status of dhimmi, that is to say, they were deprived of the rights of Muslims and subjected to special taxation, inferiority in law courts, restrictions on worship, residence and dress, and other social disadvantages. Persians, Berbers, and Kurds were among those choosing to convert, so that today they are almost entirely Muslim while still retaining their national and cultural identity. Jews and Christian communities, such as the Chaldeans in Iraq or the Copts in Egypt, became dhimmis. Meanwhile, unbelievers in unconquered countries were said to be living in the Dar al-Harb, the House of War, a phrase indicating that one day they too would be obliged by force of arms to choose between death, conversion, and dhimmitude.

Pryce-Jones's essay perfectly complements Daniel Pipes's column "Cartoons and Islamic Imperialism" on the cartoon intifada. (via Power line) The key issue at stake in the battle over the 12 Danish cartoons of the Muslim prophet Muhammad is this: Will the West stand up for its customs and mores, including freedom of speech, or will Muslims impose their way of life on the West? Ultimately, there is no compromise: Westerners will either retain their civilization, including the right to insult and blaspheme, or not. More specifically, will Westerners accede to a double standard by which Muslims are free to insult Judaism, Christianity, Hinduism, and Buddhism, while Muhammad, Islam, and Muslims enjoy immunity from insults? Muslims routinely publish cartoons far more offensive than the Danish ones. Are they entitled to dish it out while being insulated from similar indignities? The deeper issue here, however, is not Muslim hypocrisy but Islamic supremacism. The Danish editor who published the cartoons, Flemming Rose, explained that if Muslims insist "that I, as a non-Muslim, should submit to their taboos...they're asking for my submission."

Different divisions of the world have existed in Islamic religion and culture. Some are geo-political divisions that are derived from non-Qu'ranic traditions in Islamic culture. These conventions delineate several divisions of the world called "Houses" or "Dar". Other geographic divisions of the world are described in the Qur'an. *Dar al-Islam* is an Islamic term used by Muslim scholars to refer to those countries where Muslims can practice their religion freely. In the orthodox tradition of Islam, the world is divided into two components: *dar al-Islam,* the *house of Islam* and *dar al-Harb,* the house of war.

The two requirements for a country to be part of the *Dar al-Islam* are according to the founder of this concept, Abu Hanifa, the following two:

Muslims must be able to enjoy peace and security with and within this country.

It has common frontiers with some Muslim countries.

If the former does not apply then physical means such as *Jihad* can be used to correct the situation and in the latter case, individuals are required to do hijra to where they can practice their religion. Muslim scholars maintain that the labeling of a country or place as being a part of *Dar al-Islam* revolves around the question of religious security. This means that if a Muslim practices Islam freely in his place of abode despite that the place happens to be secular or un-Islamic, then he will be considered as living in the *Dar al-Islam.*

Dar al-Salam

Dar al-Islam is also known and referred to as Dar al-Salam, or house/abode of Peace.

The term appears in the Qur'an in 6.127 as a name of Paradise.

Dar al-Harb

Dar al-Harb is a term classically referring to those countries where the Muslim law is not in force, in the matter of worship and the protection of the faithful and Dhimmis. The term refers to the relationship between an Islamic state and neighbouring non-Muslim states with whom it has not signed a peace treaty or pact. In Reliance of the Traveller, point w43.2, a hadith is referred to containing the exact word Dar al-Harb. Scholars have, nevertheless, disagreed on its reliability as is commented in Reliance of the Traveller.

Dar al-Kufr

Dar al-Kufr is a term used by Muhammad to refer to the Quraish-dominated society of Mecca between his flight to Medina and his triumphant return. For much of Islamic history, the preferred term used to describe non-Islamic societies has been dar al-Harb, emphasizing various Islamic countries' aspirations to conquer such territories and render them part of dar al-Islam. A traditional Arabic saying attributed to Muhammad goes: "Unbelief is one community", or in other words, "infidels are of one nation", expressing the view that distinctions between different types of non-Muslims are insignificant in relation to the overriding distinction between Muslim and non-Muslim.

Other Ideological Perceptions and International Relations

Dar al-Hudna

Dar al Hudna (Arabic: *"house of calm"*): The land of non-believers currently under a truce, which is a respite between wars. A truce is bought by tribute by harbis. If the harbis refuse to pay tribute in exchange for the truce, hostilities are resumed. Furthermore, only treaties that conform to Islamic prescriptions are valid; if these conditions are not fulfilled, the treaty is worthless.

Dar al-'Ahd

Dar al-'Ahd was invented to describe the Ottoman Empire's relationship with its Christian tributary states. The invention of Dar al-Ahd was necessary, as the worldview prevalent at the time did not allow for a protracted peace with non-Muslim states, even those under Muslim domination. Today, the term refers to those non-Muslim governments which have armistice or peace agreements with Muslim governments. The actual status of the non-Muslim country in question may vary from acknowledged equality to tributary states.

Dar al-Dawa

Dar al-Dawa is a term used to describe a region where the religion of Islam has recently been introduced. Since the population had not been exposed to Islam before, they may not fit into the traditional definition of dar al-Harb. On the other hand, as the region is not yet Muslim, it cannot be dar al-Islam either. The most frequent use of the term *dar al-Dawa* is to describe Arabia before and during the life of Muhammad commonly referred as *Jahiliyyah period,* era of ignorance of divine guidance.s

More recently, the term *dar al-Dawa* has been proposed by Western Muslim philosophers to describe the status of Muslims in the West. The term *dar al-Dawa* may be used in conjunction with, or in opposition to, the older terms *dar al-Islam* and *dar al-Harb,* from which it is derived, or simply be seen as just another sub-category of dar al-harb.

Dar al-Amn

Dar al-Amn is a term proposed by Western Muslim philosophers to describe the status of Muslims either in the West or other non-Muslim societies. The term *dar al-Amn* may be used in conjunction with, or in opposition to, the older terms *dar al-Islam* and *dar al-Harb,* from which it is derived.

Fundamental Islam

"Fundamentalism" is a word that came from the heart of the Christian religion. It means faith that goes by the word of the Bible. Fundamental Christianity, or going with the Bible, does not mean going around and killing people. There is no fundamental Islam. There is only Islam full stop. The question is how the Qur'an is interpreted.

All of a sudden we see that the greatest interpreters of Islam are politicians in the western world. They know better than all the speakers in the mosques, all those who deliver terrible sermons against anything that is either Christian or Jewish. These western politicians know that there is good Islam and bad Islam. They know even how to differentiate between the two, except that none of them know how to read a word of Arabic.

You see, so much is covered by politically correct language that, in fact, the truth has been lost. For example, when we speak about Islam in the west, we try to use our own language and terminology. We speak about Islam in terms of democracy and fundamentalism, in terms of parliamentarism and all kinds of terms, which we take from our own dictionary. One of my professors and one of the greatest orientalists in the world says that doing this is like a cricket reporter describing a cricket game in baseball terms. We cannot use for one culture or civilization the language of another. For Islam, you've got to use the language of Islam.

Let me explain the principles that are driving the religion of Islam. Of course, every Muslim has to acknowledge the fact that there is only one God. But it's not enough to say that there is only one God. A Muslim has to acknowledge the fact that there is one God and Mohammed is his prophet. These are the fundamentals of the religion that without them, one cannot be a Muslim. But beyond that, Islam is a civilization. It is a religion that gave first and foremost a wide and unique legal system that engulfs the individual, society and nations with rules of behaviour. If you are Muslim, you have to behave according to the rules of Islam which are set down in the Qur'an and which are very different than the teachings of the Bible.

The Essence of Islam

Now let's move to the essence of Islam. Islam was born with the idea that it should rule the world. Let's look, then, at the difference between these three religions. Judaism speaks about national salvation - namely that at the end of the story, when the world becomes a better place, Israel will be in its own land, ruled by its own king and serving God. Christianity speaks about the idea that every single person in the world can be saved from his sings, while Islam speaks about ruling the world. I can quote here in Arabic, but there is no point in quoting Arabic, so let me quote a verse in English. "Allah sent Mohammed with the true religion so that it should rule over all the religions."

The idea, then, is not that the whole world would become a Muslim world at this time, but that the whole world would be subdued under the rule of Islam. When the Islamic empire was established in 634 AD, within seven years - 640 - the core of the empire was created. The rules that were taken from the Qur'an and from the tradition that was ascribed to the prophet Mohammed were translated into a real legal system. Jews and Christians could live under Islam provided they paid poll tax and accepted Islamic superiority. Of course, they had to be humiliated. And Jews and Christians living under Islam are humiliated to this very day.

Mohammed did accept the existence of all the Biblical prophets before him. However he also said that all these prophets were Muslims. Abraham was a Muslim. In fact, Adam himself was the first Muslim. Isaac and Jacob and David and Solomon and Moses and Jesus were all Muslims, and all of them had writings similar to the Qur'an. Therefore, world history is Islamic history because all the heroes of history were Muslims. Furthermore, Muslims accept the fact that each of these prophets brought with him some kind of a revelation. Moses, brought the Taurat, which is the Torah, and Jesus brought the Ingeel, which is the Evangelion or Gospel - namely the New Testament.

The Bible versus the Qur'an

Why then is the Bible not similar to the Qur'an? Mohammed explains that the Jews and Christians forged their books. Had they not been changed and forged, they would have been identical to the Qur'an. But because Christians and Jews do have some truth, Islam concedes that they cannot be completely destroyed by war [for now]. Nevertheless, the laws a very clear - Jews and Christians have no rights whatsoever to independent existence. They can live under Islamic rule provided they keep to the rules that Islam promulgates for them.

Islamic Rule and Jihad

What happens if Jews and Christians don't want to live under the rules of Islam? Then Islam has to fight them and this fighting is called Jihad. Jihad means war against those people who don't want to accept the Islamic superior rule. That's jihad. They may be Jews; they may be Christians; they may be Polytheists. But since we don't have too many Polytheists left, at least not in the Middle East - their war is against the Jews and Christians.

Two Houses

The Qur'an sees the world as divided into two - one part which has come under Islamic rule and one part which is supposed to come under Islamic rule in the future. There is a division of the world which is very clear. Every single person who starts studying Islam knows it. The world is described as Dar al-Islam (the house of Islam) - that's the place where Islam rules - and the other part which is called Dar al-Harb - the house of war. Not the "house of non-Muslims," but the "house of war." It is this house of war which as to be, at the end of time, conquered. The world will continue to be in the house of war until it comes under Islamic rule. This is the norm. Why? Because Allah says it's so in the Qur'an. God has sent Mohammed with the true religion in order that the truth will overcome all other religions.

Islamic Law

Within the Islamic vision of this world, there are rules that govern the lives of the Muslims themselves, and these rules are very strict. In fundamentals, there are no differences between schools of law. However, there are four streams of factions within Islam with differences between them concerning the minutiae of the laws. All over the Islamic world, countries have favored one or another of these schools of laws. The strictest school of law is called Hanbali, mainly coming out of Saudi Arabia. There are no games there, no playing around with the meanings of words. If the Qur'an speaks about war, then it's war.

There are various perspectives in Islam with different interpretations over the centuries. There were good people that were very enlightened in Islam that tried to understand things differently. They even brought traditions from the mouth of the prophet that women and children should not be killed in war. These more liberal streams do exist, but there is one thing that is very important for us to remember. The Hanbali School of law is extremely strict, and today this is the school that is behind most of the terrorist powers. Even if we talk about the existence of other schools of Islamic law, when we're talking about fighting against the Jews, or fighting against the Christian world led by America, it is the Hanbali School of law that is being followed.

Islam and Territory

This civilization created one very important, fundamental rule about territory. Any territory that comes under Islamic rule cannot be de-Islamized. Even if at one time or another, the [non-Muslim] enemy takes over the territory that was under Islamic rule, it is considered to be perpetually Islamic. This is why whenever you hear about the Arab/Israeli conflict, you hear - territory, territory, territory. There are other aspects to the conflict, but territory is highly important. The Christian civilization has not only been seen as a religious opponent, but as a dam stopping Islam from achieving its final goal for which it was created.

Islam was created to be the army of God, the army of Allah. Every single Muslim is a soldier in this army. Every single Muslim that dies in fighting for the spread of Islam is a *shaheed* (martyr) no matter how he dies, because - and this is very important - this is an eternal word between the two civilizations. It's not a war that stops. This was is there because it was created by Allah. Islam must be the ruler. This is a war that will not end.

Islam and Peace

Peace in Islam can exist only within the Islamic world; peace can only be between Muslim and Muslim. With the non-Muslim world or non-Muslim opponents, there can be only one solution - a cease fire until Muslims can gain more power. It is an eternal war until the end of days. Peace can only come if the Islamic side wins. The two civilizations can only have periods of cease-fires. And this idea of cease-fire is based on a very important historical precedent, which, incidentally, Yasser Arafat referred to when he spoke in Johannesburg after he signed the Oslo agreement with Israel.

Let me remind you that the document speaks of peace - you wouldn't believe that you are reading! You would think that you were reading some science fiction piece. I mean when you read it, you can't believe that this was signed by Israelis who are actually acquainted with Islamic policies and civilization. A few weeks after the Oslo agreement was signed, Arafat went to Johannesburg, and in a mosque there he made a speech in which he apologized, saying, "Do you think I signed something with the Jews which is contrary to the rules of Islam?" (I have obtained a copy of Arafat's recorded speech so I heard it from his own mouth.) Arafat continued, "That's not so. I'm doing exactly what the prophet Mohammed did."

Whatever the prophet is supposed have done becomes a precedent. What Arafat was saying was, "Remember the story of Hodaybiya." The prophet had made an agreement there with the tribe of Kuraish for 10 years. But then he trained 10,000 soldiers and within two years marched on their city of Mecca. He, of course, found some kind of pretext. Thus, in Islamic jurisdiction, it became a legal precedent which states that you are only allowed to make peace for a maximum of 10 years. Secondly, at the first instance that you are able, you must renew the jihad [thus breaking the "peace" agreement].

In Israel, it has taken over 50 years in this country for our people to understand that they cannot speak about [permanent] peace with Muslims. It will take another 50 years for the western world to understand that they have got a state of war with the Islamic civilization that is virile and strong. This should be understood: When we talk about war and peace, we are not talking in Belgium, French, English, or German terms. We are talking about war and peace in Islamic terms.

Cease-fire as a Tactical Choice

What makes Islam accept cease-fire? Only one thing - when the enemy is too strong. It is a tactical choice. Sometimes, he may have to agree to a cease-fire in the most humiliating conditions. It's allowed because Mohammed accepted a cease-fire under humiliating conditions. That's what Arafat said to them in Johannesburg. When western policy makers hear these things, they answer, "What are you talking about? You are in the Middle Ages. You don't understand the mechanisms of politics."

Which mechanisms of politics? There are no mechanisms of politics where power is. And I want to tell you one thing - we haven't seen the end of it, because the minute a radical Muslim power has atomic, chemical or biological weapons, they will use it. I have no doubt about that. Now, since we face war and we know that we cannot get more than an impermanent cease-fire, one has to ask himself what is the major component of an Israeli/Arab cease-fire. It is that the Islamic side is weak and your side is strong. The relations between Israel and the Arab world in the last 50 years since the establishment of our State have been based only on this idea, the deterrent power.

The reason that we have what we have in Yugoslavia and other places is because Islam succeeded into entering these countries. Wherever you have Islam, you will have war. It grows out of the attitude of Islamic civilization. What are the poor people in the Philippines being killed for? What's happening between Pakistan and India?

Islamic Infiltration

Furthermore, there is another fact that must be remembered. The Islamic world has not only the attitude of open war, but there's also war by infiltration. One of the things which the western world is not paying enough attention to is the tremendous growth of Islamic power in the western world. What happened in America and the Twin Towers is not something that came from the outside. And if America doesn't wake up, one day the Americans will find themselves in a chemical war and most likely in an atomic war - inside the U.S.

It is highly important to understand how a civilization sees the end of days. In Christianity and in Judaism, we know exactly what the vision of the end of days is. In Judaism, it is going to be as in Isaiah - peace between nations, not just one nation, but between all nations. People will not have any more need for weapons and nature will be changed - a beautiful end of days and the kingdom of God on earth. Christianity goes as far as Revelation to see a day that Satan himself is obliterated. There are no more powers of evil. That's the vision.

The Jews will no longer exist, because before the coming of the end of days, there is going to be a war against the Jews where all Jews should be killed. I'm quoting now from the heart of Islamic tradition, from the books that are read by every child in school. They Jews will all be killed. They'll be running away and they'll be hiding behind trees and rocks, and on that day Allah will give mouths to the rocks and trees and they will say, "Oh Muslim come here, there is a Jew behind me, kill him." Without this, the end of days cannot come. This is a fundamental of Islam.

The question which we in Israel are asking ourselves is what will happen to our country? Is there a possibility to end this dance of war? The answer is, "No. Not in the foreseeable future." What we can do is reach a situation where for a few years we may have relative quiet. But for Islam, the establishment of the state of Israel was a reverse of Islamic history. First, Islamic territory was taken away from Islam by Jews. You know by now that this can never be accepted, not even one meter. So everyone who thinks Tel Aviv is safe is making a grave mistake. Territory which at one time was dominated by Islamic rule, now has become non-Muslim who are independent of Islamic rule; Jews have created their own independent state. It is anathema. And (this is the worse) Israel, a non-Muslim state, is ruling over Muslims. It is unthinkable that non-Muslims should rule over Muslims.

Few people know that in Islam, the world is divided into Dar al-Harb and Dar al-Islam.

Dar al-Islam literally means the House of Peace which is all the lands conquered and subjugated by Islam. Dar al-Harb literally means the House of War which is all the lands currently not conquered by Islam. Islam's chief goal is to eventually conquer and subjugate all the lands of Dar al-Harb into one territory called Dar al-Islam. Only after all people and all lands of the world have been conquered and have submitted to Islam is there to be "peace" in the world. Since the very birth of Islam fourteen hundred years ago, it has set out to conquer the world by the sword. The Prophet's death came while attempting to kill and conquer pagans, Christians, and Jews in the Arabian Peninsula. After his followers finished conquering the Peninsula they moved on to conquer the whole of the Middle East. They were well on the way to conquering most of Europe and parts of Asia before they were beaten back during the Crusades.

Islam's momentum slowed quite a bit after the Crusades though it has managed to take parts of India and many countries in the Far East. However, Islam's goal remains: world domination. It was upon the discovery of oil forty years ago in the Peninsula which provided Islam with the financial muscle to restart its quest for a world subjugated under Islam. From the Philippine jungles, through the Iraqi ruins and into the heart of Europe, Islam works to bring down Dar al-Harb. The signs are clear for those who wish to see them:

Islamic armed rebellions, often using terrorist tactics, have sprung all over the World.

Terrorism against the West has continued unabated.

An influence campaign launched against our countries has succeeded in confusing and demoralizing the peoples of Europe and America.

Shari'a-like codes are being adopted and pushed for with more and more frequency.

Muslim immigration and higher birth rate is changing the composition of Europe, and even mentioning this fact is considered taboo.

Discriminatory laws (favouring Muslims) have already been mulled over.

At the same time that Islam is stepping up its military campaigns, the West has been lulled into a deep sleep by a political and social climate which has been steeped in political correctness for the last several decades. It is not polite to criticize or even question religion, as long as it isn't Christianity. We have been taught that all religions are equal, no better or worse, and questions on the subject are immediately shut down. We have further been taught that the West is responsible for the World's problems and, in this upside down universe; the West was the aggressor during the Crusades, not the Muslims. It's in this climate that we accept the oft-repeated mantra "Islam means peace" and "Islam has been hijacked by a small number of extremists" inspired by wahhabism or fundamentalism.

Western Resistance holds that while there may be moderate and peaceful Muslims, Islam itself is violent, supremacist and imperialist. Our objective is to help expose Islam and keep people abreast of current events during the War on Terror. We hope to arm people with knowledge of Islam so they can see past the politically correct version espoused by politicians, community leaders and the media. We stand against political correctness and for truth, and will promote the values which have made Western civilization great, even on a sea of timidity and confusion. We hope you will join us in our journey. We leave you with a quote from John Stuart Mill. May we avert the state he feared:

"War is an ugly thing, but not the ugliest of things. The decayed and degraded state of moral and patriotic feeling which thinks that nothing is worth war is much worse. The person who has nothing for which he is willing to fight, nothing which is more important than his own personal safety, is a miserable creature and has no chance of being free unless made and kept so by the exertions of better men than him."

4

Islam and the West
Discovering America

Muslims in other, m ore organized suburbs had felt the power of zoning when their applications to build mosques and schools had been rejected. So I wasn't surprised to see a building like this — previously used as a warehouse or for small manufacturing — stretching out beside a residential home. I was a little surprised that this is where the women would be spending the night in prayer. The imam ("leader") had a lovely voice. She stood in the middle of the line of women and recited Qur'an from memory. They listened quietly, said "amen" when she finished a passage and followed as she led them in the bowing and prostrating of prayer. Perhaps she was a *hafiz* — one who has memorized the complete scripture. In any case, it was evident that she had memorized at least a significant portion of the Qur'an, and was proficient in the art of recitation. The women were friends from the neighborhood.

All of them had been born in the Middle East or North Africa and had moved to the United States as young adults. Most of the women were in middle age; some taught at the religious school; most were homemakers. They were the kind of women who took pride in their cooking, in helping neighbors, and in maintaining a simple, but welcoming home. Whenever I visit my friend, who had invited me to the gathering when she heard I was in town, she always looks lovely and is ready to serve me homemade soup or bread fresh from the oven. They said they wanted to talk to me about being a Muslim in America. I thought this was a rather odd topic, given the length of time most of these women had been in the country. But they told me they had a hard time talking with people outside their community. They had realized, especially in the last few years that so many Americans have a very negative image of Muslims. They wanted to make themselves better known. They were not interested in giving speeches or going to organized events – they just wanted to have friendlier encounters with the non-Muslim Americans they met in their daily lives. In their experience, this was difficult, and they were convinced that their dress was the main barrier. When these Muslim women, who wear figure-flattering dresses at home, leave the house, they wear a headscarf and a long, loose coat known in Arabic as *jilbab*. This practice of *hijab* – covering one's body in public – is practiced across the Muslim world.

Its origin lies in the Qur'an and in the guidance given by the Prophet Muhammad to his community. *Hijab* is one aspect of a comprehensive system of behaviour practiced by Muslim men and women to support chastity and propriety. Some people interpret the practice of *hijab* as a way to "control women's sexuality," but this is a misunderstanding – or perhaps, an incomplete understanding. Islam requires both men and women to control their sexuality so that intimate relations occur only within marriage. But Islam does not encourage prudity nor does it demean sexuality. Sex is a vital part of marriage – it is an end in itself, not just a means to reproduction. To encourage intimacy in the home, these women change into comfortable but attractive clothes as soon as they return home. To guard this special intimate relationship, *hijab* is worn upon leaving the house. In America, we have been taught, "Don't judge a book by its cover," but as Derrida taught us, the book has no meaning except what we bring to it.

So how do non-Muslim Americans "read" a Muslim woman covered in *hijab*? What meaning do we impart to the "veiled woman"? I fear that it is difficult for many Americans to free themselves of the long sad history of orientalist voyeurism associated with *hijab*. How many books and articles about Islam use these metaphors: "unveiling Islam," "beyond the veil," "behind the veil"? In the veil we see deceit, secrets, double lives but also mystery and exoticism. This spring, *US News and World Report* played on this creepy fascination with a special issue on Islam. Entitled, "Secrets of Islam," the cover featured a close-up of a woman (or is it a man?) with her face and hair clothed in a black veil. The ambiguous gender of the model adds another level of discomfort. Perhaps this is a male terrorist dressing as a woman, or perhaps there is a more sinister aspect to the veiled Muslim woman than we realized. Unfortunately, the politicization of dress in the modern Muslim world also affects our understanding of *hijab*. In Saudi Arabia, Iran and Afghanistan under the Taliban, women were forced to adopt a particular form of dress.

Americans are given little context to understand these events. We may not be aware that these governments have also forced men to adopt certain forms of dress, nor are we aware that in most Muslim majority countries, men and women are free to dress as they like. Many women in these countries choose to observe some form of *hijab* because they believe it to be appropriate public dress. Most Americans are probably also not aware that in certain Muslim majority countries that espouse an extremist form of secularism, women are forbidden from wearing *hijab* in schools, colleges and government institutions. At Hartford Seminary, we have a number of young Turkish women who left their country because they could not continue their studies while wearing a headscarf. All these associations came to mind, as I sat with the women that night in the industrial park outside of Chicago. I acknowledged their observation that *hijab* did present an initial obstacle to connecting for many. Perhaps the most compassionate advise would be to tell the women to change their dress. But why should they have to strip themselves of something so important to them?

After all, these were not just pieces of cloth, but one aspect of a way of interacting in the world that was essential to their sense of self, family and community. So I counseled the woman about ways to engage in small talk and how to use body language to allow others to relax around them. Certainly there would always be some negative reactions, but with patience, confidence and kindness, they should be able to connect to others.

They met every month, spending the day in fasting and the night in prayer. I knew that their prayers were only for the sake of God. They did not care if anyone else knew about the rich spiritual lives they experienced behind the doors of this nondescript building. But I cared. We hear so much about the oppression of Muslim women. Certainly Islam can be used as a source of repression. But this is true of any religion and any value system.

The dominant normative discourse of any society will always be engaged to justify divergent actions and policies. In secular societies, nationalism and patriotism can as easily be used to justify oppression as Islam can be used for this purpose in Muslim societies. But this is not the essence of Islam, nor is oppression the normal experience of Muslim women. Islam is a deep source of spirituality and dignity for many Muslim women. Every place I have travelled in the Muslim world, I find women who have organized themselves to express their sisterhood and develop their own models of religious leadership. Through prayer, fasting, and other rituals of Islam, these women experience the deep joy of connecting with their merciful Creator. We do not need to rip the covers off books to understand what is inside. We can only hope to understand something about a book if we have the humility to realize that it can teach us something new — perhaps even about ourselves.

Islam is derived from the Arabic root *"salama"* which means "surrender, submission, obedience, sincerity" and consequently "being in peace" so in the religious sense Islam means, "being in a state of peace by surrendering to the will of God" and "obedience to His law". Today over a billion Muslims of the world are in a perpetual state of listlessness owing to a tirade of Islam-negative images, discourse, diatribe and stereotypes being directed at them. While the roots of Islam bashing and persecution can be traced back to the times of the Prophet (PBUH), the aftermath of 9/11 certainly saw Islamophobia reaching historic heights. Several reasons account for this disturbing imbroglio including the political policies and ambitions of the western governments, historical encounters between Islam and Christianity and agenda-setting of western media machinery; however, one of the most important factor that has lead to the current chaos and confusion is the absolute lack of understanding and scholarly guidance on what "true" Islam is within the Muslim World itself.

Islam (deen, the way of life) is based on Quran (the Revealed Word of Allah) and Sunnah (the ways of the Prophet). However, a cursory glance at the Muslim World will reveal that the Islam followed or in most cases "enforced" exhibits serious dichotomy and disconnect. Some Muslim countries have officially declared a certain form of Islam as their state religion (and they make sure that their form of Islam is enforced and strictly adhered to), while others have taken a relatively neutral stance. Yet others have declared themselves as secular Muslim countries. Many may regard this as vibrancy and plurality in Islam, but the truth is rather bitter and alarming.

For centuries, the Muslim World has been plagued by a serious dearth of intellectual discourse on Islam and its teachings. While Quran exhorts and encourages man to seek knowledge and learn; to discover himself and his Lord through this knowledge and to utilize the offerings of this universe for his blissful existence, progress and multiplication of his progeny, this trait of "pondering" and "questioning" has been consciously stifled by the pseudo-ulemas and retrogressive governments in the Muslim World. This has lead to a consistent decadence and digression of understanding of even the most basic and intrinsic Islamic principles. Similarly a mullah can be found in every mosque at every end of a street but they hardly ever do anything more than delivering war-mongering sermons on Fridays or bickering over frivolous issues like the length of the beard or the way the *takbeer* should be observed.

Borne out of this intellectual decadence and taking advantage of the void thus created, emerged a radicalized, extremist group, who took upon itself the task of "Islamizing" the Muslim society and representing (rather *misrepresenting*) the true Islam. This group loosely includes the *Taliban, Al-Qaeda* operatives, militants, *mullahs,* maulvis and their ilk whose philosophy today poses the greatest threat to the Muslim World. Their version of Islam has no Islamic authentication, their faith has no god to worship and their humanness has no humanity. They only serve to malign, defame and insult Islam. They brazenly and shamelessly use Islam to fulfill their personal and political ambitions. They are not religiously inspired, they are politically motivated. They employ religious symbolism of paradise and martyrdom to allure young minds to fulfill their destructive agendas.

Jihad is not suicide bombing, blowing up of innocent, unarmed worshippers in a mosque or killing of people who leave homes in the morning in search of livelihood; it is a pious practice of striving in the way of Allah by various means (*Jihad al-Nafs, Jihad al-Lisan, Jihad al-Yad, Jihad as-Sayf*). Similarly, women in Islam are not meant to be oppressed, mistreated and forced within the confines of their homes without providing for their physical, mental and psychological wellbeing; rather Islam empowers and encourages women to realize their true potential and lead their lives with dignity and self-respect within the parameters laid down in Islam. So burning down of girls' schools in Matta or other areas, public whipping of a young girl in Swat without ascertaining her sin, burning and closing down of barber shops and CD outlets have no precedence in Islam. It is due to this extremist and irrational behaviour that images of armed bearded men chanting and sloganeering, flogging and whipping, killing and beheading, burning and rioting are constantly splashed across the western media.

It is imperative to state that it is certainly the duty of Muslims to preach Islam to the non-believers so that truth may be distinguished from the falsehood. After that, whosoever wishes to embrace Islam may do so and whoever wishes to continue upon un-Islamic belief may do so. But under no circumstances can people be violently threatened or forced to conform to Islamic faith. Decisive evidence in this regard is the following ayah:

"Let there be no compulsion in religion; Truth has been made

Clear from error. Whoever rejects false worship and believes in

Allah has grasped the most trustworthy handhold that never breaks.

And Allah hears and knows all things." (Surah Al Baqarah: 256)

The Prophet (PBUH) spread Islam by being a practical example for the followers. He never exhibited violent behaviour even in the face of the most atrocious and barbaric cruelties directed at him and his followers. The state of Madinah was one of the most peaceful and tolerant societies the world has seen and yet these so-called forbearers of Islam "choose" to revive Islamic values not by peaceful means but violent, abhorrent devastation. Immediate corrective measures need to be taken at individual, intellectual, societal and government levels to redeem the situation. Extremism, radicalization and ultra-conservatism might push the world to the brink of "clash of civilizations" in addition to polarizing the Muslim society. The entire Muslim World needs to step back and go through a phase of introspection, self-analysis and self-realization before it even begins to counter the external threats directed at it. It needs to get in touch with the true meaning of Islam.

This can be done at the individual and collective level by ending the monopolization and "ownership" of Islam from the diktats of the faux *maulvis*, mullahs and the pseudo-scholars. The Muslim governments must end their official endorsements of a certain form of Islam and allow for open discussion, discourse and dialogue aimed at promoting and enhancing better understanding Islam and its philosophy. Every Muslim must strive to gain knowledge, read and understand Quran and Sunnah and endeavor to lead his life according to the true teachings of Islam. Islam is a religion of peace, tolerance, harmony and co-existence. Therein lays the true spirit and essence of Islam. "Islam," wrote George Bernard Shaw, "is the best religion and Muslims are the worst followers." It is about time the followers take heed and prove him wrong.

The Bible and the Qur'an

The Bible consists of two parts: The Old Testament, which is essentially the Torah (representing about 80% of the bible), and The New Testament, which is essentially four books each, is a different version but essentially the same document. This is the foundation of the Judeo-Christian world. The Bible in its format (joining the Old Testament with the New Testament) forms the legitimacy of the Judeo-Christian world. The Qur'an is a stand-alone document and is believed to be the last word of God to mankind and that it includes all God's previous revelations. In fact, a close reading of the old & new testaments reveals that there are many stories, concepts, admonitions, rulings and even sentences that are revealed word-for-word in the holy Qur'an.

The challenge to the American Muslims: The link between Judaism and Christianity is made permanent by putting their two sources together signifying one continuing history and sources. The question to the Muslims is: How Can we build a bridge to tie Judaism and Christianity with Islam to achieve a greater vision for America: The Judeo-Christian-Islamic America?

Prophet Abraham in the Bible and the Qur'an (Ibrahim)

Prophet Abraham (Ibrahim) is looked upon as the Patriarch of all prophets (The Father of all Prophets – Abu Al-Anbiyaa as revealed in the Qur'an.) Some Judeo-Christian revelations look at him as a patriarch not as a prophet. In Islam he is a prophet of God and was a Muslim; a submitter of his will to that of God. He was the first to popularize the concept of 'One God'.

Marriage, Wives and Children

In the Judeo-Christian tradition it is believed that he married the noble Sarah and later on married their servant/ slave Hagar. He had two children: Isaac from Sarah and Ishmael from Hager. In the Judeo-Christian teachings the roles of Sarah, Isaac and their off springs are heavily emphasized while that of Ishmael is very much ignored. Some schools of thought in the Judeo-Christian tradition believe that Ishmael was the illegitimate son of a slave and some right wing fanatics think that Ishmael is the anti-God. In fact Mr. Pat Robertson on his 700 Club TV program mentioned that Islam is the religion of the slaves because their original mother was Hagar!

In Islam, the emphasis is not placed on the ethnicity, genealogy, and family tree but rather on one's deeds and belief in God. So, you may find Muslims whose ancestry can be traced back to Abraham's son Isaac or Ishmael. That is because not all Muslims are Arabs (the off springs of Ishmael), while Prophet Muhammad was. In Islam it is believed that when Prophet Abraham did not get a child after his long marriage to Sarah, he married a humble wife Sarah who gave him his first child Ismail (Ishmael.) The story of Ismail's delivery is well documented and is relived every year during the Safa/Marwa part of the hajj experience. Then Sarah delivered to Abraham his second son Isaac (Is'haaq.)

The Sacrifice of Abraham's Son:

Who was the son that was to be sacrificed?

In the Judeo-Christian Tradition: It is believed that the son that Abraham attempted to sacrifice was Isaac.

In Islam, it is believed that the son was Ishmael (Ismail.)

Location of the Sacrifice Event:

In the Judeo-Christian Tradition: It is believed that the sacrifice was attempted at the top of mount "Moriah." That is; the mount where the tree of "Morr" (meaning bitter in Arabic) grows. This tree produced bitter fruits that were also used for perfume. These trees grow at the top of the mount where the Dome of the Rock is built today in Jerusalem.

In Islam, it is widely believed that the sacrifice event was attempted at the foothill of mount Arafat (an important foundation for Hajj) but there is a minority story that talks about mount Marwah (the Safa and Marwah.)

The question that needs research is: is there a possibility that Morriah and Marwah got confused and hence the general location difference between the Judea-Christian story (Jerusalem) and the Islamic story (Makkah.)

Building of the Temple (God's Sacred House of Worship):

In the Judeo- Christian story we find that all stays silent after Abraham's attempted sacrifice, then the successions of Prophets Jacob (or Prophet Israel), King David (believed to be Prophet David in Islam) and King Solomon (again believed to be Prophet Solomon in Islam.) Then we read that "King" David, who was successful in wiping out the anti-God citizens (the Philistines), and is believed to be the first founder of a nation of the Hebrews, attempted to build the temple in commemorations of Abraham's attempted sacrifice of his son Isaac and God's revelation to him. The chief Rabbis refused because David's hands, as stated by them, were full of blood. The task was given to "King" Solomon. It is believed by the Judeo-Christians that he built the first temple. It is described to be a stunning memorial in lavishness and structure.

In Islam, it is believed that the "Temple", called the Ka'baa (the cubical structure), in Makkah, was built immediately after Prophet Abraham passed the greatest of all tests; i.e. the offering of his own son – the most valuable asset he had – to God. It was Prophets Abraham and Ismail (Ishmael) who built this humble building to be the first ever masjid (Temple in Judeo-Christian language) ever built to worship God in the history of the world. Now, regarding King Solomon and the building of the Temple, the Islamic story as revealed in the Qur'an details the palace of the Queen of Sheba, which most likely is the Temple that the Judeo-Christian story talks about.

It is believed that fundamental research is needed to document and research these important historic events hoping that this will lead to our goal of a true Judeo-Christian-Islamic America.

Jerusalem and the Building of the Temple

The First Temple Period

Abraham's journey through what is called by the Gospel the Land of Jacob or the Land of Israel, and in particular his presence on Mount Moriah, consecrate the ground and impact it with national symbolism. The Book of Judges – the Bible – describes the early day people of Judaism as rebellious and troublesome, squabbling amongst them. Internal strife makes them vulnerable to the ever-growing military threat posed by the Philistines in the south.

Essentially, the primary purpose of the monarchy to manage the affairs of the "Land of Jacob/Israel" is to build and maintain the Temple on Mount Moriah. This is in commemoration of the attempted Sacrifice of Isaac (or Isma'il) by his father Prophet Abraham. The Temple was perceived, as a home for God and its construction was to mark the achievement of maturity of the Biblical child – Israel.

The two qualities, which define stable monarchy in the Bible, are:

The King must come from the tribe of Judah.

The capital city chosen by the king must be the city of Jerusalem.

City of David

David ruled his tribe of Judah from the city of Al-Khalil (Hebron). His achievement was the reversal of the unstable and archaic situation described in the Book of Judges. David began his campaign against the Philistines, inflicting the infamous lethal blow to Goliath's forehead with the slingshot. He is believed to have united the tribes of Israel.

City of Jerusalem

The city of Jerusalem was built at the foot of Mount Moriah (the tree of Morr or bitter fruits & was used as source of perfume in ancient times and it grows in Jerusalem); though David was never permitted to build the Temple. He was a soldier whose hands were stained by the blood of war. The construction of the Temple was privileged for a man of peace. That is why David resolved to pave the way for his son the Wise Solomon to perform the task. By the way, for those who care to know, Solomon as per the Bible married no less than 700 wives and kept 300 concubines. The purpose of this, as reported in Bible Research, was to establish valuable diplomatic contacts and trade ties with the fathers and kin of his wives who were the kings of the neighboring empires. The details of Solomon's temple are described in the Book of Kings. This First Temple was to stand on Mount Moriah for an era of 400 years.

The Decline of Jerusalem in the First Temple period begins with the death of King Solomon:

The Rabbis of the Talmud say that the First Solomonic Temple was destroyed because of the sins of the people. The Jews of Jerusalem were idol worshippers, adulterers and murderers. The Talmud concludes that the unique relationship between God and man was manifested in the form of destroying the city in 586 BCE. The Babylonians and the Assyrians in 600 BCE started their campaign against the city. In 586 BCE the army of Nebuchadnezzar besieged Jerusalem, pounding its fortifications and bringing it to its feet on the 9th of Av (August.) The Temple was destroyed and the city of Jerusalem was burnt to the ground. By the way NOT ONE SINGLE piece of Solomon's Temple was ever excavated. In fact only one artifact of any sort has been found. This is a small clay pomegranate, which is thought, but not for sure to have come from the Temple.

New words were introduced: Zion is Jerusalem. Zion is also mount Zion, the Biblical name of Mount Moriah, the Temple Mount, and the Dome of the Rock or Haram Al-Shareef.

Building the Second Temple in Jerusalem:

The book of Ezra and Nehemiah describes the events, which followed the conquest of Babylon by the Persian King Cyrus. Cyrus, on conquering Babylon issued a declaration permitting all the conquered nations in exile in Babylon to return to their homeland.

As Babylon declined and Persia rose, 70 years of exile come to an end. The Jewish people have their land restored to them but the Jews preferred to remain in Babylon with only a few returning to Zion. Under the leadership of Ezra and Nehemiah, they began building the destroyed city of Jerusalem and ultimately rebuild the Temple. This marks the Second Temple Period. In 332 BCE Alexander the great conquered the whole of the Mediterranean basin including Jerusalem, and shortly after he died. He created cultural homogeny in his empire by exporting the conquering culture, Greek Hellenism, which glorified the power of human physical and intellectual achievement. The Jews after 332 BCE were attracted to the Greek culture. It taught the Jews to worship themselves, to strengthen their bodies and develop their minds. The whole second temple period history of the Jewish people is conducted in the shade of Greek, and later Roman, Hellenistic culture. Jewish society in Jerusalem was bitterly divided over Jewish law, ritual, and politics and the Temple played a significant role in the struggle.

Jewish rebellion against the Romans and the destruction of the Second Temple:

After the death of Herod in CE, the tension between the factions reached the peak. In 66 CE the passion and the tension exploded into an all out rebellion against Rome. The Great Revolt, which lasted from 66 to 73 CE, had disastrous consequences. It brought about the destruction of the Second Temple in the month of Av (August) 70 CE and the total destruction of the upper city of Jerusalem, which burned for over a month. Thousands of Jews were killed in the Revolt and thousands more were taken into Roman captivity. The city of Jerusalem was left in ruins. The pile of rubble, which stood on the Temple Mount – The Dome of The Rock, was pushed aside and in its place a temple of the goddess Aphrodite was built. The vessels of the Temple were carried away in triumph to Rome where an arch, "Titus' Arch", was erected to celebrate and commemorate the victory.

Beginning of the Judeo-Christian Movement

Of all sects in Jerusalem only two, the Pharisees and the Judeo-Christians, managed to survive. The Judeo-Christians broke away from Judaism and established a new faith. Despite the radical difference between the two they both managed to incorporate the memory of the Temple as an integral part of religious life even after its physical destru-ction. In the early period after the destruction, the Judeo-Christians were a small and persecuted Jewish sect. Like the Pharisees, they adopted the policy of preserving the memory of the Temple ritual as a central motif in their religious practice.

The physical temple of Jerusalem was replaced by early Christians with the spiritual Temple of the "Upper" or spiritual Jerusalem. The ultimate sacrifice, which was atoned for all sin was the sacrifice, which Christ made on the cross. The cross became the new alter and Jesus was the last physical sacrifice.

Emergence of Christianity out of the Judeo-Christian Movement

The history of the Judeo-Christian sect as one of the Jewish factions to survive the destruction is a short one. Christianity soon took its leave of Judaism and became a separate faith. In the fourth Century, it was recognized as the official faith of the Byzantines as a result of extensive missionary activity amongst the Pagans of Roman Empire. This marks the departure of the Judeo Christians from Jewish world. Approximately 70 years after the Roman Conquest of Jerusalem, Jews began to anticipate the Messianic redemption. They believed that the master of history who rebuilt the second Temple 70 years after the destruction of the first would build the third! Rabbi Akiva hailed the charismatic military leader Simon Bar Koziva Messiah. He changed his name to Bar Kochba, "son of the star" and appointed him the leader of the Revolt, which was to overthrow Rome, establish Jewish Sate in Jerusalem and build the Temple.

The Revolt lasted from 132 to 135 CE won mass support among the Jews. They succeeded to temporarily terrorize the Roman legions stationed in Judea. They provoked a fiercer Roman counter attack. The Romans killed over 600,000 men, women and children. Rabbi Akiva himself was tortured to death by Emperor Hadrian. The Jewish name of the city; i.e. Jerusalem, was replaced by the Latin name "Aelia Capitolina" and the Jewish people along with their hopes of rebuilding the city were once again left in ruins. During the 4th century the Roman Empire underwent a dramatic change, which was to deeply affect the history of Jerusalem. Constantine the great brought about recognition of Christianity as the official religion of the Roman Byzantine Empire, whose capital was Constantinople. Christians who had spread the faith among the pagans now enjoyed a majority position in that empire. For the first time since the destruction of the second Temple, a people who considered it holy ruled Jerusalem. From the 4th Century on, Christian Byzantine rule precluded Jewish access to the holy city.

Jerusalem under Christian Rule

The physical city where Jesus had preached and spent his last days; the place where he had been tried and crucified; was of no special significance to the early Christians. The city was not a focus.

For pilgrimage and was not specially designated as a place of prayer. On account of Jesus' words the destruction of the Temple was perceived as a punishment for the rejection of Jesus by the Jews. The Temple mount became a deep anti-symbol in Byzantine Christendom. The Temple mount was to be preserved in its pitiful state as a pile of rubble and was to serve as visible testimony to God's punishment of the Jews. In its place the "New Temple" was built on the site of the new sacrifice; that was Jesus on the Cross. The Church of the Holy Sepulcher, which stood on the Mount directly facing the ruins of Herod's Temple, embodied all the holiness and glory, which had once been bestowed on Moriah. The City of Jerusalem now became a symbol of the removal of God's favor from the Jews and its inheritance by those who adhere to the Christian faith.

Christian pilgrims came from all over the empire to visit the Holy sites and to pray in the Church of the Holy Sepulcher. Jews were now granted access to the city only on one day of the year. On the 9th day of Av, the day when Jews commemorate the destruction of the Temple, they were permitted to enter the city, wearing sackcloth and ashes to mourn their humiliation.

The Christian West and the Islamic East

The "Age of Faith" is the age of the conflict between Christianity and Islam. The world was divided into "Christendom" in the West and the empire of Islam in the East.

Jerusalem in Islam

Islam, the new monotheistic faith, which evolved during the first half of the 7th century, inherited many symbols from its monotheistic predecessors. Among them, the city of Jerusalem was sanctified in Islam as the "Stairway to Heaven." This was the sight where the father Abraham had been tested and where he had been commanded to sacrifice his son, the father of the Arab people Isma'il. It was from here that Prophet Muhammad ascended to heaven and it was here that he received the order to pray. It was on the Temple Mount (Haram Al-Sharif) that Prophet Muhammad prayed with the prophets and it was from the Rock on the top of that mount that he finally ascended to heaven.

In 638 CE, six years after the death of the Prophet Muhammad, the Islamic Defense Forces reached the gates of Byzantine Jerusalem. The city fell and so began a period of Islamic rule, which was to continue almost uninterrupted through the 20th century. In the year 692 (54 years later) Abdul-Malik Ibn Marwan built the Dome of the Rock on the Temple Mount and Moriah was once again reinstated as the focal point of the City. Dome of the Rock (Qubbatul Sakhrah) often (incorrectly called the Masjid of Omar because that is where Omar prayed when he reached it) is more a sanctuary than a mosque and the Caliph Omar did not build it. The Dome stands on the rock on the Temple Mount from which the Prophet ascended to heaven in the night journey (Miraj.) The place is revered by the three Semitic religions and may have been the site of the Holy of the Holies in the temple of Solomon.

As is well known, Jesus, Moses and Solomon are prophets of Islam. It was the Original Prayer Direction

(Qib'lah) of the early Muslims before it was replaced with Makkah. The Temple Mount is often referred to as the third holy place in Islam (Thalithul Haramain) after Makkah and Madinah. The Rock itself is oblong and measures 56 ft by 42 ft (18 by 14 meters.) Below it is a chamber accessible by a stairway where one can pray in a small area set aside for that purpose (this special oratory in addition to the large area on the ground level above.) A crack in the rock, visible from the grotto, is piously explained as having split when the Prophet ascended to Heaven; the rock wished to follow. The cave is called the "Well of Spirits" (Bi'r al Arwa'aah.)

The Haram Shareef Sanctuary stands above the rock with its golden dome that dominates the skyline of old Jerusalem, was built by the Khalifah Abdul-Malik Bin Marwan 72/691. The design is noted for its Byzantine-Syrian motifs. Although Syrian craftsmen built it trained in the Byzantine tradition. It was the first major example of Islamic Architecture, whose more "indigenous" expressions would come later. When the sanctuary was built, a challenger to the Khalifah Abdullah Ibn Al-Zubair was occupying Makkah. The Khalifah Ibn Al-Zubair issued a decree whereby the Dome of the Rock, rather than the Kaa'bah became the goal of the hajj, pilgrimage. The decree was later annulled after the conquest of Makkah but this event demonstrates the sanctity that Islam attaches to the Haram Shareef.

The Dome of the Rock in Judaism (Temple Mount), Christianity (Mount Zion) and Islam (Haram Shareef):

In Judaism, only the High Priest was allowed to walk in the Holies. Since the actual position of the Holy of the Holies is now unknown, Judaism forbids access to the whole area of the Temple Mount. Orthodox Jews observe this prohibition. Sacred history and rabbinical decisions have closed the Temple Mount to the first of the three Semitic religions.

In Christianity the veil of the Temple, which separated the Holy of Holies from the rest of the Temple, was rent in twain at the crucifixion of Jesus, to symbolize the going forth of the Shechina into the world. When the Crusaders controlled Jerusalem, the Knights Templar turned the Dome of the Rock into a church and made it the model for their chapels, or "temples." The only such chapel still extant is in the Templar Castle of Tomar, Portugal, and is the small ancient church of the True Cross (la Iglesia de la Vera Cruz) in Segovia, Spain. The Dome was also the emblem of the seal of the Grand Master of the Order of the Knights Templar. When Al-Nasir Salahuddin (Saladin) recaptured Jerusalem he naturally made the Dome once more into an Islamic shrine. The area around the Dome of the Rock contains a number of minor monuments, which are built by the Ottomans who invested a lot of time, energy and resources in developing Jerusalem. At the other end of the esplanade is the al-Aqsa Mosque.

In Islam, the third and final Semitic religion which, like Christianity, is universal, makes of the Temple Mount the place where man as man, is joined once more to God through the restoration of Adam's relationship to God before the Fall, as expressed in the ascent to heaven of the Prophet; thus it is Islam that restores it as a sanctuary. With Islam in Jerusalem, the destroyed Mountain blossomed with new life as the new Temple, the Muslim Shrine, was built. With a Dome of almost identical proportions to that of the Church of the Holy Sepulcher, the golden top of the shrine on Moriah outshine the silver roof, which stood on Golgotha. The magnificent building, with its 8 walls and gates representing the 8 doors to heaven looked triumphantly on the 6 walled churches, which stood on the facing hill. The Mount, which the Byzantines prophesied would remain in ruins, was now rebuilt and splendid. For the Jews of Jerusalem, this was perhaps something of a victory too.

The War of the Foreigners

The First Crusade

The conquest of Jerusalem by the Muslims of the East in the 11th century was an outrage by the Christian West. The West concluded that it was essential to conquer the city in order to reassert the correct order in God's world. Pope Urban II, who instigated the First Crusade, gave as his primary motive for calling the Crusade the argument that it was inconceivable for the Holy city and the site of the suffering of Our Lord to be held in the hands of the "infidel." He promised atonement of sin and restoration of worldly goods to all men who would answer the call to redeem the city. The response was fanatical. The whole Western Europe was on the move. The force and enthusiasm of this movement united European Christendom. Kings, Dukes and Barons, from England, France and Germany fought side by side against the common enemy. The Catholic Church reached new heights of political power.

Europe, which has been floundering in Barbarism and economic regression, ruralization and despondency, had been given a noble cause. The execution of the Crusade was carried out with passion unprecedented in European history. On the road to Jerusalem, the Crusaders encountered the Jewish communities of the Rhineland. With the same fury and passion with which they left their homes, they massacred the Jewish communities of Mainz and Speyer. The Synagogues of Western Europe were burned down with Jews locked inside them. In 1099 the Crusader armies reached Jerusalem. They pounded at the walls of the besieged city, first burning with fiery arrows the ropes, which coated the walls so as to absorb the blows of the battering rams. They broke through and massacred everyone inside.

The Jews of the city were rounded up into the synagogue and burnt alive. So much blood was split that the rivers of it, which flowed through the city's streets reached the ankles of the horses.

1421: The Year a Chinese Muslim Discovered America

The British submarine engineer and historian Gavin Menzies gave an astounding seminar on March 15, 2002 to the Royal Geographical Society in London, with evidence to support his theory that Zheng He, a Chinese Muslim navigator in the Ming dynasty, beat Columbus by more than 70 years in discovering America. Using evidence from maps drawn dated before Columbus' trip that clearly showed America, and astronomical maps traced back to Zheng He's time, Menzies is confident that the Zheng He should be honored as the first discoverer of America. Menzies's conclusion is based on 14 years of research that includes secret maps, evidence of artifacts, and apparent proof of the voyage provided by the modern astronomy software program Starry Night. As key evidence for a voyage that will remake history, Menzies says he obtained ancient Chinese navigation charts associated with the travels of Zheng He.

The journey ran from 1421 to 1423. Menzies maintains that the ships sailed around the Southern tips of both Africa and South America. The late evening southern sky as it would have looked on March 18, 1421, from off the southern tip of South America. Reconstructed with Starry Night Software to compare with the maps found from Zheng He's voyages. "I set Starry Night up for dates in 1421 for parts of the world where I thought the Chinese had sailed," explained Menzies, a navigation expert and former Royal Navy submarine commander. He found that in two separate locations of the voyage; easily recognizable stars were directly above Zheng He's fleet. Those stars have since moved, due to changes in Earth's orientation in space. Earth's spin is slightly imperfect, and its axis carves a circle on the sky every 26,000 years.

The phenomenon, called precession, means that each pole points to different stars as time progresses. Menzies used the software program to recreate the sky as it would have looked in 1421. "I had Chinese star charts, and I needed to date the charts," he said. "By an incredible bit of luck, one of the courses they steered, between Sumatra and Dondra Head, Ceylon, was due west." This part of the journey was very near the equator in the Indian Ocean. Polaris, the North

Star, and the bright southern star Canopus, which was very nearly above the celestial South Pole, were on the charts. "From that I was able to determine the apparent shift of Polaris (due to precession). I could therefore date the chart to 1421, plus or minus 30 years." Phillip Sadler, a celestial navigation expert at the Harvard-Smithsonian Center for Astrophysics, says the estimation of a map's age based on star positions is possible. He said an estimate within 30 years, as Menzies claims, is possible.

About Zheng He: Zheng He (1371-1435), or Cheng Ho, is China's most famous navigator. He built a total of 1622 ships and made at least seven major excursions between 1405 AD and 1430 AD. He traveled more than 50,000km and visited over 30 countries, reaching Somalia and probably Europe (France, Holland and Portugal). Zheng He constructed many wooden ships, some of which are the largest in the history, in Nanjing. Three of the shipyards still exist today. In each trip, he led a troop of 27,800 people on more than 300 ships. In each trip, 62 major ships of this fleet were employed, each over 400 ft long and 193 ft wide, holding 1000 people per ship, dwarfing Columbus' Santa Maria (75 ft x 25 ft) more than six-fold. In the 1930s, a stone pillar was discovered in a town in Fujian province. It held an inscription that described the amazing voyages of Zheng He.

Zheng He described how the emperor of the Ming Dynasty had ordered him to sail to "the countries beyond the horizon," all the way to the end of the earth." His mission was to display the might of Chinese. The pillar contains the Chinese names for the countries Zheng He visited. He wrote: We have...beheld in the ocean huge waves like mountains rising sky-high, and we have set eyes on barbarian regions far away hidden in a blue transparency of light vapors, while our sails, loftily unfurled like clouds, day and night continued their course rapid like that of a star, transversing the savage waves as if we were treading a public thoroughfare. The countries and territories covered and recorded in the official

Ming history includes Java, Sumatra, Vietnam, Siam, Cambodia, Philippines, Ceylon, Bangladesh, India, Yemen, Arabia, Somalia, Mogadishu.

As a clear demonstration of his travel to Africa, among the souvenirs he brought back to China were the giraffes and lions, indigenous animals of Africa. The official history also mentioned "Franca" (which was the territory to describe today's France and Portugal) and Holland. The Hollanders were described as tall people with red hair and beard, long nose, and deep eye sockets. If he did meet with the Europeans in their native countries, then the only way would be to navigate around the Cape of Good Hope before the Suez Canal was a throughway. Unfortunately, Zheng He's magnificent accomplishment was later targeted by other courtiers as wasteful. Most of his records were destroyed and building of ships with more than three masts was considered crimes punishable by death. So, a large part of his excursion (which might include the America part) has no reports.

In Africa near Kenya today, there are tribes that are clearly Asian-looking. They also consider themselves as the descendants of Zheng He's crew. His achievements show that China had the ships and navigational skills to explore the world. Mysteriously, China did not follow up on these voyages. The Chinese destroyed their ocean going ships and halted further expeditions. Thus, a century later, Europeans would "discover" China, instead of the Chinese "discovering" Europe. China has a very old seafaring tradition. Chinese ships had sailed to India as early as the Han Dynasty. Chinese sailors had an important invention to help them-the compass. The compass, or "south pointing spoon," started out as a fortune-telling instrument used like an Ouija board. By the Song era, sailors had taken it up.

As a foreign ship captain wrote, "In dark, weather they look to the south pointing needle, and use a sounding line to determine the smell and nature of the mud on the sea bottom, and so know where they are. Chinese shipbuilders also developed fore-and-aft sails, the sternpost rudder, and boats with paddlewheels. Watertight compartments below decks kept the ship from sinking. Some boats were armor plated for protection. All these developments made long distance navigation possible. After the Mongols were overthrown in 1368, the emperor of the new Ming Dynasty wanted to assert Chinese power. Because China was no longer part of a land empire that stretched from Asia to Europe, the emperor turned to the sea. He decided to build a navy. The Chinese made elaborate plans that would not be fulfilled for many years. A shipyard was built at the new capital of Najing (Nanking).

Thousand of varnish and tung trees were planted on nearby Purple Mountain to provide wood for shipbuilding. The emperor established a school of foreign languages to train interpreters. While all this was going on, the man who would lead the navy was still an infant. Zheng He was born in 1371 in Kunyang, a town in southwest Yunnan Province. His family, named Ma, were part of a minority group known as the Semur. They originally came from Central Asia and followed the religion of Islam. Both his grandfather and father had made the Muslim pilgrimage to Mecca. Zheng He grew up hearing their accounts of travel through foreign lands. Yunnan was one of the last strongholds of Mongol support, holding out long after the Ming Dynasty began. After Ming armies conquered Yunnan in 1382, Zheng He was taken captive and brought to Nanjing. The eleven year old boy was made a servant of the prince who would become the Yong Le Emperor. It was Yong Le who renamed the boy Zheng He.

Zheng He is described in Chinese historical records as tall and heavy, with "clear-cut features and long ear lobes; a stride like a tiger's and voice clear and vibrant." He was well liked and admired for his quick wit in argument. Moreover, he was a brave soldier. When his prince seized the Chinese throne from his nephew, Zheng He fought well on his behalf. As a result, Zheng He became a close confidant of the new emperor and was given an important position at court. The

Yong Le emperor had ambitious plans. A vigorous man, he rebuilt the Great Wall to the condition in which it exists today. He also built his new capital at Beijing, next to the remains of the former Yuan capital. The emperor decided to go ahead with the sea voyages that had long been planned. He appointed Zheng He to lead them and gave him the title "Admiral of the Western Seas." At each country Zheng He visited, he was to present gifts from the emperor and to exact tribute for the glory of the Ming.

The Chinese had a unique view of foreign relations. Because China developed its culture in isolation from other great civilization, it says itself as the center of the world. The Chinese called their country "the Middle Kingdom." The Chinese emperor's duty was to attract "all under heaven" to be civilized in Confucian harmony. When foreign ambassadors came to the Chinese court, they "kowtowed" as they approached the emperor. (The required process of "kowtow" was to kneel three times and bow one's head to the floor three times at each kneeling.) In return for tribute from other countries, the emperor sent gifts and special seals that confirmed their rulers' authority. In fact, these foreign kings were officially made part of the Ming Dynasty. In 1405 Zheng He set out on his first voyage. No nation on earth had ever sent such a fleet onto the ocean. It included sixty-two large ships, some 600 feet long, larger than any other on the seas. Hundreds of smaller vessels accompanied them.

A Chinese historian described them; "The ships which sail the Southern Sea are like houses. When their sails are spread they are like great clouds in the sky." Zheng He's first port of call was in Champa, a part of today's Vietnam. He was surprised to find many Chinese living there. Merchants and craftsmen had emigrated from the coastal provinces since the time of the Tang Dynasty. They had already helped to spread Confucian ideals, and Champs's ruler willingly offered tribute for the Chinese emperor. In return, of course, Zheng He presented the king with lavish gifts that were probably more valuable. Zheng He sailed away from the coast, westward across the Indian Ocean.

The ships traveled for days out of sight of any land. Then they encountered a hurricane. The ships tossed wildly in the fierce storm and seemed to be on the verge of sinking. Then a "divine light" suddenly shone at the tips of the mast. "As soon as this miraculous light appeared, the danger was appeased," Zheng He wrote. When the Chinese sailors reached Calicut, India, their giant ships created a stir. The ruler there presented his visitors with sashes made of gold spun into hair-fine threads and studded with large pearls and precious stones. The Chinese were entertained with music and songs. One crewmember wrote that the Indians' musical instruments were "made of gourds with strings of red copper wire, and the sound and rhythm were pleasant to the ears."

On the way back to China, the fleet threaded its way through the Straits of Malacca, stopping at the large islands of Sumatra and Java. Zheng He established a base at the Straits that he would use for each of his seven voyages. There are thousands of smaller islands in this vast archipelago, and some were pirates' lairs. The pirates preyed on unwary fishermen and small merchant vessels. Zheng He, showing how the emperor treated those who disrupted harmony, attacked and destroyed a fleet of pirate ships. He captured the leader and brought him back to Beijing for execution. When Zheng He returned, the emperor was pleased. He sent his admiral on ever-longer voyages. Seven times, Zheng He's ships set sail for unknown lands. On and on he went, following his orders to travel as far as he could.

He reached Arabia, where he fulfilled a personal dream. He made the pilgrimage to Mecca that is the duty of every good Muslim once in his lifetime. He also visited Prophet Muhammad Mosque in Medina. On the fifth voyage, he reached the coast of Africa, landing in Somalia on the east coast. Zheng He organized each expedition on an enormous scale. Besides sailors and navigators, they included doctors, scribes, shipwrights, and cooks. On some voyages Muslim religious leaders and Buddhist monks were brought along to serve as diplomats in lands where people were Muslim or Buddhist. Each ship brought enough food to last the whole voyage, in case "barbarian" food was not acceptable. In addition to rice and other food that could be preserved, the ships carried huge tubs of earth on deck so that vegetables and fruit could be grown. On each voyage the fleet anchored at the Malacca base, where provisions, tribute, and gifts were stored in warehouses.

Zheng He found that foreign kings and princes particularly admired the famous blue-and-white Ming porcelain dishes, vases, and cups. Foreigners still yearned for Chinese silk, for cotton printed with Chinese designs, and for the coarse but long lasting, brownish yellow cloth known as Nankeen because it was made in Nanking (now Nanjing). The holds of Zheng He's ships were also crammed with gold and silver, iron tools, copper kitchenware, and perfumes. In exchange for such wares, and as tribute, Zheng He brought back medicinal herbs, dyes, spices, precious, gems, pearls, rhinoceros horns, ivory, and exotic animals. On the homeward voyage, the fleet again stopped at their base to sort out the foreign goods and wait for a favorable wind to return to China.

The expeditions were an important source of information about foreign countries. A crewmember described the Nicobar Islands in the Bay of Bengal off the east coast of India: Its inhabitants live in the hollows of trees and caves. Both men and women there go about stark naked, like wild beasts, without a stitch of clothing on them. No rice grows there. The people subsist solely on wild yams, jackfruit and plantains, or upon the fish which they catch. There is a legend current among them that, if they wear the smallest scrap of clothing, their bodies would break into sores and ulcers, owing to their ancestors having been cursed by Buddha for having stolen and hidden his clothes while he was bathing. In Sri Lanka, the Chinese visited Buddhist

Temple Hill, where Buddha was said to have left his footprint on a rock. They marveled at all the temples, particularly one that held a relic of the Buddha's tooth.

According to a crew member, the people of the island do not venture to eat cow's flesh, they merely drink the milk. When a cow dies they bury it. It is capital punishment for anyone to secretly kill a cow; he who does so can however escape punishment by paying a ransom of a cow's head made of solid gold. Sri Lanka seemed like a treasure island, where rubies and other precious stones were abundant. The people harvested pearls from the sea and had discovered the trick of making cultured pearls by planting a speck of sand inside an oyster's shell. The king of Sri Lanka was an ardent Buddhist who treated both cows and elephants with religious respect. However, because he did not show proper respect for the ambassadors from the Son of Heaven, he was taken back to China for "instruction."

He was returned to his island on a later voyage. When the Chinese reached the east coast of Africa, they found people who built houses of brick. "Men and women wear their hair in rolls; when they go out they wear a linen hood. There are deep wells worked by means of cog wheels. Fish are caught in the sea with nets." The Africans offered such goods a "dragon saliva, incense, and golden amber." The Chinese found the African animals even more amazing. There included "lion, gold-spotted leopards, and camel-birds (ostriches), which are six or seven feet tall." The most exciting thing that Zheng He ever brought back to the emperor's count was a giraffe. The animal came from today's Somalia. In the Somali Language, the name for giraffe sounds similar to the Chinese word for unicorn. It was easy to imagine that this was the legendary animal that had played an important part in the birth of Confucius.

Surely, it must be a sign of Heaven's favor on the emperor's reign. When the giraffe arrived in 1415, the emperor himself went to the palace gate to receive it, as well as a "celestial horse" (zebra) and a "celestial stag" (oryx). The palace officials offered congratulations and performed the kowtow before the heavenly animals. When Zheng He came back from his seventh voyage in 1433, he was sixty-two years old. He had accomplished much for China, spreading the glory of the Middle Kingdom to many countries that now sent tribute and ambassadors to the court. Though he died soon afterward, his exploits had won him fame. Plays and novels were written about his voyages. In such places as Malacca and Java, towns, caves, and temples were named after him. However, a new Ming emperor had come to the throne. His scholar-officials criticized Zheng's achievements, complaining about their great expense.

China was now fighting another barbarian enemy on its western borders and needed to devote its resources to that struggle. When a court favorite wanted to continue Zheng He's voyages, he was turned down. To make sure, the court officials destroyed the logs that Zheng He had kept. We know about his voyages only from the pillar and some accounts that his crewmembers wrote. Thus, China abandoned its overseas voyages. It was a fateful decision, for just at that time, Portugal was beginning to send its ships down the west coast of Africa. In the centuries that followed, European explorers would sail to all parts of the world. They would establish colonies in Africa, America, and finally in the nations of East Asia. China would suffer because it had turned its back on exploration.

Zheng He had started the process that might have led the Middle Kingdom to greater glory. Unfortunately the rulers of the Ming Dynasty refused to follow his lead. Zheng He died in the tenth year of the reign of the Ming emperor Xuande (1435) and was buried in the southern outskirts of Bull's Head Hill (Niushou) in Nanjing. In 1985, during the 580th anniversary of Zheng He's voyage, his tomb was restored. The new tomb was built on the site of the original tomb in Nanjing and reconstructed according to the customs of Islamic teachings, as Zheng He was a Muslim. At the entrance to the tomb is a Ming-style structure, which houses the memorial hall. Inside are paintings of the man himself and his navigation maps. To get to the tomb, there are newly laid stone platforms and steps. The stairway consists of 28 stone steps divided into four sections with each section having seven steps. This represents Zheng He's seven journeys to the West. The Arabic words "Allah (God) is great" are inscribed on top of the tomb.

5

Satan and the Soviets

With the collapse of the Soviet Empire and the demise of the cold war, the threat of Communism vanished in a twinkling of an eye. The tearing down of the Berlin Wall is one of the greatest moments in human history. Russia is now so impoverished by the arms race that it will take a long time for its economy to recover. Communism was a religion that was harsh and cruel. It murdered more people than any other ideology in the history of mankind. The atrocities committed in the name of Marx and Lenin can only be compared to Hitler and his Third Reich who fine-tuned mass murder into an art form. In the flush of victory, the West in general and Americans in particular assumed that peace had finally been established on earth. A new world order of peace, prosperity, and unity was just around the corner. We can safely dismantle our military and disarm our missiles of mass destruction. The threat to world peace is over. We can now relax our guard and rest in the confidence that World War III will not happen in our lifetime.

An Old Enemy

Thus the world is lulled to sleep while an old Enemy of truth, justice, peace, and democracy gathers its strength for an all out offensive against the civilian populations of the West. This old Enemy has attacked the West before. Its armies invaded Europe on several occasions and even reached Vienna, Austria. This evil force destroyed everything it touched and left only mangled corpses and burned cities behind it. Its blood thirst and genocide campaigns far exceed any atrocities committed by the Nazis and the Soviets. These enemies of all that is good and righteous can kill innocent women and children without mercy and shame.

They have stated time and time again that their great goal is the subjugation of the entire world to the civil laws, totalitarian political forms, and cultural norms dictated by their religion. Instead of religion being the tool of the state, the state is the tool of religion. This requires the destruction of all other religions, especially Christianity and Judaism. And, throughout history, whenever they had the political means to suppress other religions, they did so with religious zeal. This ancient enemy of freedom is the religion of Islam. It imposed itself in and beyond the Arabian Desert through wars of violence and political intimidation. It views all that is not Islam as Satan.

In this light, it makes no sense whatsoever for the West to be disarming while Islam is arming. While we are dismantling our missiles and nuclear warheads, Islamic nations are buying and building intercontinental ballistic missiles capable of showering nuclear death on any city in Europe or America. We stand in some ways like those few brave Americans and Europeans who just before World War II warned people of the Nazi threat to world peace. They took the rhetoric of Hitler at face value and saw the buildup of war and terrorism across the world. While others dismissed Hitler and his 'brown shirts' as buffoons, a few people sounded the alarm. Sad to say, their warnings were ignored. "Peace in our time" was Chamberlain's swan song and the world was lulled to sleep while the Third Reich armed itself for war.

We are in much the same situation today. The Muslim threat to the peace and security of America is as real as was the threat of Nazism and Communism. If God does not intervene, the day will come when a mushroom cloud will appear over a major American city signaling death and destruction unparalleled in U.S. history. The apostle Paul warned us that if the trumpet is not blown loud and clear, the people will not prepare for war (1 Corinthians 14:8). Ezekiel tells us that we are watchmen who have the responsibility to warn the city of an approaching army of death and destruction. If we fail to warn people of the coming war with Islam, their blood will be on our hands (Ezekiel 33:1-6). In order to convince people that Islam constitutes a clear and present danger to the peace of the world, we must first demonstrate that Islam has the will and the desire to destroy us and, second, that they now have the means to do so.

The Qur'an commands its followers to launch jihads or holy wars of conquest to force conversions to Islam:

> Fight and slay the unbelievers wherever you find them, and seize them, beleaguer them, and lie in wait for them in every stratagem of war. (Surah IX: 5)
>
> Fight those who do not believe in Allah or the Last Day, nor hold that forbidden which hath been forbidden by Allah and his apostle, nor acknowledge the Religion of Truth (i.e. Islam), (even if they are people of the Book), until they pay the tax with willing submission and feel themselves subdued. (Surah IX: 29)
>
> Seize them and slay them wherever you find them. (Surah IV: 89, 91)

At the beginning, Muhammad's armies attacked defenseless caravans during times of truce and peace. He then sent out his armies to conquer and loot small villages. Cities were later put under the sword. Ultimately, entire nations fell to the sword of Islam. Entire populations were slaughtered and great cultural treasures were either looted or destroyed. Whereas Jesus told his disciples to put away their swords, Muhammad commanded his followers make war in his name. Recorded in the Hadith, the second most important duty in Islam according to Muhammad is Jihad or Holy War.

The blood lust of Islam is thus rooted in a perverted religious impulse to kill and mutilate in the name of Allah. This is what makes it so insidious and wicked. The killing of innocent men, women, and children in the name of Islam becomes a thing of praise and a badge of honor. The more you kill, the more Allah is honored. The greater is the destruction, the greater the glory of Islam. Listen carefully to what the most influential leaders of Islam have said.

"We are at war against infidels. Take this message with you, 'I ask all Islamic nations, all Muslims, all Islamic armies, and all heads of Islamic states to join the Holy War. There are many enemies to be killed or destroyed. Jihad must triumph...Muslims have no alternative... to an armed Holy War against profane governments... Holy War means the conquest of all non-Muslim territories... It will... be the duty of every able bodied adult male to volunteer for this war of conquest, the final aim of which is to put Qur'anic law in power from one end of the earth to the other.'"

- Ayatollah Khomeini , "The U.S. is the devil on this planet." World Islamic Popular Command

"Death to America, the Great Satan!" - Muslim mobs in Egypt, Iran, Iraq, etc.

"Muslims must kill the enemies of Allah, in every way and everywhere in order to liberate themselves from the grandchildren of the pigs and apes who are educated at the table of the Zionists, the Communists, and the Imperialists." - Sheik Omar Abdel Rahman

"The United States is a den of evil and fornication... I will show all Americans that they will not be happy if they do not follow Islam." - Sheik Omar Abdel Rahman

"Any doubt about the need to struggle against the U.S. means being enslaved by the Great Satan, and losing the honor and the life the Islamic Revolution has brought to this country and the whole Islamic Ummah." - Ali Akbar Mohtashemi

"It is a matter of time... In 10 years you will have quite a number of countries united under the banner of Islamic fundamentalism." - Hassan al-Turabi

"There is fury, fury everywhere ... Islam is escalating and cannot be resisted. I pray that Allah may tear apart America just as the Soviet Union was torn apart ..." - Sheik al-Tamimi

"[I] wanted to topple one [tower] into the other and kill thousands to send a message to American that they were at war." - Ramzi Yousef, the mastermind of the blowing up of the World Trade Center

Lest you think that these statements are just a lot of wind and noise, come with me to the World Trade Center in New York City which was blown up by the disciples of Sheik Omar. Come with me to the crash sites of airplanes that were blown out of the air by Muslims. Visit the gravesites of American citizens killed by Muslim terrorists in Lebanon, Saudi Arabia, and Kuwait. In Washington DC, Muslims entered a home to kill everyone they found in the house. They took a nine-day-old baby boy and drowned him in the sink. They shot in the head his ten-year-old brother, his 23-year-old sister, his 25-year-old brother, and their mother. What can we say about the slaughter of thousands of innocent Christians in Egypt, Sudan, Iran, Iraq, Pakistan, Saudi Arabia, Kuwait, Indonesia, and Malaysia? World War III has already begun and most Americans do not know it.

Islamic fundamentalists plan on putting together an Islamic empire composed of Turkey, Iran, Iraq, Afghanistan, Kuwait, Saudi Arabia, Qatar, Oman, Yemen, Egypt, Sudan, Libya, Algeria, Morocco, Tunisia, Nigeria, the former Muslim Soviet states such as Uzbekistan, Malaysia, Indonesia, and other Muslim nations in Asia. Their plan is on schedule and they are taking over country after country while the West sleeps securely with its naive dreams of endless peace and prosperity of a new world order called the Pax Americana. Listen to politicians and other leaders trying to wake up America.

"The trial and subsequent conviction of the terrorists that bombed the World Trade Center and planned other terrorist acts should put to rest any doubt about the deadly threat to American citizens posed by radical extremists." - Henry Depippo, Federal Prosecutor of Sheik Omar Abdel Rahman

"Each day's headlines demonstrate the timeliness this important analysis of the emerging trans-national radical Islamic movement... and the growing danger that extremist Islamic elements may seek to exploit our present vulnerability to missile attack with devastating results." - Frank Gaffney, former Assistant Secretary of Defense for International Security

"The agenda of these people is to attack us for what we are... It's something very hard for Americans who live in a multi-cultured and secular society to understand."- L. Paul Bremer, former head of the counter terrorism office for the State Department

"[Muslim fundamentalists] make no secret of their contempt for democratic political procedures." - Bernard Lewis, noted Middle East scholar

"The public must always remain vigilant against acts of terrorism to ensure that terrorism does not become commonplace in this country as it has in many other countries." - William Sessions, former Director of the FBI

"Today we have no protection from even a single ballistic missile." - Ambassador Henry F. Cooper

"In short, the coming Islamic Empire will be a world power in every sense of the word, whose people will share a vibrant religion and a common Islamic culture. Like its Muslim predecessors, the Islamic Empire of the early 21st Century will also have an appetite for territorial expansion and military conquest. A modern, worldwide jihad against non-Muslim populations and societies complete with nuclear weapons promises to bring the highest casualty rates in the history of mankind. World War III, if it does come, will probably occur between the Islamic Bloc and the Western nations. It will be the deadliest war ever fought by humanity." - Anthony Dennis

"Islamic fundamentalism, like communism... is bent on the expansion of its dominion to as many corners of the world as possible." Benjamin Netanyahu, Prime Minister of Israel "It doesn't matter what they tell you - Islamic fundamentalism is a worldwide menace... Allah is rapidly equipping Khomeini's followers with a sword to carry out their master's wishes. He has offered Islam the fire in which the Qur'an says those who follow false faiths are destined to burn: nuclear weaponry. He has also provided the long-range missiles needed to use it. According to the late Imam's logic, there may be only one just and righteous thing to do: employ this technology to wipe out recalcitrant heathens like you and me." - Howard Bloom

With the break up of the Soviet military complex, the Muslims have been able to buy intercontinental ballistic missiles that are capable of striking anywhere on the planet. They have nuclear bombs that can fit into a steamer trunk and it is feared that such a device may already be in this country. There is a real danger that we will one day face nuclear blackmail just as we faced Arab oil blackmail in the 1970s.

A wise man foresees evil and takes the necessary steps to deliver him while fools will go naively on and are destroyed. The final answer to Islam is not bullets but Bibles, not missiles but missions. If they are converted, they will build up the world instead of tearing it down; they will love instead of hate; they will give instead of take. Islam is a spiritual deception and Satanic in its source and power. Only the power of the name and blood of Jesus can drive the demon of Islam out of the hearts and minds of Muslims. If Egypt will allow its Christian citizens to be butchered by Muslim fanatics, then no more American foreign aid should go to that country. If Bosnia warranted American military intervention, then how much more should we invade Sudan to bring peace to that war ravaged land?

If the U.S. wants to be the policeman of the world and invade Kuwait, Haiti, Bosnia, Somalia, and other places, then it is about time to take on the Muslims in Iran, Iraq, Libya, and Afghanistan. Financial blockades and other political measures can stop their genocide against the Christians in their nations.

Our missiles must be reprogrammed to hit Baghdad and Kabul instead of Moscow and Kiev. Muslim nations must be warned that if they commit acts of terrorism in this country, our wrath can reach their own cities. If they start World War III, they will be destroyed. We are presently unprotected from an attack launched from Iraq, Iran, or some other Muslim nation. The U.S. Constitution requires the government to protect us from our enemies. Demand that it do so. If we do not defeat Islam now, it will defeat us later. Ask yourself this question: Do I want my children or grandchildren to live under the heel of Islamic terrorism?

In the light of all these things, it is time to launch a new Crusade against Islam. But this time, the weapons of our warfare are not carnal but spiritual. They are mighty through God to the pulling down of strongholds. (2 Corinthians 10:3-5) The sword of the Spirit is more powerful than a steel blade because it cuts to the soul and brings life instead of death. (Hebrews 4:12) Islam can be defeated if we go forth in the power and demonstration of the Holy Spirit (1 Corinthians 2:4). We must boldly preach the gospel to Muslims everywhere including those in our own community. We must love them enough to share Christ with them.

The world is experiencing a resurgence of fanatical Islam, advancing and expanding as their agents attack innocents with Terror. Apologists for this madness quote convenient parts of the Qur'an which speak of kindness to strangers and other socially redeeming 'Suras' (passages). Facts on the ground speak otherwise. Wherever Muslims who believe in world dominance of Islam gather in critical mass, they habitually attack their host nation. Even in countries which are primarily Muslim, they attack in order to enforce the primitive Shariah laws as practiced by the Taliban in Afghanistan and the Saudis through the extreme Wahhabi form of Islam. These are practices of the 7th century brought to an hysterical level of cruelty in order to please Allah.

The world has seen extreme barbarism, usually with conquerors and religion joined in unholy matrimony. Some Western nations such as France and England are being deluged with Muslim immigrants whose birthrate is often triple that of their host nations. France, England, Belgium and Germany have an astonishing influx of Muslims whose children are being taught in 'Madrassas' (schools that teach only Islam). These 'Madrassas' are paid for and dominated by Saudi Arabian Muslim clerics teaching the Wahhabi form of Islam. As these children are taught to hate and kill, they become the so-called 'militants' of Islam who will subvert their host country.

It appears that in almost every nation, Muslims are releasing their heretofore hidden feelings and joining the most radical of Islamists. The continent of Africa is bristling with Muslim terrorists, following Al Qaeda or linking up with Hamas, Hezb'Allah, the PLO, Islamic Jihad, among many others. They are a multi-linked hydra who services each other's security, arms, safe houses and funding needs. Europe has become a staging ground for Terrorists to meet, plan strategies for sleeper cells and always to gather and store weapons. As Islamic extremists grow bolder in their attacks, the so-called peaceful Muslims are pulled further into their orbit of pride in successful violence. Establishing a Muslim way of life, even through violence, is not considered evil but necessary. Terrorists 'believe' they are 'doing the work of Allah' and if exploding themselves to kill non-believers is necessary for them - so be it.

Clearly, there is something in the teachings of the Qur'an, perhaps subliminal but, whatever it is, it can turn otherwise normal men like Raed Abdul Hamid Misk into homicidal killers. Raed was an 'iman' (Islamic cleric) and teacher from a mosque in Hebron, married with 2 young children, who dressed in the clothes of an ultra-Orthodox man, boarded a double bus packed with families and young children and set himself off with a chest pack of 40 pounds of explosives. He looked in their faces and murdered 21 men, women and children - 6 babies. 150 were wounded, some maimed for life, including many children and pregnant women. After the series of bombing in Baghdad, the whole world can clearly see that the Islamists are on the march. First the Jordanian Embassy bombing, then the United Nations headquarters, and at 9:10 P.M. August 19th, the Children's Massacre Bus Bombing in Jerusalem that killed 21 people, families returning from praying at the Western Wall including 6 children, with 150 wounded - many children.

That day General John Abizaid of the U.S. Central Command stated that "Terror is the Number One Threat". Islam's use of suicide killers or bombers is not new and rewards of martyrdom (paradise with 72 virgins) are always promised. The question is, what is it in the teachings of Islam that triggers a Muslim to commit suicide? What is more frightening is that the average Muslim doesn't realize that he carries within him the potential of becoming a murderer for the sake of his religion. Iraq has become a magnet for Islamic Terrorists from all over the Arab world. Syria has developed into the gateway through which are pouring Saudis, Palestinians, Egyptians, Chechnyans, Libyans, Iranians, 'et al', in an attempt to replicate pushing the Soviets out of Afghanistan. The American CIA was the prime recruiter to bring in and train Muslims in all phases of guerilla warfare to attack the Soviets.

Those we trained, like Osama Bin Laden eventually turned on us using the weapons, technology, we provided.

Iraq is to be like Afghanistan - only this time the enemy is to be America. Sheik Abed Rahman, the blind sheik, was one of America's recruiters for Muslims to 'work' in Afghanistan but, he turned against America, using his Mosque in New Jersey to recruit and subvert American Muslims. He used Ramzi Yousef to begin by using his assassins with the murder of Rabbi Meir Kahane May, 1990. Then Ramzi Yousef organized the first truck bomb under the World Trade Center February 26, 1993 - intended to topple Tower One into Tower Two. Rahman and Yousef are now in Federal Prison. Had they been audio-taped from the moment their crimes were discovered and IF the Americans had Arabic speaking agents to translate the tapes, perhaps America's Intelligence Agencies would have heard the plans for 9/11/01 and prevented it.

Now, as General Abizaid observed, "Terror is our [the Western Free World's] Number One Threat!" Regrettably, President Bush is still well behind in recognizing this fact, both in Iraq and globally. Islam is at war with America, the "Great Satan", her friends - especially Israel, the "Little Satan" and the West generally. Nothing will stop Islamists from finishing this War for Islam, Allah and all Muslims. Not kind words - not bribes - not jobs - not purchasing oil ... absolutely nothing. When will America really believe that we are at War - here - on this continent - because Muslims decided that now is their time? Bush wants to solicit Muslims in America to vote for him and so he tells us that Islam is a kindly and just religion with only a 'few bad' Terrorists who give Muslims and Islam a bad name. America and Israel, no doubt, will have to pay a bloody price for the Bush campaign for President and the oil politics that go with it.

Will it be President Bush who will prove that Terrorism pays? But, he is not alone in "reality avoidance". Most of Europe, led by France, Germany and England, are pretending that their Arab Muslims are merely those friendly folks who just happen to dislike (read: hate!) Jews and Christians. Deport all non-citizens. Any Muslim citizens convicted of a crime would be deported back to his original country. Cease giving citizenship to Muslims and wake up to the fact that Islam has declared War on non-Muslims on a Global scale. Solutions are merely theoretical when oil is King and our leaders are in the business.

Most regimes in Islamic countries in the post-war era were in one of two categories. In the first were regimes aligned to the Soviet bloc, military regimes with a socialist tendency and a strong tribal, regional or ethnic minority base; this was the case in Algeria, Syria, Iraq, South Yemen and Egypt. In the second category were regimes leaning more towards the West, as in the monarchies of the Arab peninsula such as Morocco and Jordan. Both types of regime had one thing in common. In order to have access to political or even economic power, it was necessary to have some sort of kin relationship to the ruling elite. If you were not the nephew of a general or a member of the royal family, it was very difficult for you even to have access to credit, to import anything or become an entrepreneur.

This led to very strong frustrations among the 'bazaar people', and those young professionals who had gone to the oil-exporting countries, made a lot of money and returned home only to find themselves exploited by the ruling elite. They were not as violently deprived as the Young Urban Poor, but they also longed for a different type of governance. The third important social group – you must add a third – is that which I call the Islamist Intelligentsia. These were the militant ideologues who delivered a discourse of political mobilisation to the first two groups; one that the latter would understand and translate quite differently into their social practice. They would talk about an Islamic state, and the implementation of *sharia* (religious law).

The Young Urban Poor hoped that the Islamic state would give them what they had been deprived of: respect, a job, a house, marriage. More often than not they would translate Islamic law into an attempt at revolutionary upheaval – an overturning of social hierarchies. In contrast, the Pious Middle Classes were mainly interested in ousting the ruling incumbents, encouraging the masses of Young Urban Poor to take to the streets, and withstand the violence from the regimes, in order that they might take the place of the elite. They were not really interested in a significant upheaval of social hierarchies. They just wanted to repaint the system green, and to repay the Young Urban Poor with moral rather than social rewards and retribution.

So the Islamic Intelligentsia, when they were successful, was extremely careful to downplay the social content of their message. They were extremely ambiguous, socially. If they had not kept it very vague – had they been revolutionary in their discourse – they would have pleased the Young Urban Poor, but displeased the Pious Middle Classes. Had they been too soft in their desire for social change, then the Young Urban Poor would not have 'bought it'. They were strong on political, religious and moral slogans, but they downplayed the social dimension that would divide groups. This is how that ideology shaped up and progressed the demands of two completely different groups with very different social agendas.

Three Phases of Islamism

Now, a few words about this discourse itself. By the 1960s, there were a number of ideologues and thinkers in the Muslim world who had taken up the challenge of the independent states, and tried to delegitimise them in the name of Islam: Sayyid Qutb in Egypt (who was hanged by Nasser in 1966), or Sayyid Maududi of Pakistan (who died in 1979), or Ayatollah Khomeini in Iran (who died in 1989). In spite of their differences, they held in common the conviction that the world today was not a Muslim world that evens those countries professing the Muslim were actually what the Qu'ran calls Jâhiliyya – that is, the age of ignorance which prevailed in the Arabian Peninsula before the revelation of Islam to the prophet Mohammed. To them, the modern age was a sort of 20th century remake of the *Jâhiliyya* of ancient times; it had to be destroyed as Mohammed the prophet had destroyed its predecessor.

There were a number of ways of seeing how this would come about. In Egypt, Sayyid Qutb and his followers favoured a revolutionary understanding of the need for the radical mobilisation of something they referred to as 'the Movement' to bring about an Islamic state. In Pakistan, Maududi was active mainly through elections, and legal and institutional modernisation. In Iran, it was different again, because the movement used the peculiar language of Shi'a Muslim to achieve its aims. What they had in common, however, was the use of the paradigm of *Jâhiliyya* to analyse why these states were no longer Muslim, and the resulting commitment to destroying those states. This supplied the would-be members of the Islamic cluster with what they wanted: a way to describe and decipher the present state of Islamic society explaining why it had deteriorated; and also, an alternative, something to fight for – a target.

The last three decades of the 20th century were crucial decades for this movement. Behind them lay one pivotal moment – the *jihad* in Afghanistan in the 1980s. In my view, the formation, expansion and decline of the Islamist movements correspond to three distinct phases. The first phase, from September 1970 to 1 February 1979 is the formative one. In the Arab world, the first date epitomises the demise of Arab nationalism, coinciding with the death of Nasser and civil war in Jordan. This opened a huge window of opportunity for an alternative ideology. The second date, 1 February 1979, is the day when Ayatollah Khomeini agreed to return from his exile in Paris. During this first phase, the Islamist Intelligentsia was built up mainly on college campuses, with the encouragement of powerful elements in the Muslim world that saw in these students of the Qu'ran a counterweight to leftists who were at the time prevalent.

People such as Anwar Sadat, who was assassinated by the Islamists in 1981, at first thought that they could give expression to social frustration in a religious language that would not prove dangerous, that could be reigned in much more easily than that of socialists and radicals, at a time when the Soviet Union was still a reality. The Islamic movement developed its intellectual and ideological dimensions through the 1970s. It was always ambiguous. From the October War of 1973 onwards, Saudi Arabia, which suddenly had an enormous amount of cash at its disposal after the price of oil skyrocketed, invested heavily in the movement. This was for several reasons: it was a means by which it could translate its financial clout into political power in the region, an opportunity to subsidise a movement which was turning its back on the Soviet Union, and a vehicle to spread the Islamic religious agenda into the social arena. There were various charitable programmes to buy a full Islamic outfit for Khomeini's students, and to subsidise bus journeys for female students. A wide network of charities allowed them to gain a strong following among the Young Urban Poor, providing an alternative to the derelict public services, which could no longer cope with the exploding population. But, by the end of the 1970s, the Saudi nightmare of an Islamic revolution came true, in a country in which they had almost no influence: neighbouring Iran – a Shi'a country which the Saudis considered as almost non-Muslim.

The Iranian Breakthrough

How did Ayatollah Khomeini manage it? Initially, the movement against the Shah in Iran was not led by the clerics. But the Shah had broken the backbone of secular movements – they did not have the capacity to organise. Also, Khomeini was politically astute enough to work out that seizing power for himself would involve widening his constituency of followers, and isolating the Shah even more. Khomeini was extremely careful to expand his constituency as much as possible. For example, he would address his would-be followers as *Mustazafin* – an Arabic and Persian word which means 'the ones who are weak, disinherited, the enfeebled ones'. It is a Qu'ranic term, opposed in the Qu'ran by another word – *Mustakbirin* – meaning 'the ones who are arrogant'.

These two opposing terms had been used by a predecessor of Khomeini's, namely Ali Shariati. He had lived in France during the Franco–Algerian war of 1954–62, where he sided with the Front de Libèration Nationale (FLN) and translated Frantz Fanon's *The Wretched of the Earth* from its original French into Persian. Shariati thought that its Marxist categories for 'oppressors' and 'oppressed' would not be understood, and replaced them with the moral dimension of Islamic rhetoric. In doing this, he profoundly changed the scope of these terms. Khomeini built on this change of scope, including in the category of *Mustazafin* not only the truly deprived, who had teemed in to southern Teheran from the countryside, but also the bazaar people and, by the end of 1978, even the secularists among the Intelligentsia (who also thought that Khomeini might be just the instrument to oust the Shah).

The latter, of course, then expected him to disappear into retirement in Qom where he could write poetry or preoccupy himself with Islamic philosophy. Khomeini's opening to new groups of followers was essential to the success of his revolution. Afterwards, these supporting groups were gradually eliminated until, in 1979, the hostage-taking at the American Embassy exposed the secularists, who were ousted from power. The Young Urban Poor now occupied centre stage. At that point (as in the French Revolution when the *sans-culottes* were sent to Italy to plunder and were thereby expelled from the central drama back in France), the Iranian Young Urban Poor were sent to a terrible death in the Iraqi minefields. They might defend the Iranian revolution from the outside but, henceforth, they were cut away from its centre.

Exporting Revolution

The Iranian revolution took place in the Shi'a Muslim world, and employed intensively a peculiar Shi'a political parlance. But since the Shi'a constitute only about 15% of the entire Muslim world, in order to 'export' the revolution, this linguistic element had to be replaced by a more mainstream Islamic rhetoric. Here opened a second phase of Islamist movements, running from 1979 to 15 February 1989. This was characterised by a terrific expansion of radical Islam all over the Islamic world; yet it simultaneously exposed the blatant contradictions that had been implicit in the Islamic movement from the beginning. These would be epitomised by the rivalry between the Islamic Republic of Iran on the one hand, and Saudi Arabia (backed by the US) on the other – each seeking hegemony over this very strong political movement.

Iran's view was that it must export the Islamic Revo-lution to the Muslim world in general. The new state was guided by a perspective which was extremely anti-Western, primarily targeted against the Great Satan (and even against the Little Satan, France – in spite of the hospitality that had been accorded Khomeini). Of course, this made it a worrying issue for the West. Saudi Arabia – backed by the US, and others such as Saddam Hussein (at that time the darling of the West) – took it upon them to contain and repel the Islamic Republic. Iraq attacked Iran in September 1980, leading to an eight-year war in the trenches, ultimately with millions of casualties. The Islamic Republic was contained on its western flank.

But the most important development was the *jihad* in Afghanistan, following the Soviet invasion of 1979. This was a decoy, planned and used by the US and the Saudis to kill two birds with one stone. On the one hand, it would marginalise Iran, rendering Saudi Arabia the recognised leader of the Islamist movement worldwide, particularly in the Sunni world. On the other hand, this 'counter-fire' to the Islamic revolution would direct the energies of the radical Muslims away from the Great Satan, and against the Soviet atheists that had invaded a Muslim country. For the US, *jihad* in Afghanistan was a way of inflicting a Vietnam on the USSR, accelerating its demise.

The day that the Red Army pulled out of Kabul, 15 February 1989, ultimately led to the fall of the Berlin wall in November that year. Afghanistan, to a large extent, was the graveyard of the Soviet Union. For the US – or so it was perceived at the time – the *jihad* in Afghanistan was a bargain. It cost only around $600 million a year. Moreover, no US troops were required. Not only were Afghan *mujahedin* trained and equipped (under CIA supervision) by the ISI, Pakistan's intelligence service – more importantly, recruits came from many Muslim countries, such as Algeria, Egypt, Pakistan, the southern Philippines and Turkey. These people were, in a way, members of Islamist International Brigades. This brought about a significant change within the Islamist movement itself. In the 1970s, the recruits would read books by Sayyid Qutb or Maududi. These were easy to read, written in an accessible language, and well adapted to cater for this newly-educated, literate generation.

Anyone with a high school qualification could read these, and make up their own minds whether they agreed or not. In contrast, the training camps in Afghanistan and eastern Pakistan provided a very different type of training for their militant recruits, of two kinds. Firstly, total brainwashing and indoctrination. People were not taught to discuss texts or think about them. They were force-fed the writings of medieval *ulema,* which they did not understand, but which they knew granted full authority to those in charge of the camps to direct theii actions. Secondly, they were trained and equipped in refugee camps for combat, again through Pakistan's ISI via the tutelage of the US.

Out of these camps (whose students included a then darling of the CIA, Osama bin Laden) developed a new culture of Islamist radicalism, combining the brainwashing, which shaped a very cohesive structure of forces on the ground, and the military training, which induced a particular fascination for *jihad*. This, in turn, would lead to the creation of a network called *al-Qaida*. In Arabic, the name means 'base', and indeed bin Laden and his like, who were already post-modernists, had put all the names and addresses of foreign militants on their database. This network was both a state-of-the-art system, which could easily link up militants scattered all over the world, and yet extremely cohesive, because of the deep level of commitment.

The Key Year: 1989

The year 1989 was a turning point. Iran effectively lost the war, Khomeini having been obliged to sign a ceasefire with Saddam Hussein in the summer of 1988. Nobody remembers 15 February 1989 because, on 14 February, the fatwa against Salman Rushdie was issued. Khomeini launched it on that precise day, because he wanted to be perceived as the herald of the Muslims, defending Islam against the insults of Rushdie's book – something the Saudis had been unable to do. But, at a symbolic level, it distracted people from the important event at the level of *realpolitik*, the Soviet pull-out from Afghanistan – in Islamic terms, a Saudi victory, not an Iranian one. The year 1989 is, then, in my view the peak year of these decades: one which saw not only the victory of *jihad* in Afghanistan, which would open the way to the post-Soviet emergence of a number of new Islamic countries on the southern fringe of the former Soviet Empire and the Balkans; but also the Rushdie affair and of the 'veil' fracas in France.

It was the year when the *Front Islamique du Salut* (FIS) were created in Algeria; when Hassan Turabi seized power in the Sudan; when Kashmir became a hot issue; and when, during the first *intifada* in Palestine (which started in December 1987), Hamas started to significantly challenge the former hegemony of the Palestine Liberation Organisation (PLO). Many people thought at the time that, with the demise of the Soviet Empire, the last secular messianism of the 20th century, there might now be room for a new Islamist messianism. From a US and Saudi point of view, the movement seemed to be under control. Yet from 1990, when Saddam Hussein tried to gobble up

Kuwait, a third phase opened, one which continues up to and beyond 11 September 2001.

When King Fahd of Saudi Arabia (the 'Custodian of the Two Holy Places') called US and Western troops to his rescue on 7 August 1990, this directly led to a deep split in the Islamist movement. On the one hand, the Pious Middle Classes consented to the Saudi line. On the other hand, the rebels who had fought in Afghanistan attempted to build up a guerrilla movement that could duplicate the successful *jihad* against the Soviets in Afghanistan. It was successful there, they argued, so it should be successful in Algeria, Egypt, Bosnia and Chechnya in bringing about the Islamic state they longed for. Thus, the movement, having remained largely united under Saudi guidance since the 1970s, started to fragment. There was dissent within Saudi Arabia itself. And then the guerrilla movements came into being in those different places.

From Afghanistan to Algeria – and New York

The people who started these movements were fascinated by the Afghan experience. They thought it unnecessary to waste one's time and energy building charities that could reach out to the grassroots. Theirs was a fantasy of the Afghan *jihad*, where it seemed violence was enough. It was enough to strike a military blow at the regime, which would cave in, and the local population would then welcome the new Islamic state. But it did not work out, despite the easy beginnings of *jihad* in Algeria. There, the Islamists had a promising start, managing to mobilise enough people to enable the FIS to run in the 1990 local elections, and to achieve a fair majority in the first round of the parliamentary elections in December 1991. This movement was split up, however, in the course of the subsequent civil war, and failed in its attempt to seize power.

The military coup of January 1992 deprived the FIS of their electoral victory. Many of those deprived of their democratic rights backed armed insurgency, at first. But after a while, they split along familiar lines. On the one hand, there was the Armed Islamic Group (GIA), former Afghan guerrilla fighters who mainly recruited among the Young Urban Poor, with a very radical agenda, which involved ousting the military and changing the structure of society from top to bottom. On the other hand, there was the Islamic Salvation Army (AIS), which catered to the needs of the Pious Middle Classes. Both collided with the military. But then, bloody confrontations took place between them, eventually leading to the military's successful 'divide and conquer' strategy, which defeated both GIA and AIS in 1997–98.

There is a lot unknown about the conduct of this war in Algeria, but it is necessary to remember that from the early to mid 1990s, this split in the movement – when the radical wing embarking on its guerrilla strategy caused an alienation of the middle class constituencies – ultimately led to military defeat. From the mid 1990s onwards, the bourgeois Islamists tried to find a way out of this impasse, by forging new alliances with secular-minded liberals or the middle classes, on the basis of some mix of Islam and democracy. In short, the Islamic Movement continues to exist, but it is deeply divided and militarily defeated.

And this is where terrorism enters the picture. The masses have simply failed to join the guerrilla movement. Leave aside the first attempt at bombing the World Trade Center in 1993, which is still very mysterious. The first attack traceable to the bin Laden group came in June 1996, an attack on US troops in Saudi Arabia – precisely when it was beginning to be clear that the guerrilla route was a failure and then came the Embassy bombings in Kenya and Tanzania on 7 August 1998, the very anniversary of the day King Fahd called the West to his rescue and then came the bombing of the *USS Cole* in Yemen in 2000, and, lastly, 11 September 2001. It seems clear that al-Qaida's aim was to engineer a very spectacular attack, which would prove that the enemy was weak and not worthy of being feared.

The masses they wanted to reach out to, it was hoped, would join in the *jihad* against the West to liberate themselves. But the problem is that such a closely-knit conspiratorial movement is both the basis of their success and, at the same time, the reason for their ultimate failure. They have no way to reach out to the masses. They have no charities. They do not spread the word. They have no way to deal with grassroots politics. So, they cannot mobilise. They can only use the exemplarity of symbols, and the media, to convey a message to the masses. Bin Laden became a mastermind in using the media – particularly after he singled out the new Arab media, such as the al-Jazeera channel, as the main medium of his political message.

This led to a striking phenomenon in the Middle East since 11 September, and I have frequently noticed a widespread enthusiasm for Osama bin Laden – the man who 'stood for us' – particularly among the youth, in (for example) Egypt, Syria, Lebanon and the Emirates. They were not sure about the massacre of civilians at the World Trade Center; it could not be him, 'it must have been Mossad, probably'. The suicide attacks against Israel were a different matter, because Israel is a country that has invaded Muslim lands. But what is crucial is that they were not convinced by the 'violence argument' as such. They did not go for that. In my view, this is a sign that in spite of the appearance of strength in the violent events of 11 September, with many people massacred, and the very visible threat to the West of these Islamist movements – in spite of this, the very violence of these movements is not a symbol of strength, but precisely shows that they cannot reach out to the constituencies they need to mobilise, in order to seize power.

In the first century of Islam the Kharijites, literally 'Outsiders', were a very conservative, strict and puritanical movement, seeking to recall Muslims to the basic teaching of the Qur'an and the example of the Prophet and his immediate successors. They went so far as to wage war against fellow Muslims whom they regarded as infidels, and assassinated Ali, the son in law of the Prophet. The Assassins (from the Arabic hashishiyya, suggesting 'hashish takers') were extremist, secret communities of Shi'ites, based in Persia and Syria from the 11th to the 13th centuries. They were sent one by one by their leader, the Grand Master, to kill individuals with dagger usually political, military or religious leaders of the Abbasid dynasty in Baghdad. They carried out their targeted assassinations knowing that they would be killed by their captors, and were not allowed to commit suicide.

Ibn Taymiyya (1268? 1328) was a scholar and political activist who had to move from Iraq to Damascus because of the Mongol invasion. Starting from a literalist interpretation of the Qur'an and the Sunnnah, he called for the renewal and reform of Islamic societies, pointing to the first state in Medina as the model of the Islamic state. Although the Mongols were Muslims, Ibn Taymiya issued a legal ruling (fatwa), describing them as unbelievers, kuffar, and apostates who needed to be resisted by force. He has been described as 'the spiritual father of (Sunni) revolutionary Islam' (John Esposito. 2). In the 18th Century there were a number of revivalist movements in the Sudan, Libya, Nigeria, India, SE Asia and Arabia, where the movement was founded by Muhammad ibn Abd al-Wahhab (1703 ? 1791) and known as Wahhabism.

This fundamentalist, puritanical form of Islam was later used by Abdulaziz ibn Saud in a kind of holy war to gain control of the Hejaz in 1927 and then to establish the kingdom of Saudi Arabia in 1932. In 1933 an agreement was signed with Standard Oil Company of California allowing them to extract oil. Wahhabism therefore became, in the words of Bernard Lewis 'the official, state-enforced doctrine of one of the most influential governments in all Islam the custodian of the two holiest places of Islam?' He adds that 'The custodianship of the holy places and the revenues of oil have given worldwide impact to what would otherwise have been an extremist fringe in a marginal country'.

Key Ideologues

Hassan al-Banna (1906 - 1949) was a school teacher who became actively involved in the campaign to get the British out of Egypt, and founded the Muslim Brotherhood in Egypt in 1928. Attributing the weakness of the Muslim world to its departure from true Islam and to the corrupting influence of the West, he called for jihad to implement reforms in society. Mawlana Abul A'la Mawdudi (1903 - 1979) was a journalist in the Indian sub-continent who shared the same outlook as al-Banna. He described Islam as 'a comprehensive system that tends to annihilate all tyrannical and evil systems in the world and enforce its own program a revolutionary concept and ideology which seeks to change and revolutionise the world social order and reshape it according to its own concept and ideals'. He founded the Jamaat-i-Islami in 1929 and supported the creation of Pakistan as an Islamic state. His writings were widely distributed all over the Muslim world and had a profound influence on Muslims in many different contexts.

Sayyid Qutb (1906 - 1966) worked for some years as a school teacher in Egypt and then as a government official in the Ministry of Education. While he admired many things in the West, as a result of two years spent in the US between 1948 and 1950, he became a strong critic of what he saw as degenerate Western societies. He worked with the Muslim Brotherhood, and was critical of the secularist approach of Nasser's revolution in Egypt. During the nine years that he spent in prison, he wrote one of his most important works, Signposts on the Way, which was published in 1964 after his release from prison, and which transformed the teaching of al-Banna and Mawdudi into 'a rejectionist, revolutionary call to arms' (Esposito. 5). He believed that violence and terrorism were justified in the jihad to overthrow existing governments which were not sufficiently Islamic.

Dr Abdullah Azzam, originally from Jordan, has been a strong advocate of militant, global jihad, and is significant because he was one of Osama bin Laden's university teachers in Saudi Arabia. 'Jihad,' he wrote, 'and the rifle alone: no negotiations, no conferences, and no dialogues jihad will remain an individual obligation until all other lands that were Muslim are returned to us so that Islam will reign again: before us lie Palestine, Bokhara, Lebanon, Chad, Eritrea, Somalia, the Philippines, Burma, Southern Yemen, Tashkent and Andslusia [souther Spain]'.

Significant Dates

It is hard to exaggerate the significance of the Six Day War in June 1967 in the development of Islamism. The humiliating defeat of the Arab armies which attacked Israel is seen by Muslims and Arabs as the lowest point ever reached by the Muslim world. Egypt's brief victory in October 1973 restored some sense of pride, and was followed by the Arab oil embargo. But the shame of the defeat in 1967 still remains. The Islamic Revolution in Iran in 1979 ousted the pro-West Shah and brought into existence the Islamic Republic, led by Ayatollah Khomeini. America became the main target of Muslim anger and contempt, being labelled as 'The Great Satan'.

In 1979 the Soviets invaded Afghanistan, and this was an event which had a profound effect on Osama bin Laden. The seizure of the Grand Mosque in Mecca in the same year showed the depth of hostility to the Saudi authorities. In 1989 the Soviet forces were forced to withdraw from Afghanistan, driven out by Afghan fighters supported by Osama bin Laden's Al-Qa'ida and Muslim fighters from the Arab world, and supplied with weapons from the US. Defeating the army of the second most powerful nation in the world gave an enormous boost to the confidence of these Muslim fighters, encouraging them to turn their attention to the most powerful nation of all, the US. 'The Soviet-Afghan war,' says John Esposito, 'marked a new turning point as jihad went global to a degree never seen in the past'.

When Iraq invaded Kuwait in 1990, American forces were stationed in Saudi Arabia. This was another deeply traumatic experience for Osama bin Laden, and set him on a collision course with the Saudi government. In 1996 Osama bin Laden fled from the Sudan to join the Taliban in Afghanistan, who by 1998 had taken over most of the country. In August 1998 bin Laden issued his first fatwa calling for driving US forces out of Saudi Arabia. In the same month there was the bombing of the embassies in Nairobi and Dar es Salam. A later fatwa called on all Muslims to kill US citizens and their allies.

On 11 September 2001 around 3,000 people were killed in the attacks in New York and Washington. And in March 2004 around 200 were killed in the bombings on the trains in Madrid which brought down the Spanish government. What is most significant from this brief survey is that bin Laden and those associated with him represent 'the radical fringe of a broad based Islamic jihad that began in the late 20th century' and that al-Qa'ida represents 'a watershed for contemporary Islamic radicalism' (Esposito. 8). What was new was the way in which from the 1990s America and the West became 'a primary target in an unholy war of terrorism' (Esposito. 9).

Major Grievances and Goals

The basic grievances of all Islamists can be listed as follows:

The weakness and humiliation of the Muslim world is seen as largely the result of Western imperialism in the 19th and 20th centuries. Justifying the attacks of 9/11 bin Laden said, 'Our nation has been tasting humiliation and contempt for more than 80 years'.

New forms of Western imperialism political, military, economic and religious have taken the place of the old imperialism, but which are seen as more subtle and dangerous than the old.

The failure of the ideologies imported from the West especially capitalism, communism/socialism and nationalism. These are perceived as 'bankrupt ideologies foisted on them from outside'. While some aspects of modernity are enthusiastically embraced, others are vigorously rejected.

The establishment of the Zionist state of Israel in the heartlands of Islam, carried out with the support of the West, especially by Britain and later by the US. One-sided American support for Israel since 1967 and especially since the 1980s enables Israel to hold on to the occupied territories. There is continuing, deep anger over the dispossession of the Palestinians in 1948-49 and the continuing illegal occupation of the West Bank.

The presence of foreign troops felt in Saudi Arabia since the early 1990s and the Gulf War. Sacred territory, containing the two most holy Islamic sites, is felt to have been invaded by infidels. Although American forces have now been withdrawn from Saudi Arabia, their presence in the Gulf and Iraq is seen as deeply offensive because Baghdad was 'the seat of the caliphate for half a millennium and the scene of some of the most glorious chapters of Islamic history'.

Corrupt and autocratic governments in Islamic countries are not truly Islamic and are colluding with the West. For many Islamists the main target for their anger is their own governments. 'From their point of view,' says Bernard Lewis, 'the ultimate struggle is not against the Western intruder but against the Westernizing traitor at home. Their most dangerous enemies, as they see it, are the false and renegade Muslims who rule the countries of the Islamic world and who have imported and imposed infidel ways on Muslim peoples'.

We are constantly reminded, for example, that the West will go to war to force Saddam Hussein to comply with a UN Security Council Resolution calling on him to withdraw from Kuwait, but will do nothing to force Israel to comply with similar UN Resolutions in 1967 requiring it to withdraw from occupied territory.

Islamism is therefore the angry response of Muslims who are painfully aware of the decline of Islam and the resurgence of the West. For Muslims it shouldn't be like this - that the world of Islam becomes subject to Dar al-Harb the non-Muslim world. This might be called 'the great reversal'. We should be ruling over them, not them ruling over us! The giant has been stung, wounded and humiliated, and Islamism is part of the response of the awakening giant. Those who turn to terrorism are a minority among the Islamists; but their violence has to be seen in the context of the whole Islamist movement. In the words of Bernard Lewis, 'Popular sentiment is not entirely wrong is seeing the Western world and Western ideas as the ultimate source of the major changes that have transformed the Islamic world in the last century or more. As a consequence, much of the anger in the Islamic world is directed against the Westerner, seen as the ancient and immemorial enemy of Islam since the first clashes between the Muslim caliphs and the Christian emperors, and against the Westernizer, seen as a tool or accomplice of the West and as a traitor to his own faith and people'.

Two words- Islam and fundamentalism, have become intimately linked in English usage. The *Concise Oxford Dictionary of Current English* now defines *fundamentalism* as the "strict maintenance of ancient or fundamental doctrines of any religion, especially Islam." However problematic this formula, it does acknowledge that fundamentalism in Islam is today the most visible and influential of all fundamentalisms. The nature of fundamentalist Islam, and even the use of the term, is hotly debated. But this debate is largely a self-indulgent exercise of analysts. Within Islam, there are Muslims who have created an "-ism" out of Islam — a coherent ideology, a broad strategy, and a set of political preferences. They do not defy definition. They defy the world.

What is fundamentalist Islam? Its contradictions seem to abound. On the one hand, it manifests itself as a new religiosity, reaffirming faith in a transcendent God. On the other hand, it appears as a militant ideology, demanding political action now. Here it takes the form of a populist party, asking for ballots. There it surges forth as an armed phalanx, spraying bullets. One day its spokesmen call for a *jihad* (sacred war) against the West, evoking the deepest historic resentments. Another day, its leaders appeal for reconciliation with the West, emphasizing shared values. Its economic theorists reject capitalist materialism in the name of social justice, yet they rise to the defense private property. It moralists pour scorn on Western consumer culture as debilitating to Islam, yet its strategists avidly seek to buy the West's latest technologies in order to strengthen Islam.

Faced with these apparent contradictions, many analysts in the West have decided that fundamentalism defies all generalization. Instead they have tried to center discussion on its supposed "diversity." For this purpose, they seek to establish systems of classification by which to sort out fundamentalist movements and leaders. The basic classification appears in many different terminological guises, in gradations of subtlety. We need to be careful of that emotive label, 'fundamentalism', and distinguish, as Muslims do, between revivalists, who choose to take the practice of their religion most devoutly, and fanatics or extremists, who use this devotion for political ends. So spoke the Prince of Wales in a 1993 address, summarizing the conventional wisdom in a conventional way. The belief that these categories really exist, and that experts can sort fundament-alists neatly into them, is the sand on which weighty policies are now being built.

Fundamentalist Islam remains an enigma precisely because it has confounded all attempts to divide it into tidy categories. "Revivalist" becomes "extremist" (and vice versa) with such rapidity and frequency that the actual classification of any movement or leader has little predictive power. They will not stay put. This is because fundamentalist Muslims, for all their "diversity," orbit around one dense idea. From any outside vantage point, each orbit will have its apogee and perigee. The West thus sees movements and individuals swing within reach, only to swing out again and cycle right through every classification. Movements and individuals arise in varied social and political circumstances, and have their own distinctive orbits. But they will not defy the gravity of their idea.

The idea is simple: Islam must have power in this world. It is the true religion—the religion of God—and its truth is manifest in its power. When Muslims believed, they were powerful. Their power has been lost in modern times because Islam has been abandoned by many Muslims, who have reverted to the condition that preceded God's revelation to the Prophet Muhammad. But if Muslims now return to the original Islam, they can preserve and even restore their power. That return, to be effective, must be comprehensive; Islam provides the one and only solution to all questions in this world, from public policy to private conduct. It is not merely a religion, in the Western sense of a system of belief in God. It possesses an immutable law, revealed by God that deals with every aspect of life and it is an ideology, a complete system of belief about the organization of the state and the world. This law and ideology can only be implemented through the establishment of a truly Islamic state, under the sovereignty of God.

The empowerment of Islam, which is God's plan for mankind, is a sacred end. It may be pursued by any means that can be rationalized in terms of Islam's own code. At various times, these have included persuasion, guile, and force. What is remarkable about fundamentalist Islam is not its diversity. It is the fact that this idea of power for Islam appeals so effectively across such a wide range of humanity, creating a world of thought that crosses all frontiers. Fundamentalists everywhere must act in narrow circumstances of time and place. But they are who they are precisely because their idea exists above all circumstances. Over nearly a century, this idea has evolved into a coherent ideology, which demonstrates a striking consistency in content and form across a wide expanse of the Muslim world.

Fundamentalist Forerunners

Afghani

The pursuit of power for Islam first gained some intellectual coherence in the mind and career of Sayyid Jamal al-Din "al-Afghani" (1838-97), a thinker and activist who worked to transform Islam into a lever against Western imperialism. His was an age of European expansion into the heartlands of Islam, and of a frenzied search by Muslims for ways to ward off foreign conquest.

In many respects, Afghani was the prototype of the modern fundamentalist. He had been deeply influenced by Western rationalism and the ideological mode of Western thought. Afghani welded a traditional religious hostility toward unbelievers to a modern critique of Western imperialism and an appeal for the unity of Islam, and while he inveighed against the West, he urged the adoption of those Western sciences and institutions that might strengthen Islam. Afghani spread his unsettling message in constant travels that took him to Cairo, Istanbul, Tehran, and Kabul. He visited Paris, London, and St. Petersburg as well, where he published and lobbied on behalf of revolutionary change. A contem-porary English admirer described Afghani as the leader of Islam's "Liberal religious reform movement." But Afghani—not an Afghan at all, but a Persian who concealed his true identity even from English admirers—was never what he appeared to be. While he called for the removal of some authoritarian Muslim rulers, he ingratiated himself with others. While he had great persuasive power, he did not shrink from conspiracy and violence. A disciple once found him pacing back and forth, shouting: "There is no deliverance except in killing; there is no safety except in killing."

These were not idle words. On one occasion, Afghani proposed to a follower that the ruler of Egypt be assassinated, and he did inspire a supple disciple to assassinate a ruling shah of Iran in 1896. Afghani was tempted by power, and believed that "power is never manifested and concrete unless it weakens and subjugates others." Quoting this and other evidence, one Arab critic has argued that there is a striking correspondence between Afghani's thought and European fascism. Was Afghani a liberal or a proto-fascist, a reformist or a revolutionary? Was he the forerunner of those fundamentalists who plead their case in political ways or those who open fire on the motorcades of government ministers? Afghani was athese things, and one can only wonder how today's taxonomists (and with them, the Prince of Wales) would have classified him. Some fundamentalists still pose this same intractable dilemma of classification, although most of them have far weaker "liberal" and "reformist" credentials than had Afghani.

Between Afghani and the emergence of full-blown fundamentalism, liberal and secular nationalism would enjoy a long run in the lands of Islam. Europe had irradiated these lands with the idea that language, not religion, defined nations. In the generation that followed Afghani, Muslims with an eye toward Europe preferred to be called Arabs, Turks, and Persians. "If you looked in the right places," wrote the British historian Arnold Toynbee in 1929, "you could doubtless find some old fashioned Islamic Fundamentalists still lingering on. You would also find that their influence was negligible." Yet that same year, an Egyptian schoolteacher named Hasan al-Banna (1906-49) founded a movement he called the Society of the Muslim Brethren. It would grow into the first modern fundamentalist movement in Islam.

The Muslim Brethren emerged against the background of growing resentment against foreign domination. The Brethren had a double identity. On one level, they operated openly, as a membership organization of social and political awakening. Banna preached moral revival, and the Muslim Brethren engaged in good works. On another level, however, the Muslim Brethren created a "secret apparatus" that acquired weapons and trained adepts in their use. Some of its guns were deployed against the Zionists in Palestine in 1948, but the Muslim Brethren also resorted to violence in Egypt. They began to enforce their own moral teachings by intimidation, and they initiated attacks against Egypt's Jews. They assassinated judges and struck down a prime minister in 1949. Banna himself was assassinated two months later, probably in revenge. The Muslim Brethren then hovered on the fringes of legality, until Gamal Abdel Nasser, who had survived one of their assassination attempts in 1954, put them down ruthlessly. Yet the Muslim Brethren continued to plan underground and in prison, and they flourished in other Arab countries to which they were dispersed.

At the same time, a smaller and more secretive movement, known as the Devotees of Islam, appeared in Iran, under the leadership of a charismatic theology student, Navvab Safavi (1923-56). Like the Muslim Brethren, the Devotees emerged at a time of growing nationalist mobilization against foreign domination. The group was soon implicated in the assassinations of a prime minister and leading secular intellectuals. The Devotees, who never became a mass party, overplayed their hand and were eventually suppressed. Navvab himself was executed, after inspiring a failed assassination attempt against another prime minister. But the seed was planted. One of those who protested Navvab's execution was an obscure, middle-aged cleric named Ruhollah Khomeini, who would continue the work of forging Islam and resentment into an ideology of power.

In the checkered history of Afghani, the Muslim Brethren, and the Devotees of Islam, clear patterns emerge. They saw foreign domination as a symptom of Muslim weakness, and its elimination as the key to Muslim power. Such domination could be attacked directly by jihad against foreigners, or indirectly by promoting an Islamic awakening. Those who gave priority to direct confrontation sometimes favored alliances with other nationalists who opposed foreign rule. In Afghani's anti-imperialist campaign, especially against the British in Egypt, he took all manner of nationalists as allies, including non-Muslims who became some of his most ardent disciples. The Muslim Brethren, who joined the attacks against the British presence in the Suez Canal zone, had many ties to the Egyptian Free Officers who overthrew the monarchy in 1952, but their vision of an Islamic state eventually made them bitter enemies of the new regime. The Devotees of Islam, while thoroughly anti-foreigner, never collaborated with secular nationalists, whom they deeply distrusted. Whatever their strategies, however, they all worked to redress the gross imbalance of power between Islam and the West.

They also sought to replace weak rulers and states with strong rulers and states. Such a state would have to be based on Islam, and while its precise form remained uncertain, the early fundamentalists knew it should not be a constitutional government or multiparty democracy. Preoccupied with the defense of Islam and the acquisition of power, they preferred the strong rule of a just and virtuous Muslim. Afghani, the "Liberal," did not advocate constitutional government. His biographer, reviewing the famous Arabic newspaper published by Afghani in Paris, has noted that "there is no word in the paper's theoretical articles favoring political democracy or parliamentarianism." Afghani simply envisioned "the overthrow of individual rulers who were lax or subservient to foreigners, and their replacement by strong and patriotic men."

The Muslim Brethren in Egypt also rejected party politics. Banna demanded the abolition of all political parties in Egypt and the creation of a single Islamic party. Within this party there could be elections, but electoral campaigning would be limited, voting would be compulsory, and elections would be done by list, which Banna said would "liberate the representative from the pressure of those who elected him." Banna pointed to Stalin's Soviet Union as a model of a successful one-party system. Navvab also allowed elections, but all representatives had to be "devout Muslims," who would be kept "under the supervision of an assembly of pious religious leaders in order to keep [their] activities in line with the Islamic provisions." This preference for a strong, authoritarian Islamic state, often rationalized by the claim that Islam and democracy are incompatible, would become a trademark of fundamentalist thought and practice.

The pursuit of this strong utopian state often overflowed into violence against weak existing states. These "reformers" were quick to disclaim any link to the violence of their followers, denying that their adepts could read their teachings as instructions or justifications for killing. Afghani set the tone, following the assassination of Iran's shah by his disciple. "Surely it was a good deed to kill this bloodthirsty tyrant," he opined. "As far as I am personally concerned, however, I have no part in this deed." Banna, commenting on the assassinations and bombings done by the Muslim Brethren, claimed that "the only ones responsible for these acts are those who commit them." Navvab, who failed in his one attempt at assassination, sent young disciples in his stead. For years he enjoyed the protection of leading religious figures while actually putting weapons in the hands of assassins. (Only when abroad did he actually boast. "I killed Razmara," he announced on a visit to Egypt in 1954, referring to the prime minister assassinated by a disciple three years earlier.) But despite the denials, violence became the inescapable shadow of fundamentalist Islam from the outset—and the attempt to separate figure from shadow, a problematic enterprise at best.

The fundamentalist forerunners also determined that fundamentalist Islam would have a pan-Islamic bent. The peripatetic Afghani took advantage of steamship and train, crossing political borders and sectarian divides to spread his message of Islamic solidarity. His Paris newspaper circulated far and wide in Islam, through the modern post. Egypt's Muslim Brethren also looked beyond the horizon. In 1948, they sent their own volunteers to fight the Jews in

Palestine. Over the next decade, branches of the Muslim Brethren appeared across the Middle East and North Africa, linked by publications and conferences. Egyptian Brethren fleeing arrest set up more branches in Europe, where they mastered the technique of the bank transfer.

The fundamentalist forerun even laid bridges over the historic moat of Sunni prejudice that surrounded Shi'i Iran. Iran's Devotees of Islam mounted massive demonstrations for Palestine, and recruited 5,000 volunteers to fight Israel. They were not allowed to leave for the front, but Navvab himself flew to Egypt and Jordan in 1953, to solidify his ties with the Muslim Brethren. Visiting the Jordanian-Israeli armistice line, he had to be physically restrained from throwing himself upon the Zionist enemy. Navvab presaged those Iranian volunteers who arrived in Lebanon thirty years later to wage Islamic jihad against Israel. From the outset, then, fundamentalists scorned the arbitrary boundaries of states, and demonstrated their resolve to think and act across the frontiers that divide Islam. The jet, the cassette, the fax, and the computer network would later help fundamentalists create a global village of ideas and action—not a hierarchical "Islamintern" but a flat "Islaminform"—countering the effects of geographic distance and sectarian loyalty. Not only has the supposed line between "revivalist" and "extremist" been difficult to draw. National and sectarian lines have been erased or smudged, and fundamentalists draw increasingly on a common reservoir for ideas, strategies, and support.

A resolute anti-Westernism, a vision of an authoritarian Islamic state, a propensity to violence, and a pan-Islamic urge: these were the biases of the forerunners of fundamentalist Islam. No subsequent fundamentalist movement could quite shake them. Indeed, several thinkers subsequently turned these biases into a full-fledged ideology.

An Ideology of Revolution

In the middle of this century of ideologies, the fundamentalists set out to transform Islam into the most complete and seamless ideology of them all. All-encompassing Islamic law, based upon the Qur'an and the traditions of the Prophet Muhammad, constituted their ideological manifesto and program. Many of the provisions of that law had been remote ideals, enforced unevenly over the centuries by weak states. Now fundamentalists, recognizing the enhanced coercive power of the modern state, began to imagine that this law could be implemented in its entirety, and that this total order would confer hitherto unimaginable strength on the Islamic state. Fundamentalist ideology therefore insisted not only on power, but on absolute power—an insistence, admits one advocate of an Islamic state, that "has tended to make modern Islamists into proto-fascists, obsessed with dragging their compatriots kicking and screaming into paradise."

Much of the ideological spadework was done by Mawlana Abu'l-A'la Mawdudi (1903-79), the founder of the fundamentalist Jama'at-i Islami in India and Pakistan. His many writings, translated into every major language spoken by Muslims, provide a panoramic view of the ideal fundamentalist state. In this state, sovereignty would belong to God alone, and would be exercised on his behalf by a just ruler, himself guided by a reading of God's law in its entirety. As an ideological state, it would be administered for God solely by Muslims who adhered to its ideology, and "whose whole life is devoted to the observance and enforcement" of Islamic law. Non-Muslims, who could not share its ideology, and women, who by nature could not devote their entire lives to it, would have no place in high politics.

Everything would come under the purview of this Islamic state. "In such a state," announced Mawdudi, "no one can regard any field of his affairs as personal and private. Considered from this aspect the Islamic state bears a kind of resemblance to the Fascist and Communist states," although Mawdudi rejected individual dictatorship, instead advocating a variety of one-party rule. Mawdudi was certain about what the Islamic state would not resemble: it would be "the very antithesis of secular Western democracy." Mawdudi himself never had a sufficient following to make a concerted bid for power in Pakistan, but his writings exerted a wide influence over fundamentalists better positioned to act upon his vision.

Mawdudi's ideas were carried to their ultimate conclusion by an Egyptian Muslim Brother, Sayyid Qutb (1906-66). Qutb borrowed heavily from Mawdudi's vision of an Islamic state, but he broke new ground in his analysis of how to realize it. Mawdudi had written about the need for a "revolution" to create an Islamic state, but he believed this revolution had to be prepared by a long campaign of persuasion. Qutb, confined to one of Abdel Nasser's prison camps when he wrote his major work, was far more impatient. Islam was under assault, and redemption could not wait for a bloodless revolution. Qutb urged that a believing vanguard organize itself, retreat from impious society, denounce lax Muslims as unbelievers, and battle to overturn the political order. As Qutb put it, "those who have usurped the power of God on earth and made His worshippers their slaves will not be dispossessed by dint of Word alone."

Qutb thus transformed what had been a tendency toward violence into an explicit logic of revolution. He hardly had the chance to act on his theory, for he spent almost a decade in prison before his final arrest and execution. But later fundamentalists would return to his writings, to justify their own resort to force. Qutb also placed the anti-imperialism of the early fundamentalists on an ideological footing. He attributed his own Islamic awakening to a period of more than two years spent in America from 1948. America repelled him on every level. It was, he claimed, a disastrous combination of avid materialism and egoistic individualism that commercialized women and practiced a ferocious racism. Qutb went still further, claiming that there existed something called "Crusaderism"—a systematic plan to eradicate Islam linking medieval Christianity, modern imperialism, and Western consumer culture. "Western blood carries the spirit of the Crusades within itself," wrote Qutb. "It fills the subconscious of the West." Qutb's work would later prove crucial to the fundamentalist rationale that formal independence from the West had to be accompanied by a purging of Islam's own bloodstream of all Western cultural influence.

It was Ruhollah Khomeini (1902-89) who finally wrote the ideological formula for the first successful fundamentalist revolution in Islam. Khomeini added nothing to fundamentalist ideology by his insistence on the need for an Islamic state, created if necessary by an Islamic revolution, but he made a breakthrough with his claim that only the persons most learned in Islamic law could rule: "Since Islamic government is a government of law, knowledge of the law is necessary for the ruler, as has been laid down in tradition." The ruler "must surpass all others in knowledge," and be "more learned than everyone else." Since no existing state had such a ruler, Khomeini's doctrine constituted an appeal for region-wide revolution, to overturn every extant form of authority and replace it with rule by Islamic jurists. In Iran, where such jurists had maintained their independence from the state all along, this doctrine transformed them into a revolutionary class, bent on the seizure and exercise of power. Much to the astonishment of the world—fundamentalists included—the formula worked, carrying Khomeini and his followers to power on a tidal wave of revolution in 1979.

Khomeini also revalidated the anti-Western and anti-American credentials of fundamentalism. Qutb's idea of "Crusaderism" had worked particularly well in Egypt and the Levant, where the legacy of the Crusades could be resurrected from the depths of collective Muslim memory, but it did not speak to the people of Iran, a land untouched by the Crusades. Khomeini thus drew a striking metaphor to make the same point: America, historical heir to unbelief, was the "Great Satan." This posited an absolute conflict between Islam and the West, not just in history but in eschatology. It was dramatized by the seizure of the U.S. Embassy in Teheran and the 444-day detention of its staff. In fundamentalist ideology, political conflict with the West was transformed into a timeless cultural and religious conflict with the "enemies of Islam," led by America and represented on the ground by its proxy, Israel.

Not all of Khomeini's ideas had a full impact on wider Islam. His legitimation of rule by Islamic jurists proved difficult for other fundamentalist movements to assimilate, because it assumed such jurists were inclined to take an oppositional stand. In Sunni lands, Islamic jurists usually served the state, and Sunni movements therefore tended to coalesce under lay leaders. Likewise, while Khomeini's anti-Americanism struck a deep chord, the Soviet invasion of Afghanistan in 1980 diffused its impact. Sunni movements mobilized to wage an international Islamic jihad against the Soviets, and were even ready to cooperate temporarily with America to do so. Khomeini's delegitimation of rule by nominal Muslims kings and presidents, though, found a powerful echo, and he demonstrated how a revolution might succeed in practice.

Khomeini also showed how cultural alienation could be translated into a fervid anti-foreign sentiment, an essential cement for a broad revolutionary coalition. Later it would be assumed that only "extremists" beyond Iran were thrilled by Iran's revolution. In fact, the enthusiasm among fundamentalists was almost unanimous. As a close reading of the press of the Egyptian Muslim Brethren has demonstrated, even this supposedly sober movement approached the Iranian revolution with "unqualified enthusiasm and unconditional euphoria," coupled with an "uncritical acceptance of both its means and goals." Sunni doubts would arise about implementation of the Islamic state in Iran, but for the next decade, much of the effort of fundamentalists would be invested in attempts to replicate Khomeini's success and bring about a second Islamic revolution.

The attempts to make a second revolution demonstrated that fundamentalists of all kinds would employ revolutionary violence if they thought it would bring them to power. Frustrated by the drudgery of winning mass support, full of the heady ideas of Mawdudi and Qutb, and inspired by Khomeini's success, they lunged forward. From the wild-eyed to the wily, Sunni fundamentalists of all stripes began to conspire. A messianic sect seized the Great Mosque in Mecca in 1979. A group moved by Qutb's teachings assassinated Egyptian President Anwar Sadat in 1981. The Muslim Brethren declared a rebellion against the Syrian regime in 1982. Another path of violence paralleled this one—the work of the half-dozen Shi'i movements in Arab lands that had emerged around the hub of Islamic revolution in Iran. They targeted their rage against the existing order in Iraq, Saudi Arabia, Kuwait, Lebanon, and the smaller Gulf states.

In Iraq, they answered Khomeini's appeal by seeking to raise the country's Shi'is in revolt in 1979. In Lebanon, they welcomed Iran's Revolutionary Guards in 1982, first to help drive out the Israelis, then to send suicide bombers to blow up the barracks of U.S. and French peacekeepers there in 1983. Another Shi'i bomber nearly killed the ruler of Kuwait in 1985. Some of Khomeini's adepts went to Mecca as demonstrators, to preach revolution to the assembled pilgrims. Others hijacked airliners and abducted foreigners. Khomeini put a final touch on the decade when he incited his worldwide following to an act of assassination, issuing a religious edict demanding the death of the novelist Salman Rushdie in 1989. This violence was not an aberration. It was a culmination. From the time of Afghani, fundamentalists had contemplated the possibility of denying power through assassination, and taking power through revolution. Because resort to political violence carried many risks, it had been employed judiciously and almost always surreptitiously, but it remained a legitimate option rooted firmly in the tradition, and it became the preferred option after Iran's revolution emboldened fundamentalists everywhere.

For the first time, the ideology of Islam had been empowered, and it had happened through revolution. Power for Islam seemed within reach, if only the fundamentalists were bold enough to run the risk. Many of them were. They included not just the avowed revolutionaries of the Jihad Organization in Egypt, but the cautious and calculating leaderships of the Muslim Brethren in Syria and the Shi'i Da'wa Party in Iraq. It was a seesaw battle throughout the 1980s. Nowhere was Iran's experience repeated. The masses did not ignite in revolution; the rulers did not board jumbo jets for exile. Regimes often employed ruthless force to isolate and stamp out the nests of fundamentalist "sedition." Fundamentalists faced the gaol and the gallows in Egypt. Their blood flowed in the gutters of Hama in Syria, Mecca in Saudi Arabia, and Najaf in Iraq. Yet fundamentalists also struck blows in return, against government officials, intellectuals, minorities, and foreigners.

While they did not take power anywhere, they created many semi-autonomous pockets of resistance. Some of these pockets were distant from political centers, such as the Bekaa Valley in Lebanon and several governates of Upper Egypt, but fundamentalists also took root in urban quarters and on university campuses, where Islamic dress for women became compulsory and short-cropped beards for men became customary. From time to time, impatient pundits would proclaim that the tide of fundamentalist Islam had gone out, but its appeal obviously ran much deeper. Its straightforward solution to the complex crisis of state and society spoke directly to the poor and the young, the overqualified and the underemployed, whose numbers were always increasing faster than their opportunities.

After Iran's revolution and the subsequent revolts, it was impossible to dismiss the ideological coherence fundamentalist Islam had achieved. It had succeeded in resurrecting in many minds an absolute division between Islam and unbelief. Its adherents filled with visions of power, had struck at the existing order, turned against foreign culture, and rejected not only apologetics but politics—the pursuit of the possible through compromise. Fundamentalism mobilized its adherents for conflict, for it assumed that the power sought for Islam existed only in a finite quantity. It could only be taken at the expense of others: rulers, foreigners, minorities. Fundamentalists did not admit the sharing of this power, anymore than they admitted the sharing of religious truth, and although fundamentalists differed on the means of taking power, they were unanimous on what should be done with it. One observer has written that even in Egypt, where the fundamentalist scene seemed highly fragmented, the political and social program of the violent fringe groups "did not seem to differ much from that of the mainstream Muslim Brethren," and was shared by "almost the whole spectrum of political Islam." This was true, by and large, for fundamentalist Islam as a whole.

Repackaging the Islamic State

Yet at the same time, a younger generation of thinkers added crucial refinements to the ideology, adapting it to the times. Even fundamentalists could not reject the West in its entirety. The West, despite fundamentalist faith in its ultimate decline, continued to produce technologies and institutions that gave it immense power. Muslims, to acquire that power, had to import these tools or risk being overwhelmed completely. This next generation of thinkers imagined the Islamic state not so much as a bulwark against the West, but as a filter screening the flow of Western innovations and influences. This ideological filter would admit whatever might enhance the power of the Islamic state and reject whatever might diminish the unity and resolve of Islamic society. It took a different kind of fundamentalist leader to play this role—Muslims who knew the West's strengths and weaknesses first-hand, which had themselves come through the searing fire of its skepticism with their belief intact.

Sudan's Hasan al-Turabi (b. 1932) is the most notable representative of this successor generation. Coming from a strong religious background, Turabi took a doctorate in law at the Sorbonne from 1959 to 1964. Unlike Qutb, he was not altogether repelled by his sojourn in the lands of unbelief: "I was excited by the richness and precision of the French language, the culture, the history of the revolution, the relations between church and state, and the study of the different constitutions. I was not focused exclusively on my law studies. I went to the national library, I visited museums." This unique formation has helped to transform Turabi into the maître of contemporary "Islamism," for he is presumed to know the West intimately enough to decide what should be borrowed and what should be spurned. His partnership with the military regime in Sudan, since 1989, has put him in the best position of any contemporary fundamentalist to implement an Islamic state.

Another member of this generation is Rashid al-Ghannushi (b. 1941), leader of the Tunisian fundamentalist movement. Ghannushi took to the ideas of the Muslim Brethren while studying philosophy in Damascus, where he also witnessed the Arab debacle in June 1967. Ghannushi briefly continued his preparation in philosophy at the Sorbonne in the crucial year of the 1968 student uprising. By his own account, he read not only the works of Islamic philosophers, but Descartes, Bacon, Kant, Hegel, Schopenhauer, and Althusser. But on his return to Tunisia, he preferred to teach the ideas of Mawdudi, Banna, and Qutb to an emerging fundamentalist movement. Ghannushi repeatedly ran afoul of the Tunisian authorities, and in 1989 chose voluntary exile. He is now a political refugee in Britain, where he plays the role of the foremost defender of Islamism in the West. His region-wide stature derives from the fact that he speaks knowingly from the belly of the beast.

A third figure of comparable stature, certainly among Shi'is, is Sayyid Muhammad Husayn Fadlallah (b. 1936) of Lebanon. Fadlallah, born in Iraq of Lebanese Shi'i descent, is a product of the Shi'i academies of Najaf in Iraq. But even there, he was drawn to study the forbidden knowledge of philosophers and unbelievers, as he himself later hinted: "My studies, which were supposed to be traditional, rebelled against tradition and all familiar things." Fadlallah arrived in Beirut in 1966, at a time when the city often mistook itself for an arrondissement of Paris. In this marketplace of ideologies, Fadlallah learned to package Islam in a highly competitive way. He, too, produced a nuanced argument for borrowing from the West while battling it. In the course of the 1980s Fadlallah became the oracle and mentor of Hizbullah, preaching dialogue and resistance in the same breath. Turabi, Ghannushi, and Fadlallah did not rewrite the idea of the Islamic state developed by Mawdudi, Qutb, and Khomeini.

They repackaged it. They understood that the young doubted whether the secular West really intended a crusade against Islam, and so they played down the themes of "Crusaderism" and the "Great Satan," substituting the more fashionable rhetoric of Third World anti-imperialism. This came naturally, for they had overheard the West incriminate itself during their own sojourns in and near its privileged academe. Their arguments for the inevitable triumph of Islam drew upon the dark prophecies of the West's decline that have emanated from European and American philosophers for a century. At the same time, they understood that many of the young had been influenced by notions of class struggle. This they incorporated by developing a terminology that referred to Muslims as the "dispossessed" of "the South."

Not surprisingly, fundamentalists even managed to find apologists among the West's own Third Worldists, who thought they heard an echo in the words pumped from Islamist pulpits. ("Because they hate us, they must be right," wrote a French writer in irony. "What a wonderful coincidence that the revelation of truth coincided with anti-imperialist struggle!") The genius of the new thinkers, though, was to create a climate that could sustain an altogether different analogy. They understood that many of the young had a sneaking or grudging admiration for the science and democracy of the liberal West. Thus, they claimed that elements of both could be selectively borrowed if this served to strengthen Islam. Without sacrificing any element of ideological principle, they worked to present Islamic fundamentalist movements as the functional equivalent of the "reform" movements of the former communist bloc.

This latest repackaging not only has brought new adherents to fundamentalist movements, but has persuaded a surprising number of the West's most hopeful observers of the Middle East that "Islam is the solution." They now argue that beneath a monolithic façade, Islamism has grown diverse, and carries the seed of the long-awaited reform of Islam. "Islam is now at a pivotal and profound moment of evolution," announces a journalist, "a juncture increasingly equated with the Protestant Reformation." "This is, indeed, the most exciting period in Islamic religious history since the twelfth century," gushes a professor. But who are the "reformers" who supposedly are making the first break-through in seven centuries? Where are the path finding texts without which a "Reformation" is impossible? As one Western critic of Islamist thought observes, since the writings of the founders, compiled well before Iran's revolution, "there are nothing but brochures, prayers, feeble glosses and citations of canonical authors." In works written a generation ago or more, Fundamentalist Islam became a coherent ideology, resting on a fixed canon.

The road to redemption leads through the Islamic state of the kind envisioned by Mawdudi, Qutb, and Khomeini. Turabi speaks for nearly all fundamentalists when he dismisses the need for any further thought: "Those Muslims who venture to reform Islam because they are impressed by the Western Reformation . . . did write a few books, but they did not go very far. They did not impress any Muslim." For Turabi's generation, the intellectual work of thinking through an Islamic state has already been done. It is now a matter of repackaging the vision and mobilizing Muslims for its implementation. Turabi himself puts it best: Islamist movements are today "without elitism or obsession with quality." They represent "quantity and the people." So far, there has been no "reform," and certainly no "Reformation." While fundamentalist ideology has been refashioned at its edges, its core remains consistent and stable. A decade ago, Hasan Hanafi, another Sorbonne-schooled Islamist, described this irreducible and unalterable core:

> In the past, Islam found its way between two falling empires, the Persian and the Roman. Both were exhausted by wars. Both suffered moral and spiritual crises. Islam, as a new world order, was able to expand as a substitute to the old regime. Nowadays, Islam finds itself again as a new power, marking its way between the two superpowers in crisis. Islam is regenerating, the two superpowers are degenerating. Islam is the power of the future, inheriting the two superpowers in the present.

A decade later, the Soviet Union is gone and the fundamentalists of Islam claim they pose the last ideological challenge to the last superpower. Ahmad Khomeini, son of the man who detonated the first explosion, summarized the fundamentalist point of view. "After the fall of Marxism, Islam replaced it, and as long as Islam exists, U.S. hostility exists, and as long as U.S. hostility exists, the struggle exists." This Islam, forged by a century of thought, claims the status of a world ideology. For fundame, the proof of its validity will not be found in the number of souls it wins but in its empowerment of Islam.

To achieve that, of course, Islamism must first come to state power. Given the strength of existing regimes, its leaders must build coalitions with other groups if they are to stand any chance of breaking out of encirclement. And it is here that Islamism seems to be failing. The Islamic revival was perhaps most flexible at its outset, in the preaching of Afghani. He altered his message to accommodate a wide range of political alliances, and his biographer has rightly described his interpretation of Islam as "more '`progressive' than that of the modern revivalists—more opens to new ideas and not concerned with reinforcing the Islam of the past." Guile can sometimes compensate for a lack of flexibility: Khomeini's interpretation of Islam was not "progressive," but he struck just such a posture before the revolution, allowing him to forge a coalition of diverse forces. Because the shah's state collapsed so fast, that coalition swept him to power before it unwound in recriminations and purges.

A capacity for dissimulation, such as that so effectively cultivated in Shi'i Islam, is an immense asset in the art of politics, and goes far to explain how leaders like Afghani and Khomeini found crucial allies. In contrast, today's Islamists, certainly in the Arab world, are unwilling to suspend enough of their belief to find a common ground with potential partners. Their words and deeds frighten many Muslims, even those who long for change. The reason is violence—not against the West, but against other Muslims. Even in opposition, Islamist movements cannot resist the temptation to intimidate opponents, rivals, and even lukewarm supporters.

The kind of purge Khomeini carried out once in power is being attempted by Islamist movements today, when it only serves to isolate them. Sayyid Qutb's idea of an unbelieving society, the basis of Islamism as ideology, is the congenital defect of Islamism as politics. Its deleterious effects can be seen in the continuing bloodshed between Islamic movements in Afghanistan, in the murder of intellectuals in Egypt, in the indiscriminate bombings against civilians in Algeria. Islamists claim they have been forced to follow the methods of the regimes they oppose, but if this is so, why should anyone prefer them? Regimes invoke the threat of Islamist "terror" precisely because there is a genuine dread of it in society at large. As a result, the Islamists have no allies, and without allies their chances of assuming power are slim.

There are some Islamists who know this, and who are trying (late in the day) to borrow a page from Khomeini's techniques of dissimulation. But for dissimulation to succeed, it must be consistent and seamless. As it is now practiced by many Islamists, dissimulation is no more than telling each audience whatever it prefers to hear. It is not too difficult to assemble these utterances and demonstrate their incompatibility. This is why Turabi, Fadlallah, and Ghannushi, despite protestations of pluralism, create deep unease among liberals, leftists, nationalists, and feminists, who might have been allies. They overhear the full discourse on the Islamic state—a discourse in which one can hear democracy, free expression, and equal rights denounced as Western cultural imperialism.

Turabi is the only leading Islamist whose alliance-building has given him some access to power in Sudan, but his friends are generals and colonels. In the absence of other allies, the temptation of befriending the military may also prove irresistible to other fundamentalist movements. If so, Islamism will then have filled not only the same political space as Arabism. It will have made the same fatal choice. At some point, it dawned on the military partners of the Arab nationalist ideologues that they could do without the guidance of a Sati' al-Husri or a Michel Aflaq. They could formulate ideology for themselves, whenever needed. Likewise, generals and colonels who take leading Islamists as guides are likely to discard them, even as they appropriate their ideas and language. Perhaps this will be the next phase of Islamism, as men of theory are thrust aside by new military potentates, hungry for Islamic legitimacy. Libya's Mu'ammar al-Qadhdhafi is perhaps the transitional man in this gradual shift from Arab to Islamist military rule.

But this is only speculation, and it is impossible to predict the future fortunes of Islamism. Of its many outcomes, only one seems absolutely certain. Like Arabism, Islamism may fail; and like Arabism, Islamism may fail at great cost, its adherents gradually becoming its victims. But by then, it will have launched a hundred careers and a thousand books. Of Marxism, it has been said that it failed materially everywhere but in Western academe, where its professors turned it into tenure and grants. Islamism seems destined to do the same.

6

Islam and Double Standards

Accusing Muslim leadership of using the Newsweek story to create "anti-American incitement," Lieberman asked, "Where were the protesters when Muslims desecrated Joseph's Tomb and other sites?" In an issue dated May 9, Newsweek reported U.S. military investigators found evidence that interrogators placed copies of Islam's holy book in washrooms and had flushed one down the toilet to get inmates to talk. The report prompted demonstrations across the Muslim world, with thousands rallying in Afghanistan, Pakistan Indonesia and Gaza City to denounce America. At least 15 people died in riots in Afghanistan alone.

Lebanon's most senior Shiite Muslim cleric said the alleged desecration is part of an American campaign aimed at disrespecting and smearing Islam. Spiritual leaders in Afghanistan gave the U.S. three days to respond to the accusations. The 22-nation Arab League issued a statement saying if the allegations panned out, Washington should apologize to Muslims. Qazi Hussain Ahmed, a hard-line Pakistani Islamist leader and opposition lawmaker, said Islamic groups in Pakistan, Egypt, Malaysia, Britain, Turkey and other countries would hold more rallies to protest the alleged desecration. In its retraction, Newsweek stated, "Based on what we know now, we are retracting our original story that an internal military investigation had uncovered Quran abuse at Guantanamo Bay." In a note to readers in its current issue, Newsweek Editor Mark Whitaker said the magazine's information came from "a knowledgeable U.S. government source," who, he said, later could not be sure he had read about the alleged Quran incident in the report that was cited.

Tomb Desecrated

In October 2000, after Israeli troops evacuated the city of Nablus as a peacemaking gesture, scores of Palestinians stormed into the Joseph's Tomb compound and destroyed the site believed to be the burial place of the biblical patriarch Joseph – the son of Jacob who was sold by his brothers into slavery and later became the viceroy of Egypt. The 1993 Oslo Accords put Joseph's Tomb under Israeli jurisdiction, but on Oct. 7, 2000, then-Prime Minister Ehud Barak ordered a unilateral retreat, based on a Palestinian agreement to protect the site.

Within hours of the Israeli withdrawal, smoke was seen billowing from the tomb as an Arab crowd burned Jewish prayer books and other holy objects. Palestinians used pickaxes, hammers and later bulldozers to tear apart the stone building. The dome of the tomb was painted green, and a mosque was subsequently erected in its place. Rabbi Hillel Lieberman, who lived nearby, headed by foot to the tomb when he heard of its desecration, hoping, his family said, to save any Torah scrolls or other holy objects that might have been left intact. Lieberman disappeared. His bullet-ridden body was found the next day in a cave. "[Hillel] was unarmed, wearing a tallit (Jewish prayer shawl), and he was brutally murdered by our enemies who want to erase our existence," said Yehudit Tayar, spokeswoman for the Council of Jewish Communities in Judea, Samaria and the Gaza Strip.

Hillel's father, Zevulun, a religious instructor at Yeshiva University, told WND: "If indeed the Quran was flushed down the toilet that is despicable. But now they protest that religion which actually desecrated the grave of Joseph, the great-grandson of Abraham? "Nowhere in the parameters of humanity is it tolerable to destroy a holy site. The Muslims did something even an animal wouldn't do. Only humans who are completely sick with no sense of reason can do such a thing. And only a religion that is beyond the pale of humanity can sit back and not protest such an act."

Lieberman accused Islamic leaders of using the Newsweek article to spur anti-American incitement: "These leaders, who have no conscience, they aren't upset for religious reasons. It's just an excuse." Susan Roth, director of the Eshet Chayil Foundation, one of the main benefactors of the biblical matriarch Rachel's Tomb, to which surviving artifacts of Joseph's Tomb were recently transferred, told WND: "There was almost total silence in the Muslim world when Palestinians blew up Jews at their Passover seder, when Joseph's tomb was desecrated, and even overall with regard to terrorism." Roth was referring to a Hamas suicide bombing March 2002 that killed 30 and injured 140 when a bomb was exploded in the midst of a Passover seder at an Israeli hotel.

Nathan Katz, professor of religion at Florida International University, told WorldNetDaily: "Joseph's tomb is one of many, many examples of a lack of Muslim respect for religious sites and objects, and the silence of Islamic leaders following such desecrations." He cited the desecration of the Church of the Nativity in Bethlehem by Palestinian gunmen in April 2002, and the dynamiting of 2,000-year old giant Buddhist statues at Bamian, Afghanistan, by the Taliban regime in March 2001. "In fact, those statues, destroyed by the Taliban, were first defaced when the Arabs came to Afghanistan in the late seventh and early eighth century. They cut the faces off the statues then. Later, the Taliban completely wrecked them. Like Joseph's Tomb, the Muslims were largely silent."

Israeli archeologists say they have convincing documentation of the authenticity of Joseph's Tomb's, dating to biblical times. The book of Joshua says, according to the New International Version, "Joseph's bones, which the Israelites had brought up from Egypt, were buried at Shechem (Nablus) in the tract of land that Jacob bought for a hundred pieces of silver from the sons of Hamor, the father of Shechem. This became the inheritance of Joseph's descendants." Said Daniel Pipes, director of the Middle East Forum: "This sequence of events reflects badly on everyone concerned: Newsweek, a stalwart of mainstream media, that can neither get its facts right nor its apology convincing; the U.S. government, which talked about the 'Holy Quran,' thereby falling into its old pattern of promoting Islam; and the Muslim masses, which took to the streets in lethal anger on nothing more than unconfirmed (and latterly rescinded) hearsay. This episode contains within it many lessons; let us hope they are properly learned."

"Either Muslims respect religion," Leiberman said, "and they protest their own intolerable and repeated desecrations, or they don't. They can't have it both ways." There have been and will be Muslims who do not adhere to the Qur'anic principles when responding to injustices and violence that they or fellow Muslims are subjected to, making innocent victims pay for aggressors' crimes. This form of injustice has been committed by Muslims and non-Muslims alike. History of ancient and modern violent conflicts involving various cultures and religions confirms that this is a universal phenomenon. When a violent aggressor is powerful and immune to retaliation, frustration, desperation, and anger can at times drive his victims to direct their violent revenge at innocent, vulnerable victims whose only crime is some irrelevant association with the aggressor.

One aspect of the problem of the violent image of Islam in the West is the focus on the violent reactions of some Muslims while ignoring, almost completely, the miseries that pushed them down that road. It is certainly right to condemn Muslims', and to that matter any group's, violent behaviour that targets innocent people. However, failing to acknowledge and denounce the violence that Muslims were subjected to and resulted in their violent reaction is equally criminal and condemnable. The modern term for this is "double standards." Applying double standards in any conflict can guarantee only one thing: claiming more innocent victims on all sides. I do not think those who apply double standards in any conflict can be separated from the culprits. They share the responsibility for any blood shed, child orphaned, family rendered destitute, and atrocity committed. Given that I was driven to write this book by the tragedies of September 11, I would like to cite a related event to show the use of double standards and their damaging effects.

In the middle of December 2001, TV channels and radio stations across the world broadcasted excerpts from a video tape by the anti-Islam campaigner Osama Bin Laden. In the one hour long tape, the terrorist calls the attack on September 11 "blessed" and talks at length about his version of "jihad" against the West. He cited instances of Western injustices against Muslims in various regions in the world as a justification for his and his followers' war against the USA and the West. He talked about the mass killing of innocent Palestinians, the death of more than half a million children in Iraq as a result of the sanctions, the persecution of Muslims in Kashmir, and other tragedies. What we are particularly interested in here is the comments that this speech drew from Western politicians.

The White House spokesman dismissed the speech as "nothing more than the same kind of terrorist propaganda we've heard before." "Terrorist propaganda" is how the Israeli Foreign Ministry spokesman also described it. The other comment that Western politicians rallied to make on the tape is that it proved Bin Laden's involvement in the criminal attack of September 11, 2001. As put by the British Foreign Secretary: "By boasting about his involvement in the evil attacks, Bin Laden confirms his guilt." At first glance, the response of the Western politicians might seem reasonable and understandable. After all, they exposed Bin Laden's tape as "terrorist propaganda" and, thus, neutralized any effect it could have. The reality, though, is that this response was nothing other than a complete failure to deal with the issue. Their response amounted to a non-response.

The reason that the reaction of Western politicians was effectively a non-response is actually quite simple and straightforward. Bin Laden cited the persecution and suffering of Muslims in various countries, and accused the West of being heavily involved in those tragedies, in order to urge Muslims to attack the West and Western interests everywhere. Bin Laden was not that stupid to try to recruit Londoners, Californians, or Berliners for his bloody cause. He was addressing and trying to move Muslims who have been living or following closely the years-long injustices that he mentioned. The response of Western politicians, however, was to tell Westerners that Bin Laden's tape was "terrorist propaganda"!

What Westerners thought of the tape, if they had time to listen to or read excerpts from it, was not really relevant. It is what Muslims, the overwhelming majority of whom do not live in the West, made of his speech that really mattered. Particularly important to the West was the response of those Muslims who can be vulnerable to Bin Laden's rhetoric. This audience was completely ignored by the wise politicians in the West. I cannot think of a better endorsement Bin Laden could have had from Western politicians for his message. They proved his point for him. Bin Laden used what is described in Arabic as a "right argument for a false cause." He incited feelings of hatred to the USA and the West in general, by citing their involvement in sufferings of Muslims, to ask his audience to join his campaign of brutal terror. Western politicians chose to address Westerners because they can easily overlook the facts that Bin Laden cites in front of an audience who listens only to Western media and knows little about the problems that Bin Laden mentions. They ignored the target audience of Bin Laden's message because they cannot really come up with any convincing response to an audience that is well-informed on these issues, let alone people who are living those injustices.

Western politicians cannot explain why more than half a million Iraqi children had to die because of sanctions that they imposed to punish a brutal dictator who the West decided one day to demonize and change his identity from friend to enemy. They are unable to explain why a whole people in Palestine should be driven out of their homes and forced to live for generations in camps under humiliating and brutal occupation forces that the West boastfully support. By choosing not to respond to Bin Laden's recruitment message, Western politicians chose yet again to apply double standards. We are back to square one and the vicious circle goes on and on. Muslims are left to continue to suffer away from the eyes of the rest of the world. Some would feel an urge to inflict misery on the West to take revenge and/or maybe bring a change. Innocent, vulnerable victims would then be caught up by the bloody rage. Here is another proof on the violence of Islam, we would then be told!

The Quran has instructed us to weigh and measure exactly whether we are receiving the goods or selling them. The Quran does not consider it enough to mention this instruction just once. Rather, it repeats this command several times and in different context and manner. In fact the practice of cheating at the scales or while measuring is declared a sin. From that, one can gain an idea of the importance the Quran places on this practice. Please reflect on the following verses:

(Be just), fill the measure to its full and weigh accurately. (6:152)

So, give the full measure and weight, and do not defraud and deprive people of their rightful things. (7:85)

And do not decrease (cheat at) the measure or the scale (11:84)

Employ the measure and the scales correctly! Do not shortchange people in their goods! (11:85)

When you measure, be exact (do not curtail); and when you weigh, use the correct and proper scales (do not diminish). (17:35)

"Fill the measure to its capacity. Do not inflict a loss (by supplying reduced amount)." "And weigh with an accurate balance." (26:181-182)

He raised the sky far above, and set up a (perfect) balance. So do not transcend the balance. Administer the weight (and measure) with justice. Do not inflict a loss to others (by cheating) at the scales. (55: 7-9)

Emphatically and unambiguously the Quran stresses the need to be fair while weighing and measuring. That is an indication that the Quran considers unfair weighing and measuring practices as one of the basic ailments, and the root cause of many major evil that afflicts societies. The messengers of God came to this earth to stamp out this practice. The question to consider is this: is cheating at weights and measures to be taken just literally in a narrow and limited manner? Is its meaning confined to when an actual weighing instrument and a measuring device is in use, like when a vendor tinkers with his scale and shorts the goods he sells to his customer? Or when a vendor measures an inch or so less than a yard, but charges for a full yard? Of course this is the minimal, specific and the direct meaning of these verses. But just reflect upon the mode and manner in which this evil practice is mentioned in the Quran. The meaning is not confined just to the physical process of doling out specified quantities of products according to an established standard of weights and measures. It encompasses all situations when a person curtails the rights of another, or withholds from another what is due and just.

Actually the word "scale" is used as the symbol of fairness and justice and the granting of due rights. For this reason the word 'scales' is sometimes used in conjunction with the word 'divine book'.

Allah it is, Who has revealed the Book with the truth and the balance (42:17)

And in Surah Hadeed this matter has been clarified still further:

We have certainly sent Our messengers with clear proofs. We revealed to them the scriptures and the scales, so that you may establish justice. (57:25)

Of course the messengers did not come to the earth holding a 'scale' in their hands. Clearly the word 'scale' here is a symbolic reference to justice and balance that the messengers of God came to establish in the society. By associating the word "scale" with the word "book" the Quran indicates something far more important: it signifies that the divine book provides the ideological guidance, and the words and deeds of the messengers present to the world the verifiable 'scale', the criteria which draws a clear line of distinction between the truth and falsehood. In this 'scale' of the messengers all matters can be adjudged and weighed to perfection. It is obvious that cheating at the scales has a broader meaning, and a wider scope. Curtailing and violating the rights of any and all kinds are included in its meaning. Any one who neglects to fulfill the rights of another to the full extent is guilty of shortchanging the 'scales' of justice.

It is just as hate worthy and condemnable an act as that of a vendor who cheats at the physical scales and hands out lesser amount than transacted. Every one considers the later disgusting and despicable. The injunction of the Quran al-kareem concerning fairness at the scales described above covers all those whose liability it is to fulfill the rights of somebody else. For the husband it means that he should fulfill the rights of his wife to the fullest extent. To the wife it says not to withhold any of the rights of the husband. In the context of the government, it means that there ought to be no encumbrances upon the rights of the citizens. The citizen is being commanded not to deduct anything that is due to the government. The employee is being asked not to shirk the responsibility that he has contracted to shoulder, and for which the management has agreed to pay his salary. The management is being commanded to respect the rights of the employee and to deliver to him his due, in return for which it is benefiting from his hard work. In short there isn't any two-way relationship in the world that this noble verse does not address and guide.

The Quran goes a step further and says that the worst form of cheating at the scales is to have a double standard. It means that when it is time to give, a person cheats and gives less than due. But when it is time to receive, he wants to receive the full measure, and is not willing to forego even half an ounce. For such one the Quran al-kareem has sounded off a dire warning.

Woe to those who weigh and measure less! Those who insist upon receiving the full measure, when they are the ones receiving, But when they measure and weigh for others, they (short change and) give less than due. (83: 1-3)

The verse mentions those who 'weigh and measure' less than what they contract to transact. In its wider meaning all kinds of violation at the 'scales' of fairness is included. Interpreting this verse, Hazrat Abdullah ibn Abbas (radee allaho unhuma) says:

"To weigh fully or to weigh short can be in any matter"

This verse primarily condemns those who go through life with double standards. They have one standard for receiving their rights, and quite a different standard for granting them. They are swift and smart while seeking their rights, but quite stingy and sparing when granting them. They spend their days and nights augmenting their assets and their wealth, and in the process they trounce every principle of fairness and justice. They are oblivious of the torture, humiliation and disgrace that await them when they shall be brought up before Allah SWT. It is so sad and shameful that today at the 'scales of justice', in the matter of rights and responsibilities, we employ a self made double standard. We have set aside the scales of balance sent down by Allah SWT, and have thus included ourselves as those for whom the Quran al-kareem sounds off the serious warning. If anyone squeezes out additional work from a laborer beyond the appointed time, and without his free will and fails to compensate him for the extra labor, then he is one of those deserving of the above warning of the Quran because of his double standard. The excess service he forced out from the laborer is the illegitimate benefit. It is 'haraam' for him!

Conversely, if the laborer or an employee is indolent, shirks his duty, or attends to his personal chores and errands during duty hours, but still expects and accepts his full salary, is also covered in the above warning of the Quran. The salary paid for the time he spent on personal chores is illegitimate or 'haraam' for him. In fact during duty hours, while his job is not yet complete, an employee cannot even engage in acts of non-obligatory worship, like 'nafl' salat or the recitation of the Quran. Such acts are not allowed according to Islam. His liability is to perform his assigned duty with attention and honesty. As long as the subject has cropped up, it is appropriate to mention here that even in matters of worship our society is given to immoderation; there is overindulgence as well as negligence among us. Some employees indulge in acts of non-obligatory worship during duty time, even though they still have some unfinished job-related assignments. On the other hand, there are some folks on the management who forbid their employees the opportunity to perform even the obligatory prayers. That prayer is absolutely essential in every situation and the management definitely has the responsibility to provide their employees the opportunity to perform the obligatory acts of worship. It is true that the employee has contracted to work eight hours, but attending to the demands of the mundane bodily needs is included in the duty hours.

Fardh salat, the obligatory prayer, is also as essential as the physical needs and time spend on it too is included in the duty hours, albeit with a caveat: the employee must not spend excessive time on it, and must not perform the 'nafl' salat. That was a little off the subject. Actually I wished to emphasize that all of us should see if we are also guilty of failing to fulfill the rights of others, while demanding our own rights to the fullest. Do we also have double standards? Are we demanding from others that, which if we were in their shoes we would never agree to grant? Unless we assess and change our attitudes, and until we fear being included among the group whom the Quran al-Karim has threatened with dire consequences, the violations and trampling of each other's rights will continue unabated. The corruption and chaos will made life miserable, and everyone will continue to look over his shoulder all the time. The entire society will remain edgy and restless. He who violates the rights of dozens of people himself fears dozens who are ready to trample his rights at the drop of a hat.

The first revelation to the Prophet Muhammad (Pbuh) was about gaining knowledge. It consisted of five verses; "Read in the Name of your Lord who created. Created man from (a substance) that clings. Read! Your Lord is the most bountiful one who taught by the pen, taught man what he did not know". Prophet Muhammad (Pbuh) himself was unlettered. He descended from the cave of Hira with the first revelation and within a course of 23 years made the leaders of the world out of camel grazers. He declared that gaining knowledge was compulsory for every Muslim male and female. He said that the ink of the pen of a scholar was better than the blood of a martyr. He told that a scholar is 70 times superior to a worshipper. He freed the war prisoners if they could teach 10 Muslims reading and writing. He ordered his followers to obtain wisdom from whomsoever it came considering it their own lost heritage.

The subsequent revelations of Qur'an told a Muslim that the Qur'an was the Word of God while the universe was a Work of God. The wisdom they acquired inspired them to explore the universe with the same devotion as if they were studying the Ayahs (verses) of The Book. Within 300 years, Cordova, Grenada, Baghdad and Cairo became the most important centres of seeking knowledge in the world. There were more than 200 bookshops per street on many streets of Baghdad in the 10th Century AD where the students from Europe visited to buy books. Among the top 132 scientists of the world 121 were Muslims at one time while the rest were educated in Islamic universities. When Muslim army entered a city, the terms of peace with the conquered invariably included a clause that they should be given possession of all works of Greek knowledge, a clause to which the conquered readily agreed as they were a useless heap for them.

It was the peak of intellectual heights when in 12th century, Iran and Iraq fell to Tatarian Genghis Khan and Halakoo Khan. History has never witnessed such scenes of indiscriminate murder and destruction as at the hands of Tatars. Millions of Muslims were murdered. They literally drank toasts on the towers erected of human skulls. The terror of Tatar was such that a Tatar woman ordered a man in the street to stay put, came back with a sword and beheaded him. The water of the rivers turned red. The Tatar destroyed all treasures of knowledge, books and libraries in Baghdad. They made bridges by dumping books in the river. The Tatarian attack changed the course of all creative progress in Muslim states. Possession and safe keeping instead of creativity and evolution became their psyche. The downfall continued till the early 20th century. The most revered religious scholars of the darkest Muslim era (19th and early 20th century) ruled that the women were forbidden education.

While they still talked of the golden era with pride, they declared the universities were the abattoirs of humanity. They ordered to shut all eyes from whatever wisdom came from the West. They classified knowledge into the worldly knowledge (rejectable) and the knowledge pertaining to Hereafter (attainable). The Prophet's classification of knowledge was Ilm-e-Nafey (the knowledge that benefits) and Ilm-e-Ghair Nafey (the knowledge that does not benefit the humanity). Whatever knowledge was there in the languages other than Arabic, Persian, Turkish and Urdu was taboo. The list is very long. All this happened in the name of Islam through the most revered scholars of Islam.

The Muslims have started learning. It is a transitional phase. The out of context Islam and Qur'an, by those alone who had no scientific knowledge of the universe and their self proclaimed exclusive right to interpret has given rise to many contradictions. The colonization, suppression and discrimination of the have-nots by those yielding power have driven some Muslims youths of a resurgent community in the third world to take to terrorism in the name of Jihad. Islam is a very powerful tool and a powerful tool when used by those who do not understand it well is very dangerous. Those aggrieved now are themselves to be blamed. They have inspired them to use Islam against their adversaries for their own political motives and now they cannot do anything. They cannot wipe Islam out. If it could be wiped out it would have vanished in the last centuries. The only proper course is not to use misguided religious elements by any power to gain political mileage against anyone. They should instead help Muslims educate and gain wisdom which was once their hallmark.

The dilemma of a majority of sane Muslims is two-fold—their attitude towards the interpretations of the clergy of the recent past and their attitude towards the aggrieved champions of democracy and freedom who have scant respect for the freedom and democracy of others. We are rightly indebted to the clergy who have safeguarded Islamic texts and tenets through the centuries to pass on to us unadulterated but misinterpreted, some unadulterated texts in the socio-political compulsions of the past. We shall always revere them but a rational sense has to be prevailed to correct their mistakes. Secondly we have to convince the advance democratic nations to respect and strengthen the democratically elected governments of the developing world by not supporting, inciting and aiding the unpopular kings, autocrats, dictators and separatist movements for their immediate gains.

We are confident that we shall overcome and Islam will emerge once again a very strong tool for peace and benevolence. When a country wishes its criminal deported to it, it has to satisfy the system of justice of the other country about his crime where the criminal has taken refuge. In the absence of any evidence thereof such requests are not granted. True, the killing of thousands of innocent Americans by terrorists was a most heinous crime. We want the culprits to be brought to justice. True again that the publicized credentials of Bin Laden by the Western media paint him as a hardcore terrorist. Accepted that his statement of justification of the terrorists' attack mark him a fanatic but those facts do not prove his involvement in the crime the least. Many Non-Muslim governments including China have dismissed the American government's projected evidence against him as rubbish. Killing thousands of innocents and rendering millions, crippled, starving homeless to apprehend that one person against whom the American justice system has secret evidence is also a most heinous crime bigger than the crime of the deplorable terrorists.

If Bin Laden has planned or executed the terrorist attack in the US, he should be apprehended and killed, but sorry, the American justice system is the most unreliable when American ego is hurt. The evidence of this is printed with blood in all the newspapers of the world. As far as our study goes, it is illegitimate for Muslims to seek subsidy on Haj journey from the Government of India. More so in a secular country like India where the Government is supposed to respect all religions and favour none, such subsidy is totally undesirable and should be withdrawn. It has already attracted criticism from the VHP and other Hindutva bodies. Despite their anti-Muslim rhetoric, let us be fair in accepting this criticism. Let us put the whole question of Haj Airfare Subsidy in the socio-political and purely economic context. Last year nearly 90,000 Indian pilgrims went for Haj and the government of India paid out nearly Rs. 120 crore (Rs. 1200 million) to the Air India towards subsidizing the airfare. It is reported that the Haj airfare costs Rs. 29,000 but each individual pilgrim pays only Rs. 12000 towards the air journey to the Haj Committee which takes him to Jeddah from anywhere in India, say from Mumbai or Kolkata or Srinagar.

Remainder of the money i.e., Rs. 17,000 is borne by the Government of India. The fact is that even a Delhi-Bangalore-Delhi air journey would cost an individual something like Rs. 14,000. Going by the current fares, a Muslim pilgrim is paying for an international trip even lesser than what he would pay for a domestic two-way journey. There is one more aspect to it. While a person travelling on Delhi-Bangalore-Delhi uses two flights, the journey of pilgrims to Jeddah actually involves four flights. It is because all the chartered flights that take the pilgrims from say Kolkata to Jeddah have to return empty. Similarly, after 40 days the planes have to fly empty to Jeddah to bring back the pilgrim to Kolkata. Looking from this angle, the Rs. 12,000 airfare is highly subsidized and should in no case be done by the government. Even if the Air India allows 33 per cent discount (because the tickets are booked in bulk), the airfare of Rs. 12,000 will be unfairly low and unviable for the kind of air operations.

But at the same time let us be reminded that Indian Muslims did not demand the airfare subsidy. This was begun after the ship voyages to Jeddah were phased out. But now since the subsidy is in force since 90s, several Muslim organizations demand that it should continue. It is unfair and any such demand should be held illegitimate. Considering the plain terms in which the Holy Qur'an lays down the obligation of Haj, the government subsidy is untenable and should be discontinued. Moreover, the cheaper Haj journey is encouraging people to repeat Haj performances. Haj is obligatory just once in a lifetime. It does not add to one's piety to do it repeatedly. Nor should repeat performances become a status symbol. However this should not bar the Muslims from exploring the ways to make the Haj operations cheaper.

One way this can be done is by amending the Central Haj Act and forming a Haj Corporation. This could mobilize deposits from aspirants of Haj pilgrimage, do some business, make profits, which could then go into making their Haj cheaper. It could as well go into buying planes which could be leased out to other airlines for eight months and do the Umrah and Haj trips during Ramazan and between Zul Qaidah and Muharram. Any operation that involves an international pilgrimage by 100,000 people annually could make a sound business proposition. The Muslims of India should demand suitable amendment in the Central Haj Act and put some business minded members on the Central Haj Committee. The current Haj management leaves much to be desired. There is a serious apprehension that a lot of bungling and corruption is involved in booking of accommodation in the holy sites.

We can take a leaf from Tabung Haji Corporation in Malaysia which has involved some business principles in making the pilgrimage cheaper for its pilgrims. Finally, let us mobilize Muslim opinion to demand withdrawal of airfare subsidies for Haj in best traditions of secularism. Such a partisan largesse to Muslim is all likely to kick up demands from other communities. This will not be in the interest of this nation. The Quran prescribes clean earth as the agent of Thayammum (partial dust-bath), (4: 43, and 5:6).

The word saeed meaning 'earth' always appears along with the qualifying word thayyib, meaning "Pure and pleasant" in the Holy Qura'n with respect to the subject of Thayammum. This means that the earth or the material akin to it must be free from filth, obnoxious or offensive elements. The Fiqh authorities have said that the dust gathered on materials not akin to "earth" such as pure metals etc., is good Thayammum material, for, the dust emanates from the earth. But that was in olden days when the environment was comparatively clean. Today, in most of our mohallas, the dust that collects anywhere, even if it be on the painted walls of mosques, emanates from the dirty black silt that the Municipal workers scrape from the gutters and dump all along our lanes and bylanes.

Similar is the fate of the traditional arrangement in certain mosques where some sand is kept in a flat container along with a signboard indicating that it is the place for Thayammum. Whether there is a lid over the sand or not, it is nevertheless open to the outside dust. And that sand, in all probability, has not been replaced for decades! Most of those who avail of it, are people afflicted with communicable diseases. Even the common cold virus is transferable through such a medium. Now, how can this be considered safe, let alone clean and pleasant? Such a predicament is due to our tendency to hang on to hearsay and tradition, without subjecting them to the litmus test of the Qur'an. For, here, the qualifying word thayyib - "clean" shines out throughout!

Considering most urban environments of the world, and worse still, the phenomenon of progressive urbanization underway everywhere, it seems scientifically sound, and quite in accordance with the Qur'anic wisdom that the universally available commercial Talcum Powder is the answer! For, Talcum Powder is nothing but powdered soap-stone which is part of the earth, like other kinds of stones, pebbles, rocks, sand, clay, etc. Of course, commercial Talcum includes traces of chemicals for added perfumery or medicinal value. Not only is this powder pure and pleasant, it is untouched by hand. What is poured out, is never returned to the container. There is no risk of any contamination whatsoever. In olden days such a precaution was unnecessary due to easy and quite obvious access to and availability of clean Thayammum material. Today in our extremely contaminated environment, Allah has endowed us with the easy availability of the knowledge and technique to overcome it.

Al-Qur'an guides us to the wisest path, a path that is most pleasant, most easily accessible, and most scientific! It is the duty of the Ulema to give Fatwas in the light of Holy Qur'an so that people are not put to inconvenience as regards 'ibadath! The Pentagon has acknowledged five instances in which guards or interrogators at the detention facility in Guantanamo Bay, Cuba, handled the Qur'an in such a way as to cause offense to some who believe it is the revealed word of Allah. Three are said to have been three deliberate and two unintentional.

Amnesty International has put the United States high on the list of countries it says are guilty of prisoner and human rights abuses because of the way suspected terrorists are treated. The chairman of the joint chiefs of staff, General Richard Myers, rebutted the notion of inappropriate treatment of detainees last weekend when he told Fox News Sunday that these are people who would "slit our throats, our children's throats" were they to be set free. Islamic countries apply a double standard when it comes to the treatment of "holy books" and people who differ in faith and practice from Islamic dogma. While Islamic groups in the United States are engaged in "sensitivity training" sessions for non-Muslims that have included federal workers, the Ohio National Guard and U.S. Air Force Academy, there are no such training sessions directed at Muslims to teach them tolerance for non-Islamic faiths.

While the slightest verbal or physical slight of any Muslim in America is immediately condemned by activist groups and sometimes the U.S. government, the denigration of Jews and Christians throughout much of the Islamic world is theological and political business as usual. Jews are regularly referred to as "apes and pigs," mostly because that is what the Qur'an calls them. According to the

MEMRI-TV Monitor Project, which observes the way Jews, especially, are portrayed throughout the Middle East, a Jordanian produced program titled "Stories From Before the Verses Came Down" was aired in February on Saudi Iqra TV. The soap opera contained familiar anti-Semitic stuff, including blaming ancient Jews for distorting their own Torah to make it seem like Mohammad could not be the "true prophet" and portraying a Jewish character saying, "We are the slayers of prophets, and we live off their blood! We live for destroying them."

According to a report authored by former CIA Director James Woolsey for Freedom House, the government of Saudi Arabia has made it a practice to disseminate propaganda about Jews, Christians and America through mosques in the U.S. and through schools, many of which are funded by the extremist Wahhabi Islamic sect. The 89-page report titled, "Saudi publications on hate ideology fill American mosques," concludes that propaganda collected from U.S. mosques shows a "totalitarian ideology of hatred that can incite to violence." The report also says such mosques are in the minority, but how many are needed to train terrorists who might attack the U.S. with biological, chemical or nuclear weapons?

Throughout much of the Islamic world, the practice of Christianity and Judaism is severely restricted, if not outlawed. The Freedom House report said Saudi publications "state that it is a religious obligation for Muslims to hate Christians and Jews" and that, under Saudi law, Muslims who convert to any other faith "are to be put to death." In a column four years ago, The Washington Post's Richard Cohen wrote, "The Arab world is the last bastion of unbridled, unashamed, unhidden and unbelievable anti-Semitism. Hitlerian myths get published in the popular press as incontrovertible truths. The Holocaust either gets minimized or denied. How the Arab world will ever come to terms with Israel when Israelis are portrayed as the devil incarnate is hard to figure out." Little, if anything has changed since he wrote those words.

Despite the Western diplomatic talk about Arabs and Palestinians living in peace with even a geographically reduced Israel, the Arab world demonstrates no intention of coming to terms with Israel or the Jewish (or Christian) people, unless those terms involve their complete subjugation to Islam, or their deaths. The State Department acknowledged for the first time during the Clinton Administration that Christians — from China, to the Sudan, to the Middle East — have become the most persecuted faith group in the world. Yet those persecutors are not pressured into the kind of sensitivity training Muslim groups in America demand at the slightest slight, whether actual, imagined or concocted. To accept this Islamic double standard creates a significant threat to the United States.

7

A Failure of Modernity

During the huge public discourse, especially in the aftermath of 11 September 2001, Muslim mind-set toward modernity frequently came into question. A whole theology has came into being on the question whether Islam and modernity are compatible to each other. Neither the question nor the arguments are new. Similar debates arose in the nineteenth century when the Western nations colonized Muslim lands. Unfortunately, the terror and violence that accompanied modernization distorted the image of modernity. Today also, the debate on modernity is deflected by the political events that are marred by violence, terror and destruction. The focus of debate shifts the emphasis from the quest of modernity to political concerns. It is in the wake of such concerns that modernity is defined in universalistic and essentialist terms and Islam and Muslims are characterized as incompatible to modernity.

It is in this sense that there is not one but several modernities; various traditions transform into varying modernities. Second, the Western and Muslim societies were not always as self-righteous as they are today. In fact in the early nineteenth century when the Western nations landed on the shores of Muslim lands, they were fascinated by the mystique of the orient. In India, for instance, Warren Hastings chose the title of Nawwab Bahadur for himself.

English historians are fond of telling the stories of 'English Nabobs' who lived and dressed like Indian Muslims. More than 500 Europeans mastered Urdu language to the extent that they are acclaimed as Urdu Poets by the historians of Urdu literature. The' English residents of Delhi frequently visited Shah Abdul Aziz the famous scholar in the city. James Skinner requested amulets from Shah Abdul Aziz for the health of her children.

Some of Shah's contemporaries raised questions about one of the Shah's relative who had taken employment with the British. Shah could however, satisfy these inquirers that Islam did not forbid relations with the English because they were people of the book. He could also explain that a Muslim could sit and eat with the English. I am not saying that the Muslims and the English had no problems. Of course, on both sides there were also people who were reluctant, but the significant fart is that an Islamic scholar and a religious leader could justify cultural relations between the Muslims and the Westerners. Today also, the number of Muslim citizens, not immigrants and temporary labour, in the Western countries is significantly higher than ever. On the other hand, the presence of Western culture in Muslim societies is equally evident in daily urban life, in schools, in media and in various cultural aspects. In the following pages, I would like to analyze three aspects in Islamic tradition that have provided Islamic intellectual tradition the cultural flexibility sufficient to cope with contemporary challenges: secular sciences, jihad, pluralism and human rights.

Secular Sciences

We may say that Islam's encounter with the West began quite early when Greek intellectual tradition came to the Muslim society in the ninth century under the Abbasid caliph Mamun. It generated a debate about the legitimacy of studying Greek sciences but the fart that a movement in favour of Greek sciences continued to flourish throughout the Islamic history is by itself an evidence of Islam's cultural compatibility. This movement generated a controversy deep into the religious issues about the nature of the Qur'anic revelation and the role of reason. Opposition to this movement finally triumphed as "orthodoxy", but not without recognizing the necessity of studying Greek secular sciences. Al-Ghazali, a twelfth century Muslim thinker, who wrote a refutation of this philosophical movement in Islam and who separated purely "religious" from other sciences, was also responsible for introducing Greek logic in the "pure religious sciences". The science of Kalam (roughly, Islamic theology) born out of the need to refute foreign ideas was regarded as the science of Da'wa and Jihad. This science relied heavily on Greek logic, rhetoric and metaphysics.

The science of Kalam continued to engage Muslim philosophers in the controversy about reason and revelation in Islam. The controversy came to be known in Europe through Latin translations of Averroes. Islamic philosophical investigations into revelation attracted the European religious thought to appreciate the rationalist tradition. No doubt, opposition in the Muslim community to rational sciences continued, but at the same time a considerable number of Greek texts or their Arabic adaptations on Astronomy, Geography, Calculus, Mechanics etc., became part of the Muslim religious curriculum. They were called "Ma'qulat" (rational sciences) in contrast to pure religious text studies, which were called "Manqulat". Abu'l Hasan Ali Nadwi, a twentieth century Muslim educationist in India, in bis book on Islamic encounter with the West, admired the Muslim way of adapting Greek sciences to the need of Muslim society in the ninth century as a model for assimilation of modern Western sciences into Muslim education today.

The Greek sciences, especially logic and metaphysics shaped the Muslim worldview, which Muslim modernists like Jamal al-Din Afghani and Muhammad Iqbal found responsible for Muslim stagnation. Iqbal argued that the classical Greek thought of statism was opposite to the Qur'anic dynamism. It is paradoxical that some religious institutions of learning insisted in the nineteenth and twentieth century on preserving traditional curricula which include some of the Greek secular sciences, but refused to introduce new sciences. The situation is gradually changing and these institutions are adopting new secular sciences as well. Often, the modernists have argued that modern sciences are in fact Muslim sciences which came to Europe in the middle ages. In the twentieth century the dispute about whether Muslims should learn Western sciences was settled with reference to Da 'wa and jihad. Some Algerian students approached Mufti Abdul Aziz b. Muhammad b. al-Siddiq in Morocco in 1985. They narrated that some Ulama forbade studying secular sciences because they would influence young Muslim minds in favour of the West.

The students asked if migration to Europe for work and for studies was permissible. Mufti al-Siddiq recited the Qur'anic verse "Let not the unbelievers think that they have surpassed, they could not be weakened. Against them make ready your strength to the utmost of your power (8: 59-60). He explained that the verse requires Muslims to travel to the West and learn the sciences and technology that gives west the superiority. Muslim must learn these sciences to build their strength. I must add that this verse is very basic to the modern Jihad discourse. It is used to justify the continuous obligation of jihad. Here, the Mufti employed it to justify modernization of Islamic education. The verse is also employed to justify the need for modernization of society, state and particularly the Muslim armies.

Jihad

The above mentioned verse was also cited to justify modernization of Ottoman armies, warfare and weapons. A Muslim jurist Mufti Shihabuddin Alusi (d. 1853) was reluctant to allow the use of firearms. It was, for him, against the conventional warfare. Other jurists disagreed because it would put Muslim army in a weak position. Resistance to seeking help from non-Muslims, especially hiring non-Muslim army instructors to train Muslim soldiers was also easily dismissed on similar grounds. Rashid Rida (d. 1935) insisted on modernizing Muslim armies. How could Muslims remain restricted to the use of arrows and swords against an enemy who used guns and rifles? To Rashid Rida, the Qûr'anic verse obliged Muslims to build up strength superior to their enemies. No modern Muslim scholar is today opposed to the modernization or Westernization of Muslim armies. In fact, the directors of a panel of researchers in the Third Mediterranean Social and Political Research Meeting, Florence March 2002 proposed to explore the reference to jihad as justification of modernizing armies in the following words:" The study of the founding discourses and the ideological controversies that presided over the creation of modern armies raises questions about the foundations of Nizam legitimating, in the light of the generic mission of Jihad".

The notion of Jihad was thus quite naturally used for justifying modernization and reform of Muslim society. The principle of jihad was extended even to things and matters, which were other wise, prohibited. It opened space for modernization of Muslim society, especially legitimizing women's place for women in public as nurses and teachers. The principle of Jihad also gave birth to the movement of reform in Muslim societies in eighteenth century and afterwards. These movements condemned social practices that promoted superstition, extravagance, pessimism and annihilism. They also initiated reforms within Islam that challenged the religious authority of traditional schools of Islamic law and the Sufi orders. Some of these movements in Africa revolted against the traditional political systems and established Islamic states.

The principle of Jihad became the mainstay for the struggle for independence against the colonial rule. The traditional Ulama who were reluctant to join politics were obliged to participate in the struggle in the name of Jihad. The Western capitalism also found Jihad useful in the cold war. It became the rallying point against communism and socialism. The word Mujahidin became a common word in the Western societies. Alliance of the Mujahidin with the West introduced to them new ideas and technology and the need modernize Muslim societies. The need for change of political system with militant force led these Mujahidin groups to reconstruct a new ideology of Jihad. It advocated militant solutions of political conflicts. After the collapse of the Soviet Union, the West was no longer interested in Jihad or Mujahidin. The rise of this extremist view of Jihad led to its privatization and sectarian violence.

Private Jihad

One of the many setbacks to Islamic law during the colonial period is its privatization. Unfortunately, this privatization continued after the independence of Muslim countries. The idea has become so entrenched in the modern Islamic thinking that it has gravely damaged the conception of its role as a public and international law. I will illustrate this point with reference to a university dissertation on Jihad. 'Ali b. Nafi' al-Ulyani, in his doctoral thesis in 1984, defines Jihad as follows: "The word in simple usage means killing infidels for the supremacy of the word of God and cannot be interpreted otherwise unless there is an evidence for a different meaning". The aims and objectives of Jihad, according to him, include making people submit to God alone, protection of Islamic state, killing infidels, and terrorizing infidels and to humiliate them, among other things.

In his words: "In modern times, some persons trained by the colonialists and who have chosen the life of humiliation and helplessness to that of honor and Jihad, have doubted the role of Jihad in the spread of Islam. They assume that it was due to peaceful preaching without Jihad that Islam spread in the early period and it is the best way today as well. They have rather extended their argument to claim that spread of Islam by Jihad is an allegation against Islam that must be defended. Their teachers in this intellectual distortion are the Orientalists. The most famous among them is the evil-minded Orientalist Thomas Arnold who wrote a book entitled "Preaching of Islam". This book was aimed to kill the spirit of Jihad among the Muslims". Al-'Ulyani describes that Jihad is generally divided into two types. *Jihad al-talab wa'l ibtida*, which means to call upon (*tatallub*) the infidels in their land to Islam, and fighting (killing) them if they do not submit to the rule of Islam. This type is regarded as *fard kifaya* (collective duty) and becomes individual duty, when there is a general declaration of war or the Imam calls for it. *Al-jihad al-difa 'i* (defensive Jihad) is the second type, which is regarded as *fard 'ayn*. He questions this division and concludes that *Jihad difa 'i* (defensive Jihad) is a *bid'a munkaru* (a reprehensible innovation).

He then condemns the following as those who committed this heresy of defining Jihad to be defensive: Abd al-Wahhab al-Khallaf, Mahmud Shaltut, Muhammad Abd Allah Diraz, Wahba Zuhayli, Muhammad Izza Darwaza, Hamid Sultan; Ali Ali Mansur, Jamal al-Banna, Abd al-Khaliq al-Nawawi, Muhammad Ra'fat Uthman. I need not to stress that all of them are well known religious thinkers and are respected for their scholarship. This trend of privatization can be traced to the inclusion of *Amr bi 'l-ma 'ruf* in the books on Islamic Criminal Law. I illustrate here with reference to 'Abdul Qadir 'Awda's (shahid 1954) *Al-tashri' al-Jina'i al-Islami*, which has become popular text in law faculties.' Awda argues that *Jihad, Zakat*, and enforcement of *Hudud* (penalties) are not only duties of a state but also of an individual. It is an individual obligation to use physical force to correct evil. He, therefore, allows an individual to inflict punishment on convicted criminals. He argues that enforcement of *Hudud* is an obligation for the Muslim Umma as a whole, not only for the state.

The Islamic legal principle of *Ihdar* (violability, meaning loss of rights and protection) is not available for non-

Muslims and apostates. Islamic law provides legal protection only on the basis of *Iman* (faith) and *Aman* (pact), 'Awda maintains. The life and property of a non-Muslim are violable if he or his people have no agreement of protection with Muslims. An apostate, a Muslim who forsakes Islam, also loses all rights and becomes violable. According to 'Wada, any Muslim can kill a *Harbi* (a non-Muslim without a pact of protection) or an apostate without criminal liability. 'Awda extends the law of violability also to persans sentenced in the Hudud crimes. If a Muslim kills a person convicted for *Zina*, rebellion and robbery, he is not criminally liable for murder.

'A wda's concept of the principle of violability (*Ihdar*) of life differs significantly from the classical jurists. For instance, according to Hanafi School, a person who kills an apostate must be punished for taking law into his own hands. The Maliki school calls for punishment in this case in addition to *diya* (compensation for murder. Similarly, according to Maliki, Hanafi and Hanbali schools, the murder of a persan convicted for *Zina* may not be treated as homicide but may be punished for taking law in his own hands. The Shafi 'i jurists regard the person criminally liable for murder. 'A wda disagrees with the views of these schools and justifies, in a sense, taking law into one's own hand: " If courts do not sentence an apostate, as it commonly happens in Muslim countries today, these institutions have no authority to punish a person who kills an apostate (in obedience to *Sharia*). The killer cannot be accused of violating the authority of these institutions because they have not undertaken the responsibility of enforcing *Shari 'laws*. Since they have forsaken *Shari a,* individuals cannot be held responsible if they implement these laws on their own".

Muslim orthodoxy condemned these views as religious extremism. Muslim governments started taking legal actions against these movements. These groups were however too well organized and financially too strong to be controlled by Muslim governments. While the governments in Egypt, Pakistan and Saudi Arabia banned these extremist Jihad organizations, the Ulama were engaged in distinguishing jihad from extremism, militarism, violence and terror. These inner controversies in the Muslim world on Jihad came to be known to the world only after the 11 September. In fact this debate was already going on in Muslim societies. That is why the condemnation of the terrorist attack was immediate and unanimous. Sa'id Ramadan al-Buti, in bis Al-Jihad fi 'I Islam (1993) rejected the use of Jihad for political change, revolution, and to change the government.

The right Islamic legal term for this activity was Baghy (revolt and disobedience). Islamic law allowed revolt if it could be justified rationally. The use of violence and force without specific political objective was also distinct from Jihad. Islamic law called it Haraba (terror) which was a crime and condemnable. In Iran the Shi'i thinker Mutahhari refuted the extremist argument that Jihad was an absolute obligation and that the Muslims must always be at war with non-Muslims. Jihad was a positive concept. That is why in Iran the term Jihad was used for social reconstruction. Jihad Sazindagi (1979) aimed at modernization of rural Iran, roads, schools, health, electricity, etc.

Pluralism

Pluralism favours the freedom of individual. It questions the traditional monopoly of certain persons, groups or institutions to prescribe ethical values authoritatively. Pluralism derives its legitimacy and acceptance by justifying universal values in local contexts. This is particularly significant in today's world of globalism. A powerful group, nation or country cannot impose its values on others without generating the feelings of frustration and resentment among the weaker groups and countries. Globalism can succeed only on the basis of ethical pluralism. Generally, Islamic law is regarded as the only Islamic moral tradition. Islam as a moral tradition has never been monolithic. Quite early in its history, it developed several approaches to moral issues.

These approaches vary in their sources of authority, methods of interpretations and emphasis. They sometimes oppose one another but often continue to function side by side, even complementing each other. It is therefore well in order to review, even if briefly, these various moral traditions in Islam.

The Hadith literature reflects a very significant moral tradition. It offers the Prophet Muhammad and his companions as models for moral behaviour. This tradition does refer to the pre-Islamic tribal Sunna but only to elaborate its approval or disapproval by early Muslims. The outstanding aspect of this ethical tradition is that it is essentially religious and authenticity oriented. However, the fact that this tradition produced dozens of compendia, each of them accepted by Muslims as authoritative, stresses the principle of ethical pluralism within the tradition itself. Pre-Islamic tribal values like manliness, honor, forbearance and tolerance were part of the Arab Sunna tradition that operated at the level of custom and usage in the literary moral tradition called Adab. The Adab tradition represents a humanist moral approach to morality. Most probably, writings in this tradition were initiated by Ibn Muqaffa' (d. 756), and carried on by several other writers like Ibn Qutayba (d. 889), al-Mawardi, (d. 1058) and Qalqashandi (d. 1418). The Adab tradition expresses itself in the literary genre. The Adab literature is composed as guides for the rulers or civil servants, or mirrors for the prince. It lays down the ideal model behaviour for them.

This tradition is more open as it derives its ethical values from diverse sources: pre-Islamic Arabic as well as Persian literature, Qur'an, history of Islam, ancient Persian history and Greek and Indian Literature. Ibn Muqaffa' translated into Arabic *Kalila wa Dimna,* a book on moral stories originating in India. The Adab tradition continues in arts and literature but also as etiquette literature providing code of ethics for various professions such as musicians. The philosophical tradition in Islam dealt with the ethical issues on a more abstract level than the Adab tradition. One of the essential questions with which this tradition engaged itself was about the question of ethical obligation and its origins. The issue was whether it was only religion that defined rights and obligations or the human reason on its own could also differentiate between ethically good and bad. The Muslim philosophers explored the nature, of Prophethood, revelation, role of reason and other such themes.

From Ibn Sina (d. 1037) to Ibn Rushd (d. 1198), the Muslim philosophers generally argued that there was no conflict between reason and revelation. The most interesting example of the discussion of this problem is the treatises by the title *Hayy bin Yaqzan* (The Living, son of Awake) by Ibn Sina and Ibn Tufayl (d. 1185). Ibn Tufayl's story presents Hayy as a human child growing up on an island among animals, without any contact with humans. By instinct and experience he develops a moral code for himself. Later, he finds out that his moral values were not different from the religious values in the neighboring island with human habitat. Jurist philosophers like Abu Ishaq al-Shatibi and Shah Waliullah also hold that human reason reaches similar conclusions during the absence of revelation.

Rushdi Rashid has argued that Algebra presented a new rationality that provided a new intellectual strategy to find new solutions. It opened new vistas into the realm of the impossible. Algebra, employing the multidisciplinary methods of geometry and arithmetic, demonstrated that approximate and impossible solutions could also be true solutions of a problem. The philosophical tradition developed a system of practical or applied ethics that came to be known as *Akhlaq*. It received its recognition as Islamic ethics proper as early as eleventh century. It is a synthesis of pre-Islamic Arab moral values, Qur'anic teachings and has Persian, Indian and Greek elements in it. Miskawayh's (d. 1030) *Tahdhib al-Akhlaq* offers a comprehensive and systematic treatment of ethical values in this tradition. It is quite obviously influenced by Greek ethical literature. Miskawayh explains that Greek ethics is more in accord with Islamic teachings than the pre-Islamic Arab morality. Jalal al-Diu al-Dawwani (d. 1501) and Nasir al-Diu alTusi (d.) followed Miskawayh in their writings on ethics. Their books, popularly known as and respectively, were used as textbooks in the religious institutions.

The Sufi moral tradition is more popular than the other Islamic moral traditions. The Sufis were critical of the literal and exoteric approach to obligations by the jurists and theologians. Al- Harith al-Muhasibi (d. 857) wrote *Kitab al-ri 'ava fi huquq Allah* (The book of observance of the rights of God). He treats ethical obligations as surrender to the will of God. He speaks of moral values such as *Taqwa* (fear of God), *Tawba* (retum to God), and *Mahabba* (love) etc. Muhasibi stresses abiding by the laws of prescription and prohibition in the Qur'an and Sunna, but he stresses on a more conscious effort to contraI the self from its propensity toward evil. Ghazali (d.llll) also followed Miskawayh in his ethical writings. His books on ethics, namely *Ihva 'Ulum al-Din* and *Kimivai Sa 'adat* have been more popular among Muslim readers than bis other works. The Sufis became more and more critical of legal and theological approach to obligations in later local traditions. The folk literature stresses on inner and humanist meanings of obligations, and on tolerance, love and sincerity.

Kalam (theology) is another tradition that dealt with the moral questions. This tradition also came to engage very early with the question whether the ethical values of good and bad were known only by revelation and religion or human reason can also discover them. The Mu'tazila school maintained that the ethical values were rational and the revelation never contradicted them. The Mu'tazila developed an entire system of theology and jurisprudence on this basis. They believed in the principle of justice to the extent that they argued that it was an obligation even for God. The revelation, specifically the Qur'an, was not sempitermal because it conformed to the findings of human reason. The Mu'tazila came into conflict with other Muslims, especially the Hadith groups who accused them of denying Divine Attributes. Asha'ira, a group of theologians that broke away from the Mu'tazila denounced the theology of human reason. The Mu'tazila lost the caliphal support they had in the initial period and other groups gained strength. The Kalam tradition, however, is not monolithic; it also developed multiple voices. It was not pluralist in the strict sense as each group claimed authenticity only for itself.

Fiqh (legal ethics) developed initially as multiple local customary legal traditions. The plurality of views in the Fiqh traditions is proverbial. The Hadith tradition questioned the authenticity of Fiqh traditions and described it as mere opinions (*ra 'y*) as opposed to the Hadith which was based on scientific knowledge (*'ilm*). The Fiqh traditions produced more than nineteen schools, all of them recognizing each other's legal validity. The multiplicity of views continues within the schools and is regarded as a blessing. The principle of legal reasoning (*ijtihad*) encourages difference of opinion considered religiously rewardable even in case of error. Adherence to these different schools of law is reflected in the diverse personallaws in Muslim societies. It is significant to note that the caliphs in early Islamic history were quite apprehensive about the conflicting views of the Muslim jurists that produced diverse court judgements. Several Abbasi caliphs and later other Muslim rulers tried to unify laws.

Resistance to such attempts often came from the Muslim jurists themselves. They feared that such attempts would mean state interference in this tradition. They wanted to preserve their freedom. They did consider their works enforceable by the state, but they never agreed to codify them as state laws. As a result, Muslim societies have been continuously practicing legal pluralism before the advent of modern nation state. The rural and tribal areas continued their local customary laws, sometimes even non-Muslim laws (as for example in Mughal and Ottoman villages). In cities as well, there were different type of courts. The courts of complaints differed from ordinary courts even in their procedural laws. Different state institutions like police also had their own legal system and procedures. The Hisba (public sensor) courts had jurisdiction in business ethics in the market as well as in offences against public marals.

Fiqh soon came to stand for Shari'a (Divine law) and defined moral as well as legal obligations. This position of the Fiqh came about, mostly with the jurists functioning as Muftis. A Mufti, even today, may be asked about any matter under the sun and he is supposed to explain God's law on the points in question. Consequently, Fiqh assumed a dominating position. A Mufti's response, called Fatwa, offered a social construction of Shari' a, as most often it referred to a concrete social question. Fatwa reviews a moral practice with reference to the Shari'a ideal. Most often we find Muftis also adjusting ideals to practice in view of the prevailing social conditions. These practices are frequently assimilated in the tradition in such a way that they are sometimes hard to distinguish. I shall refer to some fatwas to illustrate this point in the next section.

To conclude, Islam as a moral tradition favours pluralism on two bases. Firstly because it appeals to human reason. The Qur'an attaches pivotal significance to individual rational choice and responsibility. "There is no coercion in religion. The truth stands out clear from Error" ... (Qur'an, 2:256). "By the soul, and the order given it, He has inspired it to its wrong and to its good" (Qur'an, 91: 7-8). "To each is a goal to which he turns it. Then strive for what is good..." (2: 178). "Say, 'The Truth is from your Lord', then believe who wills and deny who wills (18: 29). The emphasis here is not so much that ethical values are rational and scientific but that they are reasonable to be understood as such by humans. Since the level of understanding may differ from person to person and from community to community multiplicity of views is inevitable. The second basis of pluralism is social acceptance of these values. This basis also regulates the dissent. The Qur'an calls good Ma'ruf (well known) and evil Munkar (rejected) which points to the fact that normativity is based on social acceptance or rejection. The social dialectics develop the acceptable definition of ethical values.

Human Rights

There are two Muslim declarations on Human rights: The Universal Islamic Declaration of Human Rights (UIDHR) issued by the Islamic Council, a non government Muslim organization in London, in 1981 and the Cairo Declaration of Human Rights in Islam (CDHRI), issued by the Foreign Ministers of Muslim countries in Cairo in 1990. Compared with the Universal Declaration of Human Rights 1948, the area of common grounds between the Muslim documents and UDHR is larger than that where they differ. The two documents share respectively 20 and 14 themes of rights with those mentioned in the UDHR. It is also significant to note that UIDHR, which is a non-state declaration, has more in common with UDHR than CDHRI which is a state document.

The themes where the Muslim documents differ with UDHR are as follows: Freedom of thought and expression, protection of life, penal laws, marriage, and holding of public office. On the whole, I find in both documents an attempt to come closer to the global community. The same trend is reflected in numerous Muslim writings on Human rights which stress on a larger area of common perspectives. They suggest uniformity with an emphasis on diversity. In other words, diversity in these writings stresses the possibility of localizing the universals. Here, universal rights are mentioned in Islamic language, often claiming that Islam is the first religion to award these human rights.

In my view, these debates on Islam and human rights have been missing a very essential point: the ethical aspect of the human rights. A movement for global ethics hopes to fill this gap. I find Muslim anxieties emerging from the perspectives of national sovereignty and security on the one band and from religious and cultural perspective on the other band. Most human rights are restricted or violated by Muslim governments in the name of national security, and they object to international criticism as a violation of their national sovereignty. Concern for national security cannot justify violation of the freedom and dignity of man. However, when the US, Britain, and Israel, to name a few current examples, violate human rights and justify them in the name of national security, the question arises: what is global, national interest or ethical principles? UDHR document is quite ambivalent; it stresses the universality of human rights as well as the principle of the sovereignty of the nation and nation state.

It is a challenge for us all to define and apply human rights as truly universal principles, and not as an instrument for cultural, economic and political hegemony of the powerful. For this purpose Human Rights have to be rooted in ethics that protects the weak and the poor also. There is a wide range of diversity among Muslim scholars on human rights. This diversity is informed by a very complex under-standing of tradition and change. One notices three major trends in the Muslim writings on this subject: Neo conser-vative, Islamic modernists and Progressive Muslims. Neo-conservative Muslim thinkers that emerged in probably 1970s and their full impact was visible in 1980s. They are closer to conservative in sharing same cultural values. They differ with them however, because they have developed a new jurisprudence and they frequently use modern Western thought categories presenting and justifying their conservative values. Abdul Wahhab Abdul Aziz al-Shishani's book on Human Rights in Islam represents this group. Shishani speaks about a major paradigm shift in the concept of state in the modern period. This concept stresses protecting the rights of the individual.

Revising the authoritative sources of Islamic law Shishani adds six more to the classical four: the Qur'an, the Sunna (the rulings and practice of Prophet Muhammad), Qiyas (analogies from the above two), and Ijma' (consensus of the jurists). Normativity of Islamic laws is grounded on the principles that suit human nature; they are not based on customs of a people. This explanation illustrates this neo-conservatism. Unlike traditional jurists, who regard revelation by itself normative, this new trend justifies it on the basis of its suitability to human nature. AIso, unlike modemists, this trend dismisses historicity and social process as an explanation for the development of Islamic law. Also, unlike traditional conservatives who insist on continuing the legal tradition of the schools of law, this new trend calls for Ijtihad (legal reasoning beyond the confines of schools).

In contrast to conservatives, Islamic modernists believe that modernity is compatible to Islam. Like Neo-conservatives they stress on Ijtihad against strict adherence to the Islamic legal tradition, but they define it as "reinterpretation" or reconstruction. They believe that the classicallegal doctrines were product of historical and social contexts and therefore there is a need for reform. Their methodology consists of explaining the historical and social contexts of the basic Islamic texts, including the Qur'an, and to reinterpret them in view of modern needs. Progressive Muslims describe themselves as distinct from conservative and liberals because they regard Muslim liberals have relativised Islamic values and operate in a framework informed by the Western impact. They are committed to three basics: social justice, pluralism and gender justice.

A progressive Muslim engages with tradition in light of modernity, but at the same s/he is critical of the arrogance of modernity. Progressive Muslims are contesting injustice, exposing violations of human rights and freedom, standing up to increasing hegemonic Western political, economic, and intellectual structures that perpetuate an unequal distribution of resources around the world. Progressive Muslims distinguish themselves on the one band from conservative Muslims who adhere to the authority of the schools of law, and from neo-conservatives, including Wahhabis and neo-Wahhabis, the followers of fourteenth century Muslim Syrian thinker Ibn Taymiyya and an eighteenth century Arabian reformer Muhammad b. Abdul Wahhab. Safi describes Wahhabi as a reactionary theological movement based on a trivial ideology. On the other band, Progressive Muslims distinguish themselves from secularists and "modernists", who look to the prevalent notion of Western modernity as something to be imitated and duplicated *in toto.*

Progressive Muslims have developed a methodology which is different from other groups. They call it "multiple critiques", because it is critical of bath tradition and modernity. For example, veiling or *hijab* is not subjugation of women in all cases. In most cases, veiling is accepted as a strategy of negotiating the rights to work. "In Iran and Egypt, for example, as in other parts of the Muslim world, the wearing of the *hijab* has neutralized public space for many traditional families, thus making it more acceptable for women to occupy such space". Coming back to the public discourse on modernity with which I began this essay, I must note that this discourse expressed its concern about not only the Muslim attitude but also about the Western ambiguity in its commitment to modernity. The twentieth century had seen the end of the cold war and the beginning of a peace process in the various parts of the world. The humankind was supposed to be moving in the twenty first century to an era when conflicts would be resolved by reasoning and negotiations, not by use of violence.

No one could expect the 11 September colossal violence against humanity to happen in this era. Most of us could not expect a war also. The perception that Islam was not compatible with modernity and that the Muslims were opposed to the values and symbols of Western civilization, was not sufficient to justify a war against Muslims. It was claimed that the war on Afghanistan was not a war against

Islam, but' it was still a war. In spite of this explanation and despite the fact that almost all Muslim countries allied with the USA in this war the image of Islam as the main obstruction to modernity looms large. Fortunately, this voice did not dominate the public discourse this time. A considerably sizeable segment of this discourse remains critical of how the West, particularly the government agencies in the United States have functioned during this time of crisis. The way the wars were imposed on Afghanistan and Iraq has damaged the fragile achievements of modernity.

This criticism has insisted that the resort to terrorizing the terrorists has only proved that the West also did not believe in the values of modernity. Refusal to negotiate with Afghanistan, marginalization of the United Nations, and the use of the extremely destructive weapons against a country that had been already devastated by long wars and against the people who were already on the verge of extinction by famine, do not reflect a commitment to the values of modernity. The culture of modernity upholds that killing criminals cannot eliminate crime. That is the reason why modernity opposes capital punishments. Islam's incompatibility with modernity is also explained on the ground that Islamic penal law allows corporal punishments. The discussion in this public debate urges for investigating the causes of terrorism in order to eliminate terrorism. The debate suggested that terrorism was caused by the frustration felt on the failure of political solution. The US hegemonic foreign policy, especially its indifference to the political impasse in the Middle East, contributed to this frustration. Islam alone cannot be blamed for the failure of modernity today.

Islam and modernity is about the relation and compatibility between the phenomenon of modernity, its related concepts and ideas, and the religion of Islam. In order to understand the relation between Islam and modernity, one point should be made in the beginning. Both Islam and modernity are not simple and unified entities. They are abstract quantities which could not be reduced into simple categories. The history of Islam, like that of other religions, is a history of different interpretations and approaches to Islam. "There is no historical Islam that is outside the process of historical development." Similarly, modernity is a complex and multidimensional phenomenon rather than a unified and coherent phenomenon. It has historically had different schools of thoughts moving in many directions.

European Influence

Modernity swept through Europe in the 18th and 19th centuries. Power shifted from religious leaders to a growing civil service, with a deliberate separation of church and state. Respect for science grew with each new discovery. This led to scientific ideals such as rationality and empiricism being applied to society itself, changing industry, schools, and commerce. The Crimean War marked a major alliance between Christian and Islamic powers. The Ottoman Empire co-operated with France and Britain against Russia, and benefited from outside ideas about weapons and medicine. After the war, Muslim scholars became more interested in the west. This interest went beyond military technology and included European law, science, and art.

Islamic Modernists Until 1918

Turkey was the first Muslim country where modernity surfaced, with major shifts in scientific and legal thought. In 1834, Ishak Efendi published *Mecmua-i Ulum-i Riyaziye*, a four volume text introducing many modern scientific concepts to the Muslim world. Kudsi Efendi also published *Asrar al-Malakut* in 1846 in an attempt to reconcile Copernican astronomy with Islam. The first modern Turkish chemistry text was published in 1848, and the first modern Biology text in 1865. Eventually, the Turks adopted the metric system in 1869. These shifts in scientific thought coincided with Tanzimat, a reform policy undertaken by the Sultans of the Ottoman Empire that was inspired by French civil law.

This reform confined sharia to family law. The key figure in the Turkish modernist movement was Namik Kemal, the editor of a journal called *Freedom*. His goal was to promote freedom of the press, the separation of powers, equality before the law, scientific freedom, and reconciliation between parliamentary democracy and the Qur'an. In 19th century Iran, Mirza Malkom Khan arrived after being educated in Paris. He created a newspaper called *Qanun*, where he advocated the separation of powers, secular law, and a Bill of Rights. Jamal al-Din al-Afghani, also educated in France, proclaimed that Europe had become successful due to its laws and its science. He became critical of other Muslim scholars for stifling scientific thought, and hoped to encourage scientific inquiry in the Muslim world.

Muhammad Abduh became a leading judge in Egypt, after political activities and studies in Paris. He pushed for secular law, religious reform, and education for girls. He hoped that Egypt would ultimately become a free republic, much like how France had transformed from an absolute monarchy. Muhammad Rashid Rida also became active in the Egyptian modernization movement, although he was born and educated in Lebanon. *Al-Manar* was his journal, through which he advocated greater openness to science and foreign influence.

He also stated that sharia was relatively silent about agriculture, industry, and trade, and that these areas of knowledge needed renewal. Qasim Amin was another reformer in Egypt heavily concerned with the rights of women. Khayr al-Din al-Tunisi was similarly educated in Paris around the same time. He surveyed the political systems of 21 European countries in an effort to reform Tunisia. Other major Islamic modernists included Mahmud Tarzi of Afghanistan, Sayyid Khan of India, Achmad Dachlan of Java, and Wang Jingshai of China.

Impact of Early Islamic Modernists

The influence of modernism in the Islamic world resulted in a cultural revival. Dramatic plays became more common, as did newspapers. Notable European works were analyzed and translated. Legal reform was attempted in Egypt, Tunisia, the Ottoman Empire, and Iran, and in some cases these reforms were adopted. Efforts were made to restrict the power of government. Polygamy was ended in India. Azerbaijan granted suffrage to women in 1918 (before several European countries). At the recommendations of reform-minded Islamic scholars, western sciences were taught in new schools. Much of this had to do with the intellectual appeal of social Darwinism, since it led to the conclusion that an old-fashioned Muslim society could not compete in the modern world. Just as the Bible had been deconstructed and criticized in light of modern science, so too was the Qur'an.

1918-1968

The aftermath of World War I resulted in the fall of the Ottoman Empire and the domination of the Middle East by European powers such as Britain and France. Intellectual historians such as Peter Watson suggest that World War I marks the end of the main Islamic modernist movements, and that this is the point where many Muslims "lost faith with the culture of science and materialism". He goes on to note that several parallel streams emerged after this historical moment. In some parts of the world, the project of Islamic modernity continued from the same trajectory before the Great War. This was especially the case in the new Republic of Turkey, under Mustafa Kemal Atatürk.

Political Islam

Certain groups and thinkers openly criticized European ideas, which they saw as a corrupting influence on Islamic thought. By the 1920s this stream of thought began a surge in power, emphasizing a modern society that would not abandon traditional Islamic law. In British India, the Muslim League had co-operated with Hindu leaders in the Indian National Congress for a few years, with the goal of an independent and unified India. But once the Indian National Congress rejected the idea of separate electorates for Muslims, the divisions with the Muslim League became stronger. Muhammad Iqbal, a philosopher and poet educated in the West, was elected president of the Punjab Muslim League in 1930.

Iqbal believed that Islam had traditions that were inseparable from social order, and thus rejected the notion that Muslims ought to blend with other peoples in a secular society. He emphasized traditional rules guided by Islam, along with a philosophy of free will inspired by Nietzsche. This philosophy was a driving force behind the creation of Pakistan as a Muslim state. In Egypt, Hassan al-Banna founded the Muslim Brotherhood. This can be seen as a predecessor to more militant Islamic fundamentalist groups in the late 20th century. On the other hand, Arab socialism of Arab Socialist Ba'ath Party and Nasserite movement emerged as a stream of thought that played down the role of religion.

1968-Present

The Six-Day War ended in a decisive loss for the Muslim side. Many in the Islamic world saw this as the failure of socialism. It was at this point that "fundamental and militant Islam began to fill the political vacuum created".

The Middle East, Modernity and the proliferation of Islamic fundamentalism:

Liberal movements within Islam have attempted to reconcile Islamic sharia law with feminism and human rights norms of international law. Numerous efforts have been made in Iran among other countries to make democracy and religion compatible. Mohammad Khatami voiced concepts like civil society, democracy and tolerance in Iran and other parts of Islamic world. Modern efforts in Indonesia, Afghanistan and the proposed state of Palestine have often emphasized the traditional role of women's control of the household finances. In Bangladesh the Grameen Bank has been involved in microcredit financing of small businesses run exclusively by women.

Modern Islamists movements are considered the 'dominant' voice today, though this belies the reality. Some Islamists (the word itself has yet to be well-defined, since there is no overall global "Islamist" movement) have entered the limited democratic processes in the Gulf States, and others, such as those in Pakistan, have long been on the political stage. The vast majority of Muslims remain within, what has been termed, Traditional Islam, which is largely apolitical and accommodationist (and so a subject of criticism from certain activists). Advocates of violence, like Qutb, were opposed to the traditional scholars of al-Azhar, because they regard them as complicit in the crimes of the secular state. One general feature of Islamist movements is that they advocate creation of "the Islamic state", though this often means "Islamisation" of the modern nation-state.

In general, the first two trends are more commonly understood in the Islamic World whereas the latter trends are more known in non-Muslim and Muslim-minority nations, or ones receiving substantial aid from developed nations. Some argue that this suggests that these trends are insincere and that alternations between fundamentalism and secular military dictators are somehow inherently part of the politics of the Arab World in particular. One response is that such trends were likewise observed in other regions, e.g. Latin America, with Communism as a form of fundament-alism, and that those regions often democratize once outside interference is limited.

In recent years the world has witnessed the proliferation of Islamic extremist groups all over the world and in the Middle East, who are voicing their dislike of concepts such as democracy and modernity. This is due to the fact that democracy and modernity as concepts in the Middle East, are most commonly associated with imposing Western secular beliefs and values. If considering that about 95% of the population of the Middle East is Muslims and keeping in mind the imperial past of the region, it should come as no surprise that the spread of secularism has caused great concerns among many Islamic political groups. It has indeed been the reasoning for the 'islamisation of politics and protest' which has been seen happening across the region. To reiterate, for Islamic countries in the Middle East, there is not necessarily a problem as such with modernity, however, 'the problem is when modernity comes wrapped with wersternisation, with absolutely and utterly rampant materialism'.

In the book, *Political Islam: Religion and Politics in the Arab World* (1994), the author N. Ayubi continues this debate by explaining, what he believes to be the two main concerns of Islamic political movements and extremist groups in the Middle East; namely the Western belief in a bureaucratic state and secondly, what is mentioned above, the secular values and beliefs associated with concepts such as modernity.

These concerns are exemplified in an interview with the well-known Islamic fundamentalist, Osama Bin Laden who states, after being asked about the message he wants to send to the West:

Their presence [in the Middle East] has no meaning save one and that is to offer support to the Jews an Palestine who are in need of their Christian brothers to achieve full control over the Arab peninsula, which they intend to make an important part of the so called Greater Israel...They rip us of our wealth and of our resources and of our oil. Our religion is under attack. They kill and murder our brothers. They compromise our honor and our dignity and if we dare to utter a single word of protest against the injustice, we are called terrorists.

After September 11, the Western media often has its focus on personalities such as Usama Bin Laden for condemnation, and exaggerate what are often unknown terrorists into forerunners of "Islamic jihad." This causes the creation of stereotypes of Muslims in the Middle East and moreover, results in the grants of prominence to Islamic fundamentalists who might otherwise have been insignificant political characters, and legitimises extremist opinions and views which might otherwise have been shunned by mainstream Muslims. However, as John Esposito notes:

> The tendency to judge the actions of Muslims in splendid isolation, to generalize from the actions of the few to the many, to disregard similar excesses committed in the name of other religions and ideologies…is not new.

Yet, the number of militant Islamic movements 'calling for an Islamic states and the end of Western influence is relatively small.' Nevertheless, these groups are causing great fear among people in the Middle East and in the West. Finding a solution to this problem of fear will depend not only on how Islam deals with concepts such as modernity, but on how the West deals with Islam.

To understand the relationship between Islam and modernity, it is important to begin with an understanding of the religion itself. Generically, Islam is a religion which brings the mission of liberation and salvation. Islam came to the world in order to bring a set of new morality because of its metaphysical and humanitarian characters. It brings not only vertical dimension teachings, but also horizontal aspects for humanity. It is a teaching deriving from God and oriented toward humanity. Thus, Islam highly respects the dimension of humanity. The presence of Islam as a moral source can be observed in its achievement in transforming pre-Islamic Arabic nomads into civilized communities with values and morality. With the presence of Islam, these communities, being used to living in open deserts and highly susceptible to inter-tribal wars and conflicts, achieved success becoming sensitized to elevated values and morality. Inter-tribal wars and conflict occurred because of their lack of values and morality, which terminated after Islam spread its teachings. The Qur'an, Muslims' holy book and reference, has manifested itself in a language laden with aesthetics, which has the power to influence the nomads' emotions and awareness in shaping society's humanitarian vision.

Linguistically, Islam derives from the root words implying the meaning of peace, salvation, maslahah (well-being) and justice. Islam is a metamorphosis of a three-letter root word (tsulatsi), i.e. salima-yaslamu-salaaman, meaning safe and peaceful. The four-letter root word (ruba'i) namely aslama-yuslimu-islaman means to save and to bring peace. Linguistically speaking, Islam has a very fundamental concern for peace, justice, and well-being. These values should be inwardly internalized by each and every Muslim in the first place. The feeling of being secure and safe in the mind of every Muslim individual is a basic capital for transcending the same feeling to others, making them sensitized to society's needs and interests.

This feeling generally grows along with the process of ritualism and ritual practices, which will strengthen one's commitment and vision on the equality of all human beings. Islam teaches that there is no hierarchical structure among Muslims, all are equal before God. The combination of spiritual and ritual practices will produce Muslims who have balanced personalities, inwardly and outwardly, vertically and horizontally.

Islam, Modernity and Modernization

Is Islam compatible with modernity? How do Muslims respond to the continuous change of the world which has grown at a rapid and unprecedented rate in the last century? How do we resolve the problem of maintaining the legacy of the past in our religious tradition and integrate change into society and our lives? How do we introduce change smoothly, which is rare and difficult, without disrupting societies and dislocating values? These are some questions that may trigger a discussion on the relations between Islam and modernity. There are various responses to this problem, depending on our point of view. An economist has one kind of answer, a sociologist perhaps another. A secularist has a certain type of answer, which may be different from a fundamentalist's. Modernity and modernization are words that are continuously contested in contemporary Islamic discourse.

Modernization, the introduction into society of the artifacts of contemporary life such as communications, technology, or household equipment, has permeated into virtually all societies including Muslims. But modernity, a way of thought and of living in the contemporary world and of accepting change, as part of political and cultural processes by integrating new ideas into society, may not always be present. One may be using modern technologies and modern communication system, but maintains a past-oriented closed mindset and resists new ideas of modernity such as democracy or pluralism. The opposite can be true; one may lack modern facilities and live traditionally but adopt the attitudes of modernity. These people assume an attitude of enquiry into how people make choices, be they moral, personal, economic, or political. This problem of rational choice is central to modern people. Choice, query and doubt—which imply rationality, debate, discussion and disagreement—are part and parcel of modern mindset.

Muslims' Responses to Modernity

How do Muslims react to modernity? There are several forms of reactions, but for simplicity purpose they will be grouped into two: the reformist/modernist and the fundamentalist. The modernists are devout, knowledgeable Muslims whose mission is threefold: first, to define Islam by bringing out the fundamentals in a rational and liberal manner; second, to emphasize, among others, the basic ideals of Islamic brotherhood, tolerance, and social justice; and third, to interpret the teaching of Islam in such a way as to bring out its dynamic character in the context of the intellectual and scientific progress of the modern world. The modernists sincerely endeavour to reconcile differences between traditional religious doctrine and secular scientific rationalism, between unquestioning faith and reasoned logic, and between continuity of Islamic tradition and modernity.

Reformists/Modernists

Many consider Jamal al-Din al-Afghani (1838-1897) as the father of Islamic modernism. He was foremost a belief in the transcendence of God and in reason. Independent judgment and interpretation, the so-called ijtihad, is a necessity and the duty of man is to apply the principles of the Qur'an afresh to the problems of the time. He extremely critical of traditional ulama (religious scholars) who discouraged any new and creative thought and convinced that this type of medieval mentality was primarily responsible for the decline of Muslim power and influence in the world. Islam must be active and energetic. Al-Afghani supported this principle by quoting the Qur'an that "God changes not what is in a people until they change what is in themselves.' He argued that Europeans had integrated change, and Muslims must do it in their own way by becoming better Muslims. He thought that Europeans had modernized because they were no longer really Christian; and Muslims, conversely, were weak because they were not really Muslims.

He questioned the division of knowledge into two categories: Muslim knowledge and European knowledge. He argued that knowledge, which is a noble thing, has no connection with any particular group. Islam is the closest religion to knowledge and learning and there is no contradiction between (modern) knowledge and the basic principles of Islam. Al-Afghani strongly recommended acquiring Western knowledge, technology, and services, as long as borrowing from the West was selective and served the basic needs and aspirations of the Muslim people. In this undertaking, which he believed would raise the standard of living of all Muslims; al-Afghani struggled to initiate an Islamic reformation similar to the successful Christian Reformation sparked by Martin Luther.

The seeds for ijtihad (logical reasoning) planted by al-Afghani were sustained by his most prominent Egyptian student and ardent follower, Muhammad Abduh (1849-1905), who insisted that Muslims could improve their lives and their society only by carefully studying the Qur'an in the light of reason and rationality. He taught that the Qur'an gives all Muslims the right to differ even with the ulama, if the latter were unreasonable or irrational. Abduh constantly encouraged Muslims to approach problems in the true spirit of Islam: through analysis, reason and logic. Because of his emphasis on reason and rationality, he considered Islam and constructive science twin offspring of reason, which "God gave to guide us in the right path."

The reformers of Islamic thought and practice such as al-Afghan, Abduh, or the more contemporary like Mahmud Muhammad Taha of Sudan, Muhammad Abed Al-Jabri, Ali Shariati of Iran or Abdurrahman Wahid of Indonesia, are knowledgeable not only about Islam but also about modern non-Islamic Western ideas. They believe in the convergence of Islamic and universal ethics and eager to introduce them into their own societies. Hence, unlike the fundamentalists, modernists do not fear or dislike Western ideas and practices. On the contrary, they welcome non-Islamic ideas and practices that they consider beneficial to the progress and prosperity of Muslim societies. They imaginatively synthesize Islamic and Western ideas to produce a reasonable and relevant reinterpretation of Islamic thought with enlightened cosmopolitan, liberal, and realistic perspectives. Modernists believe that this tolerance for diversity and willingness to adjust rapidly to a changing environment contributes to the emancipation of the individual Muslim and to the progress of Muslim societies.

Firstly referred to in the U.S. in the early 1920's in connection with the battles of leading evangelical Protestants against liberal and progressive spirits of the age, fundamentalism is now observed to exist in all religions. The term has recently been used reluctantly and apologetically to describe new radical Islamic movements, or to offer substitute terms such as 'revivalists,' 'religious nationalists,' 'Islamic radicals,' 'political Islam,' 'Islamists,' or 'extremists.' For all the controversy, it is clear that fundamentalism can lead to superficiality and reductionism in one's under-standing of the religion. Deeper spiritual dimension of the religion cannot be captured and reflected because funda-mentalisms tend to refer to religious texts rigidly and literally. Fundamentalist thinking is no more relevant in the currently fast changing world because human problems are so complex and diverse. Religious texts need to be reinterpreted by putting at the forefront the goal of the religion (maqasid al-syari'ah).

Two tasks are relevant in understanding fundamentalism: to ascertain why it has emerged in the larger cultural-historical sense—what is the common cause with which fundamentalism is associated; and to explain the particular-ities of its emergence—why here and not there, why now and not then, why among these groups and not those, and so on. Almond et al. categorize fundamentalist movements into four: 1) world conqueror, 2) world transformer, 3) world creator, and 4) world renouncer. To the first group they classify, on top, Al-Qaeda. Others include, inter alia, the Revolutionary Shi'ism in Iran, the Sunni radical movements in Egypt (Muslim Brotherhood), the Ulster Protestants (sparked by the entrenched ethnic conflict between Scot and English-derived Protestants and Irish Catholics), the Sikh militants, and the Sri Lankan Buddhist extremists. Meanwhile, the world transformer group comprises among others of the U.S. Protestant fundamentalism and the Pentecostalism in Guatemala.

Ideologically, fundamentalism is marked by several characteristics. First, it reacts against marginalization of the religion. Fundamentalist movements form in reaction to, and in defense against, the processes and consequences of secularization and modernization that have penetrated the larger religious community. Protestants, Catholics, Muslim, Jews, Hindus, Sikhs and Buddhists are losing their members to the secular world outright or to relativism—the assumption that any given religion is culture-bound and thus relatively true or false. Second, fundamentalists demonstrate moral Manichaeanism, a dualistic worldview which uncompromisingly divides the world into two: the light (the world of the spirit and of the good) and the darkness (the evil). Third, they are selective. For example, they accept much of the modern science and modern technology such as radio, television, computer, and so on but refuse the concepts arising out of modernity such as democracy. Fourth, fundamentalists are absolutist and inerrant. They steadfastly believe in the infallibility of certain religious interpretation and oppose hermeneutical methods developed by secularized philosophers or critics.

Modernity is the common denominator of the outside forces, which is often viewed as an external threat by the fundamentalists. Failure of modernizing secular state is evident by political decay, the decline of politics into authoritarianism, patrimonialism, corruption, and the dissatisfaction with the project of the post colonial secular states. The growing saliency of religion in the politics of countries throughout the world is a struggle for cultural liberation in search for authentic identity, political representation, and more equitable development in third world countries. The unbalanced pace of modernization and development has led many Muslim countries into developmental crises. The rapid changes through a process of technological, economic, political, social, and cultural innovation, however, have not been followed by the development of their people. In contrast to modernization, development denotes the relative welfare of a nation's population. In most Muslim countries, appropriate development has not happened because it is neither holistic nor healthy.

Modernization and development have become paradoxical. Modernization has occurred rapidly, while appropriate development has not. In the West, modernization accompanied the growth of a middle class. Because of its relative success in the West, modernization has become identified with Westernization and secularization. The unhappy predicament of the nation-building, modernizing, and secularizing Muslim world has given rise to a number of crises, afflicting the fragile nation states of developing world. Of the five developmental crises—identity, legitimacy, penetration, distribution, participation—the identity crises is often the precipitating crisis, triggering political chaos and national catastrophe. Rapid modernization has broken the familiarity of traditional society, uprooting people from their traditional communities and moving them to new social environments where they oft become victims of the development. These conditions are fertile grounds for the breeding of fundamentalism.

Needs to Focus on Women

During the last three decades the world has witnessed a growing process of Islamization or re-Islamization, the application of Islamic principles and values to personal and public life. Along with greater religious observance among many individuals of their prayer, fasting, dress code and so on, there grows as well as the creation of new institution such as Islamic banking, insurance companies, and finance houses. Although many speak of the failure of political Islam, a more widespread and significant reality exists. Islam is becoming a more visible and dynamic force in Muslim life and societies. While this growing Islamization has had an impact on states, societies, and communities, women seem to be impacted the most. More than anything else, gender-related issues present some of the most difficult and complicated challenges to contemporary Islamic law.

Islamic legal system regulating women-related issues, the family law (al-akhwal al-syakhsyiyyah), has remained static and immutable since its codification a thousand years ago. Time and space have changed, and Muslims are currently living in a completely different socio-cultural and political context, but the conventional shari'a on gender and women remain unchanged. This same law has been used as a reference on issues like gender relations, polygamy, divorce, inheritance, women's leadership role, etc. which, unsurprisingly, reaffirms the already patriarchal attitudes of many Muslim males. Under the guise of uplifting Islamic law, the war against women is launched demonstrating the misuse and abuse of God's authority in order to impose a suffocating patriarchy among Muslim society. It is imperative that Muslim legal specialists develop critical ways of dealing with these issues. The resurgence of Islamic fundamentalism in the last decades has been signified most obviously by its perseverance in reviving Islamic doctrines on women's status. Fundamentalists appear to share a common sense of threat from changes in gender relations, triggered by the spread of capitalism and modern concepts of feminism. They believe in the doctrines that put restrictions on women.

On the basis of shari'a and kodrat (nature) women have to be controlled, subjugated and live in the domestic sphere. Hasan al-Bana, founder of Muslim Brotherhood in Egypt, expresses his fear of women's liberation and equality by saying that women's place is the home, and their primary roles are mother, wife, and housekeeper. Social mixing between men and women is prohibited. Another fundamentalist Muslim, Abul A'la al-Mawdudi, founder of Jamiat-I Islami from Pakistan, says that one of the basic human rights is respect for women's chastity. To preserve chastity women must be kept household and in purdah. Cases of discrimination and violence against women in the name of Islam can be documented from worldwide. Experiences of formalization of shari'a in Muslim countries like Saudi Arabia, Afghanistan, Sudan, Iran, and other gulf countries show that women are systematically marginalized, forced to veil themselves, may not go out without a guardian, or work in public places. Women are made to become detainees in their husbands' homes.

In pursuit of Islamic Feminism

"Feminism" is a contested term even in their birthplace, the West. Historical literature is filled with different types of feminists who would certainly find difficulties identifying common ground. Likewise is the notion "Islamic feminism." Scholars and activists are divided in terms of acceptance of this term. Some consider it problematic as they find it impossible to reconcile between Islam and feminism. They believe that the power structure in Muslim societies is so male dominated that the epistemology of Islam is contrary to women's rights. Some activists who truly work to promote women's rights in Islam refuse to be called Islamic feminists because of their reluctance to be identified with Western feminism.

Increasing pressures on women following the Islamist movement have induced the birth of Islamic feminism. Contrary to secular feminists, Muslim feminists keep the faith in the religion and religious teachings while trying to promote egalitarian ethics of Islam by using the female supportive verses of the Qur'an in their fights for women's rights, especially for women's access to education. In Iran the failures of the Islamic Republic of Iran (IRI) to deliver its promise to honour and protect women has led to the emergence of the Islamic challenge, or what the Iranian Muslim feminist Ziba Mir-Hosseini calls "an indigenous locally, produced, feminist consciousness."

In Indonesia, the emergence of Islamic feminism has been triggered by the growing conservatism in the last decades along with the growing Islamism that has threatened women's relatively good position and status in society. This movement neither adopts Western feminism nor follows Middle Eastern model of gender relations but refuses both secularism and Islamism, and is purely based on values and tradition of Islam prevalent in Indonesia. The ultimate goal of the movement is to pursue justice for women, justice that is promised by Islam to all humankind.

8

The Wahhabi Teaching

Wahhabism and the Occult Conspiracy

British Channel 4's *Dispatches* has produced a scathing documentary, called *Undercover Mosque,* about the negative influence of Saudi Arabia, through its promotion of Wahhabism, among the Muslim community of Britain. But the video is clear to point out that, "Wahhabism is opposed to the traditional tolerant beliefs of classical Islam". What the video does not cover, however, is that the spread of the Wahhabi interpretation of Islam is part of a larger Western agenda, involving the CIA, to denigrate Islam. The Wahhabis insinuate themselves as legitimate members of the Muslim community, but Wahhabism was created by the British, in the eighteenth century, to undermine Islam. It has since been promoted by the state of Saudi Arabia, which was originally established by the British to achieve Western control of the world's primary oil resource.

In modern times, the Wahhabis have aligned themselves with a still more pernicious deviation from Islam, the Salafi. These name themselves accordingly because they claim to follow the earliest generations of the Muslims, known as the Salaf, and therefore, to be nearest to the purity of the original faith. Nothing could be further from the truth. Salafism was the result of a policy, at the turn of the century, of the Oxford movement, headed by Lord Palmerston, Benjamin Disraeli and Edward Bullwer-Lytton, to spread Scottish Rite Freemasonry in the Middle East (Robert Dreyfuss, *Hostage to Khomeini*). Lord Palmerston was a fellow member of the Palladian Rite, along with Albert Pike, who originally devised a plot for three world wars, culminating in a third against the Muslim world. Bulwer-Lytton was a leading occult figure, heading the English Rosicrucians, which evolved directly from the Shabbatean heresy, through the Asiatic Brethren.(author, *Terrorism and the Illuminati*, "The Salafi")

The agent of this strategy was a notorious impostor by the name of Jamal ud Din al Afghani, the Grand Master of the Freemasons of Egypt. According to K. Paul Johnson, it was Afghani, as head of the occult Hermetic Brotherhood of Luxor, or HB of L, who was responsible for teaching Helena Blavatsky her central doctrines (*In Search of the Masters*). Helena P. Blavatsky, the famous medium and mystic, was the godmother of the occult revival of the late nineteenth century. According to Manly P. Hall, a leading Masonic historian:

The Secret Doctrine and *Isis Unveiled* are Madame Blavatsky's gifts to humanity, and to those whose vision can pierce the menacing clouds of imminent disaster it is no exaggeration to affirm that these writings are the most vital literary contribution to the modern world. No more can they be compared with other books than can the light of the sun be compared with the lamp of the glowworm. *The Secret Doctrine* assumes the dignity of a scripture.

Numerous other leading occultists affiliated with Bullwer-Lytton's English Rosicrucians travelled to Egypt at the time, and on their return, established branches of the HB of L, out of which emerged the *Ordo Templi Orientis* (OTO), the most notorious member of which was Aleister Crowley. The Nazis were the result of a merging of the O.T.O of Crowley and the Thule Gesselschaft of Germany. It is presumably for this reason that Hitler, when he wished to create an arm of German Intelligence in Egypt, contacts a leading Salafi and Freemason, named Hasan al Banna.

It was eventual head of the CIA, Allen Dulles, after WWII, who spearheaded the move to hire ex-Nazis to train the terrorists. This was part of the same plot that created the Stay-Behind or Gladio network, that were behind the "Strategy of Tension" that used the Red Brigade to destabilize Italy throughout the seventies. In 1954, after it was discovered that the Muslim Brotherhood was responsible for an attack on his life, President Gamal Nasser of Egypt ordered a crackdown. Interrogations revealed that the Muslim Brotherhood functioned virtually as a German Intelligence unit. As well, as divulged by Miles Copeland, a former CIA operative specializing in the Middle East, in his autobiography, *The Game Player*:

Nor was that all. Sound beatings of the Muslim Brotherhood organizers who had been arrested revealed that the organization had been thoroughly penetrated, at the top, by the British, American, French and Soviet intelligence services, any one of which could either make active use of it or blow it up, whichever best suited its purposes. Important lesson: fanaticism is no insurance against corruption; indeed, the two are highly compatible. Fleeing members of the Muslim Brotherhood were then shuttled to the CIA's ally, Saudi Arabia. When John Loftus, a Justice Department official in the eighties, was permitted to peruse classified government documents, he discovered that the British Secret Service convinced American intelligence that the Arab Nazis of the Muslim Brotherhood would be indispensable as "freedom fighters" in preparation for the next major war, which was anticipated against the Soviet Union. There, according to Loftus, "they were given jobs as religion education instructors."

Among those transferred to Saudi Arabia by the CIA was Mohammed Qutb, brother of the executed head of the Brotherhood, Sayed Qutb, who then befriended Osama bin Laden, and recruited him into the organization. The first important strategy which they served in, at the height of the Cold War, was as pawns in the US's strategy against the Soviet Union. The US sought to covertly undermine the USSR by dragging it into its own version of Vietnam in Afghanistan. The CIA accomplished this by beginning to fund members of the Muslim Brotherhood in the country, following which the Soviets had no choice but to intervene. What ensued was a 20 year brutal struggle, after which, again through CIA support, the fanatical and Wahhabi indoctrinated Taliban were brought to power.

Being the largest covert operation in CIA history, it was all secretly financed through the Iran-Contra affair. The regime in Iran itself was also brought about through Western conspiring with members of the Muslim Brotherhood in that country, culminating in the establishment as ruler of British agent Ayatollah Khomeini. Arms were sold to Iran, traded with the right-wing Contras of Nicaragua for Cocaine, then brought to the Mena, Arkansas, under Clinton's supervision, before being distributed to LA street gangs, thus igniting the so-called Crack Epidemic of the eighties. Funds accumulated were then transmitted to Afghanistan, to fund the "Mujahideen", headed by Gulbuddin Hekmatyar, who was also responsible for the CIA's opium cultivation in that country.

The novelty of the ruse of the Wahhabis is that they do not present themselves as a sect of Islam, but merely as a group within the majority, known as Sunnis, committed to orthodoxy. In Western countries, as pointed out by Stephen Schwartz, in *The Two Faces of Islam*, the Muslim communities there are newly created, and do not have long-standing traditions of classical Islam. It is possible, therefore, for Saudi Arabia to move in and dominate the burgeoning communities. Through their immense oil wealth, they have financed the construction of mosques, printed the majority, if not all, of the Muslim literature in English, and have financially backed all the so-called "moderate" organizations which purportedly represent the interests of the Muslims.

The purpose of promoting Wahhabism is not merely to create the mindset of the terrorist, but to indoctrinate certain

Muslims to become aberrations of human beings, exemplifying all that is despicable, including misogyny, ignorance, intolerance and bigotry, as the video painfully exposes. The intent is to create an egregious image of the Muslims, to secure their identity with the prevailing prejudices against them, in order to bring about a *Clash of Civilizations*, or the so-called *War on Terror*, in other words, the War on Islam. This video will certainly inflame hatred among the bigoted right in America and elsewhere, who will surely claim "I told you so". But more importantly, the message provided in this video is a wake-up call for the Muslims, to recognize the vipers hiding their midst's who have hijacked their religion. It is high time for Muslims to return to the noble principles of their religion, and start acting like the examples the world is waiting to see.

Born out of the extremity of the Arabian dessert, the Wahhabi school of thought and its puritanical adherents have sought to define the political and religious trajectory of the Arabian Peninsula for the past three centuries. Through a symbiotic political relationship with the al-Saud royal family, they have been largely successful, and a historic comparison of this relationship sheds light on the intricate history of a kingdom fighting to remain austere. However, this success has paralleled great and often grudging compromises between the two parties that threaten the fabric of their relationship and the society they have built.

Today these historic compromises divide the Saudi royal family between a faction that is loyal to the conservative clerics, and those who support a comparatively more pluralistic system. This division, which would regularly be of little significance, is amplified globally by the oil-funded expansion of Wahhabi beliefs throughout the Muslim world. If the Wahhabis stay their current course of intolerant puritanical conservatism—exporting their beliefs with the aide of oil revenues—the future of Saudi Arabia and the gulf region as a whole is deeply troubling. The future of Saudi society is inextricably linked with the compromises and power plays required to balance the will of the Wahhabi puritans with any hopes of modernity.

The Puritans 1703-1744 Wahhabism derives its name from its ideological founder, Muhammad ibn And al-Wahhab. Al-Wahhab was born in the isolated central Arabian province of Nejd at the beginning of the 18th century. Nejd, a desert plateau in central Arabia, is a land of extreme and fundamental contrast—day and night, hot and cold, dessert and oasis. These contrasts were the basis for al-Wahhab's new interpretation of Islam that contrast belief and unbelief, monotheism and idol worship, and right and wrong in the same uncompromising nature. Al-Wahhab lived in a unique and by many accounts deficient intellectual setting, removed from the pressures and currents of mainstream Islamic scholarship, but was nonetheless heavily influenced by past fringe Islamic scholars. This can again be attributed to al-Wahhab's home, Nejd province, which lacked strategic and economic value, historically allowing it to avoid colonialism and invasion.

The ideology and worldview of al-Wahhab was not created by an uneducated tribal puritan isolated from Islamic scholarship, as argued by the movements many critics and enemies, nor was it a legitimate derivative of mainstream Islamic thought, as proposed by adherents to the creed. Al-Wahhab's early education was provided by his father, a descendent of a long line of Hanbali jurists, the most conservative of the four schools of Sunni Jurisprudence. This began al-Wahhab's exposure to conservative Muslim scholarship, which formed the basis of his later revisionist ideology. Al-Wahhab traveled widely throughout his youth, spending time in Medina studying the work of Ibn Taymiya, a 13th century Islamic scholar. Taymiya's father was a refugee of the Mongol destruction of Damascus, and he watched with disdain as the Mongols created a cosmopolitan and tolerant society based on Sufi mysticism and Sh'ia doctrine. This disdain was reflected in his writing, which stressed an absolute and literalistic commitment to *tawhid*, or the oneness of God expressed in the universal call to Islamic faith, *"there is no God but God and Muhammad is his messenger."*

While absolute tawhid is a fundamental tenant of Sunni revivalism, Taymiya is most notably remembered for his reinterpretation of jihad. The Hanbali school of thought and the overwhelming majority of Muslim scholars hold that there is a division between jihad kabeer, lesser military struggle, and jihad akbar, greater interpersonal struggle. Taymiya rejected this consensus and in doing so set a precedent for an independent and literal interpretation of the *Qur'an* and *Hadith*, as opposed to traditional reinterpretation of past Islamic scholarship. He stated that *"jihad against disbelievers is the most noble of actions and moreover it is the most important action for the sake of mankind."* This inability to accept the division of jihad is the second tenet of more militant Sunni revivalism. Together, these two tenets, and the precedent of puritanical reinterpretation of scripture formed the basis for the scholarship behind al-Wahhab's doctrine.

While al-Wahhab gained his scholarly inspiration from the fringe works of Taymiya, conditions at home incited his puritanical rhetoric. As Islam spread after the time of the prophet, it was fused with various religions and customs of the era to create a composite belief structure. Out of this composite belief structure arose practices in Sunni Islam derived from Christianity and Shi'aism—among these the veneration of saints and notable Muslim leaders, as well as general disregard for what Wahhab saw as true Sharia in favor of more traditional tribal law. These practices offended al-Wahhab's notion of tawhid, as he perceived them to defile the purity of Islam. For al-Wahhab, the logical answer was a return to a simpler, more pure Islam specifically that which predominated after the death of the prophet under the rule of the four rightly guided caliphs. Al-Wahhab had now experienced all the factors responsible for the creation of his doctrine: historically conservative scholarship, a precedent of literalistic reinterpretation, the concept of absolute tawhid, a militarized interpretation of jihad, a puritanical worldview, and most importantly a perceived decay of societal morality.

Al-Wahhab first published this doctrine in *Kitab al-Tawhid* (*The Book of Unity*) that declared the necessity of absolute tawhid, rejected progression in Islam, and laid out a four-step plan for salvation that demanded total loyalty to religious leaders and armed jihad against non-believers. Al-Wahhab took an uncompromising stance in *Kitab al-Tawhid* regarding Muslims who followed more pluralistic traditions as a function of their composite belief structure or other schools of jurisprudence. Breaking with traditional Islamic interpretation that held these persons to be fellow Muslims, al-Wahhab declared them nonbelievers living in a state of willing *jahilya,* the ignorant times before Islam. Under this new interpretation, Shiites and non-Wahhabi Sunnis were transformed into those *"who have known the religion of the prophet and yet stand against it, prevent others from accepting it, and show hostility to those who follow it."* These people, by al-Wahhab's definition, should be *"denounced as infidels and killed."*

Al-Wahhab returned to Nejd and attempted to implement his religious doctrine without the sponsorship of a local ruler. He failed. Recognizing the shortcoming of his past attempts to spread tawhid to be a lack of political influence, al-Wahhab formed the first and lesser of his two religio-political alliances with Ibn Mummar, a local tribal Sheikh. This alliance was sealed by the marriage of al-Wahhab to Mummar's aunt, the first of al-Wahhab's two attempts to gain continual influence through family lineage. While under the protection of Mummar, al-Wahhab delivered three religious rulings that have become symbolically representative of Wahhabism. He ruled in favor of cutting down a sacred tree, destroying the tomb of a revered Muslim leader, and stoning an adulteress, all in line with his ardent belief in absolute tawhid and his literalistic interpretation of Sharia law. With the extreme and revisionist nature of these decisions, al-Wahhab broke from the traditional implementation of Islamic law and threatened the established clerical structure or *ulema,* which used its influence to challenge al-Wahhab.

The protection of Mummar was no longer sufficient to insure al-Wahhab's safety, and in a journey later compared to the prophet's pilgrimage between the holy cities, he traveled to Dariya. There he gained the favor and conversion of the local ruler Muhammad Bin Saud, forging the second and more significant of his religio-political alliances. In 1744 this alliance was formalized in a symbiotic relationship wherein al-Wahhab retained the position of imam while relinquishing political rule to the emir Bin Saud. The alliance was sealed by the marriage of al-Wahhab's daughter to Bin Saud's eldest son, creating the Saud-Wahhab lineage. Bin Saud at the time of the alliance possessed few favorable traits to differentiate himself or his territory from the countless other warring sheikhdoms of the area. However, the religious legitimacy and zeal for proselytizing conquest attained through Saud's pact with al-Wahhab would propel the religio-political alliance towards a regional dominance that still exists to this day.

The First State 1744-1819

Bin Saud began a reconquest of Nejd through military dominance, extorting a tribute from conquered rulers under the guise of *zakat,* the obligatory giving of charity that represents one of the five pillars of Islam. While al-Wahhab held radicalized views concerning fellow Muslims who failed to follow tawhid, he preferred to contact neighboring leaders and peacefully convince them to accept the Wahhabi creed rather than gain coerced submission. Despite al-Wahhab's attempt at peaceful alliance building few rulers accepted and Bin Saud continued in conquest until his death in 1767. His son Abd al-Aziz, who, compared to his father and the ultra-conservative Wahhabi clergy, emphasized materialism rather than religious zeal and piety, succeeded him. This perhaps is the reoccurring theme of the Wahhabi-Saudi relationship—the influence of a more conservative religious leadership in constant opposition to their perception of growing materialism and modernity within the political leadership.

In 1773 al-Wahhab stepped down as imam under questionably coercive circumstances and was replaced by Abd al-Aziz, who assumed the dual role of emir-imam and in doing so permanently returned ultimate religious authority to the political ruler. In 1773 Abd al-Aziz conquered Riyadh, relocating his capitol and uniting the entire Nejd region. From 1780-1800 Abd al-Aziz continued to conquer territory along the eastern Arabian coast in a manner intended to resemble the initial conquest of Arabia in the time of the prophet. As the conquest gained momentum, legitimate religious zeal morphed into less than holy attempts to justify the large economic and material advantages of conquest through faith. In 1802 Abd al-Aziz conquered the Shiite town of Kerbala in modern day Iraq, massacring its inhabitants as well as desecrating the tombs of several companions of the prophet under the precepts of tawhid. In 1803 after gaining control of the holy cities of Mecca and Medina, a Shiite taking revenge for the Kerbala massacre assassinated Abd al-Aziz at prayer, leaving his son Saud to succeed him.

Saud was a talented military commander, and sought to reinvigorate the religious conquest of Abd al-Aziz. He dispatched copies of Kitab al-Tawhid to local sheikhs, using any hostility or failure to implement the doctrine as an excuse for conquest. One such sheikh, upon refusing to implement the Wahhabi creed that had little legitimacy within more mainstream Islamic scholarship, commented that *"it is a small book that legalizes the murder of all Muslims who dissent from them (the Wahhabis), the appropriation of their property, the enslavement of their offspring, and the marriage of their wives without first being divorced from their husbands."*

After gaining control of most of the modern kingdom, Saud began raids into current day Iraq, Jordan, and Syria. These raids, combined with the loss of control of the holy cities, agitated the Ottomans, and in response, Sultan Selim III sent an Egyptian force to rout the Saudis in 1811 regaining control of Mecca and Medina in 1814. Shortly thereafter, Saud died of fever, creating a succession struggle between his oldest son Abdullah bin Saud and a descendant of the original Saud-Wahhab family pact, Abdullah bin Muhammad. Abdullah bin Saud was victorious; however, the struggle significantly weakened the state and divided its military forces, allowing a revitalized Egyptian force to conquer Riyadh in 1818. Abdullah bin Saud was extradited to Istanbul to stand trial, where he was executed.

The Ottomans found little value in the Arabian Peninsula beyond the holy cities, and discontinued their occupation of Nejd. The withdrawal led to a reversion to century old patterns of tribal warfare and local conflict. During this era, Wahhabism was largely maintained and perpetuated by tribal zealots rather than religious institutions, allowing it to survive the transition between unified Saudi states. The first Saudi state had been a grand experiment, combining traditional tribal conquest with fanatical religious zeal. It was a largely effective formula that would be repeated again with equal success, but the over-ambitious nature of the zealots towards external powers had detrimental effects to the longevity of the state.

The Second State 1824-1897

Turki bin Saud, the son of Abdullah bin Saud's challenger, retook Riyadh in the name of the original alliance in 1824. Turki relied heavily on the prestige of his family name—which was still associated with religious purity and political capability—for the legitimacy that he used to incite a new religious fervor for expansion. Learning from the lessons of the past Saudi realm, Turki focused his conquest east, away from the holy cities and their Egyptian protection.

In 1833 Turki had established control over the entire Persian Gulf coast of the Arabian Peninsula with the blessing of the British Empire, which hoped unification would quiet the warring sheiks of the region. Internal strife began to tear apart the second Saudi realm. In 1834 Mishari bin Saud, with the support a disparate group of tribal sheikhs, lead a rebellion against his cousin, Turki. The rebellion failed and Mishari was imprisoned; however, Turki was subsequently assassinated. Mishari, in the absence of Turki's eldest son Faisal, was named ruler by the Wahhabi clerics who were reluctant to suspend political unity while waiting for Faisal's return.

The clerics were comprised of descendants of the al-Wahhab lineage known as the al Sheikh. A precedent was set mandating that endorsement by the al Sheikh was necessary for political legitimacy. The precedent was played out again, gaining a dimension of appeasement in exchange for endorsement. Faisal returned from conquest and defeated Mishari, agreeing to uphold, spread, and enforce the more conservative tenants of Wahhabi doctrine in exchange for the blessing of the al Sheikh. In 1838 the Egyptian pasha Muham-mad Ali defeated Faisal in an attempt to build a Cairo-centered Islamic empire to rival that of the failing Ottomans. Ali installed Khaled bin Saud—the brother of Abdullah bin Saud, who was captured at the first Egyptian conquest of Riyadh 20 years earlier—as the Saudi king. In 1841 Ali's empire failed, leaving Khaled as the ruler of the second Saudi state.

In 1843 Faisal returned from Cairo, deposed and executed Khaled, and began a revitalization and transformation of Wahhabism. Wahhabi doctrine was codified as law, transforming the initial revolutionary zeal of the Wahhabis to ultra-conservative Islamic jurisprudence that was implemented throughout the Kingdom. Faisal's reign brought with it relative stability, but compared with the consolidated unity of the first state, internal conflict and divisions ran high. Faisal, still cautious of upsetting foreign powers, continued to focus expansion toward the east, fighting and entering into a British-brokered truce with Bahrain in the years before his death in 1865. Intense family rivalry caused the Saudi royal family to begin a slow disintegration. The position of emir was shuffled between close relatives of Faisal eight times in the 11 years after his death. Eventually Abdullah bin Faisal, Faisal's first cousin, gained a semblance of stable control in 1886.

A northern Sheikh, Muhammad bin Rashid, capitalized on the weak Saud authority, capturing Riyadh in 1887. In 1891 Rashid exiled the remaining Sauds to Kuwait, ending the second Saudi State. The second Saudi state was capable of controlling zeal for conquest and in doing so avoided the agitation of the Ottomans and other external powers influential in the region. This control was achieved at a costly price, appeasing the Wahhabi religious zealots with a long-term commit-ment to implement Wahhabi doctrine as codified law. Inter-family tribalism as well as the political divisions and chaos it created allowed a relatively inconsequential Sheikh from the north to conquer the kingdom and exile its ruling family.

The Ikwahn

Wahhabism, as a primarily verbally transmitted ideology, had survived the five-year transition between the two unified Saudi states with surprising continuity. Easing this transition was the retention of control of small sheikdoms by representatives of the original alliance. Contrasting this ease of transition were the significant changes undergone by Wahhabism during the transition from the second Saudi state to the modern kingdom. Wahhabi doctrine, at the fall of Riyadh, had been transformed from the radical oral ideology of the first state, to a codified system of Islamic jurisprudence. This has been attributed to al-Wahhab's emphasis on the importance of personal learning that stemmed from conceptual and thematic understanding of the *Qur'an*, rather than root memorization that had been common. However, while al-Wahhab did place emphasis on learning, the Wahhabi transition was one of necessity.

As the unified second state concluded its phase of conquest, the need for a stable legal system superceded the need for proselytizing zeal, and the Wahhabi doctrine evolved. This shift in Wahhabi doctrine made it nearly impossible for it to survive the fall of the second state and the subsequent exile of the royal family with the same continuity as did the original doctrine. After the fall of the second state the preservers of the faith in Nejd became the Artaib and Harb, Bedouin tribes. These tribes formed the *Ikwahn* or the brotherhood, and upheld the tenets of Wahhabism in their most conservative and puritanical forms.

The Ikwahn abandoned the traditional Nomadic lifestyles of their tribal heritage in exchange for the hujar, an oasis community that became the basic unit of the modern kingdom. The Ikwahn become the cavalry and zealots of Wahhabism under the renewed territorial expansion of Ibn Saud. In doing so they led the revival of the proselytizing zeal of Wahhabism and the parallel reversion from a comparatively more moderate and scholarly version of the doctrine. Ibn Saud's strategic need for the zealots as warriors would outweigh the need for rational scholarship and the moderation of the doctrine.

The Unification 1902-1932

Faisal's eldest son Abd al-Aziz Ibn Saud began the reunification of the Arabian Peninsula from Kuwaiti exile in 1902. With the support of the Kuwaiti emir, Ibn Saud launched a legendary covert attack on hostile Riyadh. Ibn Saud led a small outfit of cavalry through the southern desert to Riyadh, where they slipped through the city's defenses under the cover of darkness and infiltrated the royal palace. At daybreak Ibn Saud and his men massacred the members of the royal court along with the governor of Riyadh, seizing control of the city. From his new central stronghold, Ibn Saud aligned himself with the Ikwahn zealots, and declared jihad on the non-Wahhabis of the region. In 1902 and 1904 Ibn Saud, who had gained control of all of Nejd, fought inconclusive battles over the control of the northern Qassim province with the Ottoman-backed Sheikh Rashid, of the lineage that originally conquered Riyadh from Saud control.

Ibn Saud nominally became a Ottoman vassal, demonstrating his strategic foresight in postponing military action until internal pressures forced the over-extended Ottomans to withdraw from Qassim. Ibn Saud lost a major battle in 1910, and two years were required to forcefully displace the internal rebellion that occurred the same year. Ibn Saud entered into a treaty with the British Empire in 1915, recognizing the legitimacy and sovereignty of the Sharif Hussein of Mecca in exchange for British favor and support against the Ottomans. Ibn Saud continued to clash with Hussein, who ostentatiously declared himself King of all Arabs with British support. Ibn Saud and Hussein signed a British-mandated armistice in 1920; however, shortly after, the balance of military power shifted significantly towards the Saudis.

Ibn Saud, who recognized the military potential of the Ikwahn when he first regained control of Riyadh in 1902, had implemented a policy to strengthen their forces and expand their membership. Other tribes were encouraged to abandon their nomadic ways and settle in oasis regions, building deeply fundamental religious communities with the help of Wahhabi clerics dispatched by Ibn Saud. Until the treaty of 1920, the highly-motivated religious zealots of these hujar com-munities had remained an untapped military resource. However, the Ikwahn forces, estimated at 30,000 strong, soon played an integral role in the conquest of western Arabia that brought Ibn Saud to the gates of the Hijaz province, the dominion of Sharif Hussein that contained the holy cities. In 1924 Ibn Saud and his Ikwahn Calvary conquered Mecca and in 1925 Medina was brought under Ibn Saud's influence, nominally concluding his territorial acquisition.

Ibn Saud moved to consolidate his rule over the disparate tribes of his north central Arabian kingdom and was forced to choose between the Bedouin tribal tribute system based on continued conquest that had been employed by his family for two and half centuries in the region, or a more centralized model offered by his British allies. After questioning the sustainability and longevity of a truly tribal state, he chose the latter, and in doing so significantly eroded the position of the Wahhabi Ikwahn, who desired continued conquest and proselytizing jihad in society. The Ikwahn approached Ibn Saud with complaints in 1927, including the unholy relationship with Britain, the introduction of new communication technologies, and the tolerance of Shi'ism.

The Ikwahn's continued raids outside the borders of the modern kingdom posed the same threat to Ibn Saud as did the continued raids of the first kingdom, which proved to be its eventual undoing. Ibn Saud attempted to suppress the more extreme elements of Ikwahn militancy, leading to a revolt in 1929. Ibn Saud questioned the religious legitimacy of violent suppression of fellow Wahhabis, and looked to the ulema, which represented a more institutionalized Wahhabism, for a sanction to contain the Ikwahn. In exchange for a revitalized commitment to the Wahhabi creed in the modern kingdom, the ulema issued a fatwa sanctioning the suppression of the Ikwahn. Ibn Saud, with this newfound religious legitimacy, routed the Ikwahn at the battle of Siblia in 1929.

While the Ikwahn had been suppressed, the political necessity that had prompted the first transition from revolutionary Wahhabism to institutional Wahhabism in the second state again arose anew. The transition in its infancy drew from the radical Ikwahn ideology rather than the already moderated ideology of the second state. While the Ikwahn were suppressed as a military force, its ardent followers still remain a powerful conservative fringe of Saudi society. In 1932 Ibn Saud declared the modern kingdom, naming himself King and giving the newly formed state, Saudi Arabia, his family name. Ibn Saud, to cement his rule, took a wife from each of the tribes of his new kingdom and the prominent families comprising the Al-Sheikh. He fathered more than 45 legitimate sons with his 20 wives, and every King of Saudi Arabia has since been a son of Ibn Saud.

With the foundation of Saudi Arabia, the Wahhabi doctrine—conservative scholarship, literalistic reinterpretation, absolute tawhid, a militarized jihad, a puritanical worldview, and opposition to decay in societal morality—had been institutionalized as the moral, religious, and legal principles of the land. The Saudi royal family would be faced with the daunting challenge of running a state on the principles of puritanical zealotry and tribalism, while integrating it into the modern world.

Oil and Infidels 1933-1953

Ibn Saud faced two secular and pragmatic realities upon the kingdom's unification: fiscal stability and security. The true challenge of his reign occurred not only in facing these realities, but doing so in such a way as to appease the clerics and still prominent tribal sheikhs of nascent Saudi Arabia. Ibn Saud's charisma coupled with the religious uniformity and zeal provided by Wahhabism had led the Saud-Wahhab family alliance to provincial prominence. However, this alliance, operating in a resource scarce desert, would have gained little regional or global significance without the discovery of oil, which took place in 1931 in a failed attempt to locate water.

Ibn Saud, who recognized the importance of foreign investment and expertise in the developing oil industries of his neighbors, invited foreign prospectors to the kingdom. The ulema resisted, declaring the invitation extended to foreigners by Ibn Saud as an attempt to bring infidels into the holy land of Mecca and Medina. The power of Ibn Saud's personality overpowered the challenge of the clerics. A group of senior clerics supposedly visited the court of Ibn Saud, where he challenged them to provide justification for their resistance to foreigners. Before allowing them to respond Ibn Saud cited the instances from the *Hadith* in which the prophet used Christians and Jews for his advancement. He paralleled these instances to his invitation to foreign oil firms to develop the Saudi petroleum industry. Ibn Saud was indifferent as to which Western nation's oil firms received the concessions and they were awarded to the highest bidder, the United States, which paid $170,000 in gold in 1932.

ARAMCO, the Arab American Oil Company, began operating in the kingdom and was controlled by the four major American oil firms of the day: Exxon, Mobil, Texaco, and Socal. Ibn Saud had won a victory for fiscal reality with the clerics; however, there was no compromise concerning the push for modernity and more importantly the moderation of the state or its religious institutions. Oil revenues would only exacerbate the division between the modernizers and the puritans. Saudi Arabia, in its infancy, demonstrated no significant political or military strength to differentiate itself from the short-lived first and second states, which fell to external regional pressures. Further validating security concerns were the hostile neighboring Hashemite kingdoms of Jordan and Iraq.

The Hashemite were the same group that controlled the Sharif of Mecca before Ibn Saud's conquest. To avoid Hashemite conquest, Ibn Saud chose to exchange the large fiscal potential of his kingdom for long-term security, without the transitional phase of militarization. Ibn Saud met with President Roosevelt, who was sailing from the Yalta conference, in 1945. The meeting took place aboard the USS Quincy in the Suez Canal, where what has come to be known as the *"Oil for Security Deal"* was forged. The United States agreed to provide for the territorial security of the kingdom, and established the Dahran military base in return for insurance of easy access to Saudi oil. In the eyes of the clerics, the man who had massacred the Ikwahn, a potent but uncontrollable Wahhabi cavalry, was now contracting the defense of the kingdom to the Americans.

Ibn Saud died in 1953, separating his authority between his two sons, Saud, the eldest and Faisal, the third. Saud received the crown but proved to be largely inept and apathetic.

Faisal managed foreign affairs and proved to be much more competent than his elder brother. From the military conquests of his youth to the directional and existential decisions of unified rule, Ibn Saud had, by force of personality, defined Saudi Arabia. ARAMCO and oil revenues brought with them Western opulence and materialism. Saud, whose father was a Bedouin tribal warrior, eagerly adopted this lavish lifestyle and lived a life of grand and opulent comfort. The transition from Bedouin subsi-stence to Western materialism within the royal family was instant, occurring just as abruptly as the discovery of oil. The ulema, a generally elderly body still accustomed to traditional Bedouin living, was vehemently opposed to Saud's lifestyle.

Adding to the ulema's disapproval, Saud was an ineffective and incompetent ruler, and while kept strictly within the family, had developed severe alcoholism. Ibn Saud's sons recognized the threat that Saud, without the consent of the religious institution or political capabilities, posed to Saudi stability. In 1964 they gained the ulema's sanction for Saud's exile, and for Faisal's ascension to the throne.

Appeasement of Exportation 1964-1989

Faisal was a descendant of the original Saud-Wahhab alliance and was intimately intertwined with the religious establishment. Faisal nonetheless perceived a necessity for modernization; however, the implementation of modern technologies and institutions would require the constant appeasement of the ulema. Faisal's first reform that met significant resistance from the clerics was the introduction of female education, which the ulema viewed as a violation of Islamic decency. Faisal approached the problem both gradually and institutionally. He began to implement female education first in the more liberal urban areas, allowing a generation of conservative rural Bedouins to become accustomed to the concept. He also separated the ministries responsible for male and female education, giving the ulema oversight privileges into the curriculum.

Faisal began a transformation of the Saudi ministry system, which had been simple and absolute under his father's rule. Ibn Saud had three ministries: foreign affairs, finance, and defense. Under Faisal's reign this system swelled to 23 ministries. The control of many newly created ministries was ceded to the al Sheikh and the ulema. To gain further legitimacy with the clerics, Faisal allowed the kingdom to become a refuge for regional extremists, including expelled leaders of the Egyptian Muslim Brotherhood: Sheikh Omar Abdul Rahman—later convicted of involvement in the World Trade Center bombing of 1993—Ayman al-Zawari, al-Quaeda's ideologue, and Abdullah Azzam, a prolific fundamentalist. These extremists integrated into the Wahhabi- controlled Saudi education system, teaching their violent jihadi interpretations to Saudi children and university students.

In 1965 Faisal approved television broadcasting in spite of the strong opposition of the clerics, who objected to the depiction of the human form and the content associated with television pro-gramming. To counter the second concern, Faisal had a *Quaranic* recitation filmed and broadcast const-antly, thus demonstrating that while television did have a potential to propagate immoral content, it had an equal potential to propagate learning and religion. While the mainstream ulema had been convinced, the ultra-conservative fringe was not. Faisal's nephew was involved with a demon-stration held outside a Saudi television station. The demon-stration became violent and when riot police intervened Faisal's nephew was killed.

For Faisal the increased fervor of the religious estab-lishment was a useful tool to counterbalance the socialism of pan-Arab nationalism. In 1962 a conference of Islamic scholars in Mecca was convened to create the Muslim World league, effectively a conservative proselytizing institution. Later in 1972 he created the World Assembly of Muslim Youth, an organization designed to fund Wahhabi-style education across the Muslim world. Both these organizations were inspired by the beliefs of the grand mufti, a descendant of the al-Sheikh and a close advisor to the king. The grand mufti viewed the Saudi as the inherent leaders of Islam due to their control of the holy cities. As such they had an equal duty and right to export their belief structure through their vast wealth. For the first time since al-Wahhab's initial reversion to fundamentalism, Wahhabi rhetoric had been focused on change rather than puritanical consistency. This was a natural progression but nonetheless a fundamental change in Wahhabi doctrine.

Faisal was assassinated in 1975 in a revenge killing by his nephew, brother to the nephew who was killed in the protest over television broadcasting. The division within the royal family was one of violent tribal tradition. Faisal's brother Khaled bin Abdul Aziz, Ibn Saud's second son, succeeded him. In 1975 the oil revenue of Saudi Arabia was greater than $22 billon annually, and the pace of construction and development was very great. This exterior change was not paralleled by moderation of the Wahhabi outlook, and as the royal family became more extravagant, they became more contradictory to the Wahhabi clerics. Dr. Saad al Fafih, an ultra-conservative dissident cleric, stated that the royal family is *"corrupt in every sense, in Islamic sense, in financial sense, in administrative sense...the only way to save the country, in every sense, even the basic human sense, is to change the whole royal family."* Rapid construction within the kingdom was a façade of modernization that covered the increasingly pressured and fragmented religio-political institutions of 18th century puritanical tribalism.

This pressure boiled over in 1979 with the seizure of the grand mosque in Mecca by descendants of the Ikwahn, led by Juhayman al Utayba. Utayba and his followers demanded that the kingdom return to puritanical tawhid. They rejected all progress and modernization, and believed one of their members to be the messiah. The Saudi royal family could not intervene in the grand mosque without a fatwa from the ulema, and after an 18-day standoff, the clerics issued a fatwa allowing the royal family to remove the apostates from the holy mosque. Along with the fatwa came the greatest transfer of power to the ulema since the original religiopolitical alliance was formed. The clerics were given control over the extraordinarily well-funded education system; the minister of education was chosen from within the al Sheikh. The al Sheikh and the more conservative clerics used their increasing influence in the education system to perpetuate the view that the Wahhabi doctrine was the only true form of Islam.

The clerics attained full media oversight and censorship and began to play an integral role in monitoring the "morality" of society. As a whole, the royal family viewed the conservative reversion that occurred after the seizure of the grand mosque as a means through which to stabilize the country. In reality it only forfeited whatever gains were made over the past half century to the Wahhabi clerics. King Khaled in a move to bolster religious credibility and shift the dissenting focus of the clerics from the morality of the monarchy, expanded Faisal's initial exportation. Funding for Wahhabi schools abroad through the International Islamic Relief Organization, the action arm of the Muslim World League, increased exponentially as oil revenues were pumped into the organization and other Islamic charities. A puritanical understanding and implementation of Islam was promoted throughout centers of Islamic thought globally, especially in renowned institutions in Egypt.

Khaled died in 1982 and was succeeded by Ibn Saud's fourth son Fahd. Fahd, like Faisal, was devoutly religious; he changed his official title to *"Custodian of the Two Holy Mosques"* and viewed his power as a mandate to strengthen and spread Islam. The Soviet invasion of Afghanistan in 1979 offered the great impetus to exercise this mandate and disseminate Wahhabi beliefs. The Saudis in total offered nearly $4 billion in official foreign aid to the Mujahideen, not including the private funding of the princes or Islamic charities. To Fahd funding the Muslim Afghan resistance was the silver-bullet solution to a multitude of internal and external challenges. Aiding in the fight against infidels invading Muslim lands offered Fahd immense religious credibility, while allowing Saudis to volunteer for jihad in Afghanistan offered an outlet for the frustrations of indoctrinated youth, another way to ensure that a crisis similar to the 1979 seizure of the grand mosque would not occur again.

The two most radical and ideologically-Wahhabi factions received the majority of the funding, and many of their members morphed into the Taliban at the conclusion of the conflict. While formal Saudi aid into Afghanistan was terminated upon the conclusion of the conflict, Saudi charities continued to fund Wahhabi education in the mountainous Pashtun badlands of the Afghanistan-Pakistan border. A considerable portion of this funding went to create Jamaat Ulama Islami and Jamat-I-Islami madrasas, virulently radical religious seminaries that provide free *Quranic* education to Muslim youth. These madrasas spawned the Taliban and are largely considered the breeding grounds of global Islamic terror. It is unclear to what degree the royal family was aware of the implications of its actions; however, the desire for global Wahhabi proselytizing efforts is clearly evident.

This desire translated itself into a global network of Saudi charities designed to inspire puritanical piety and preach jihad against the oppressor, often synonymous with the West. Mosques and madrasas were constructed in the former Soviet republics, notably Kyrgyzstan and Uzbekistan, and there was a significant effort to support Muslim causes in Chechnya and the Balkans. The 1970s and 1980s were an era of continuity for the royal family. Faisal, Khaled, and Fahd were continually forced to appease the ulema.

In exchange for their grudging sanction of modernization, the kings ultimately began to fund, export, and perpetuate the Wahhabi mission. The royal family had discovered a formula for limited sovereignty from the religious establishment—an Islamic agenda abroad would buy complacency for modernization at home. While this allowed the Saudi state to modernize, the tensions that arose from the failure of religious institutions to moderate were simply projected through oil funds onto a largely unsuspecting Islamic world. It would require an instance of existential pragmatism for these tensions to disrupt the Saudi balance.

Reactionary Clerics 1990-2005

This instance of existential pragmatism presented itself in the invasion of Kuwait by Sadaam Hussien's Iraq concerning foreign debt and oil production. This invasion imminently threatened the kingdom, which had failed effectively to increase its military potential since unification. King Fahd's only avenue for military victory was to accept an open-ended defense offer from the Untied States; however, he first needed the sanction of the ulema. A conference was convened in Mecca, and a fatwa was issued by Sheikh Abdul Aziz bin Baz, allowing the U.S. intervention in order to defend Islam. The United States subsequently used Saudi Arabia as the staging ground for Operation Desert Storm, driving Iraqi forces out of Kuwait. Despite the approval of the religious institution, the presence of hundreds of thousands of U.S. troops in the holy lands offended the religious sensibilities of many conservatives. Upon the conclusion of combat, the majority of U.S. troops withdrew from Saudi Arabia.

The disgruntled clerics first voiced their opinion to the royal family in 1991. An open letter was signed by 400 clerics and demanded among other things the repeal of non-sharia laws, a more equitable use of oil revenue, and an Islamic foreign policy independent of Western influences. In 1992 a more in-depth version entitled *"Memorandum of Advice to King Fahd"* called for more sweeping reversion, including official veto power for the ulema. This document was signed by the 17-member senior ulema and the grand mufti, posing a serious threat to royal legitimacy. Fahd condemned the document, demanding that the senior ulema do the same. While 10 clerics including the grand mufti caved under Fahd's pressure, seven did not and Fahd subsequently dismissed them. These seven joined a younger more hard-line group of clerics who had been educated and radicalized by the foreign extremists harbored by the Saudi royal family. In doing so their former stature added scholarly legitimacy to the hatred of the West that these hard-line puritanical zealots espoused.

Many members within the radical segment of the ulema began to question and preach against the policies of the royal family alongside their already powerful messages of hate towards non-Wahhabis. Most prominent among them were Sheikh Safar al-Hawali and Sheikh Salaman al-Auda, who held vehement views concerning the supremacy of Islam and the necessity of a indivisible and total jihad. These clerics were arrested in 1994 for disseminating sermons by illegal means and preaching against Saudi foreign policy. They were released a month later under the condition that they remain loyal to the royal family, and the authorities seemed apathetic to their ideology if the vehemently violent rhetoric was not directed towards the Saudi government. A new tension-causing factor had arisen in Saudi society, this time within the organization whose worldview was based on continuity, the ulema.

In 1995 King Fahd suffered a debilitating stroke and his half brother Crown Prince Abdullah took over the kingdom's government. Abdullah began slow but comparatively sweeping reforms within the Saudi system. He liberalized trade, relaxed repressive religious laws, opened the doors to more prominent roles for women, combated the funding of extremist clerics, moderated the education system, and implemented population control measures. Abdullah was capable of effecting much of this reform through the more moderate grand mufti of Saudi Arabia, Sheikh Abdul Aziz bin Baz, who commanded great respect within the ulema, even from the radical clerics. Sheikh Baz died in 1999, opening the door for a resurgence of hard line clerics to gain prominence within the ulema.

Wahhabism and the Future

Saudi Arabia was affected by the events of September 11, 2001, but it was truly rocked by a six-month string of terror that started with the bombing of a residential compound in Riyadh in November 2003. The attackers were disgruntled about Abdullah's reforms, especially his relationship with the West. Most of their activities were linked to radical clerics and were conducted by men who had once traveled to Afghanistan to fight with the Mujahideen. These attacks caused a reversion in Wahhabi doctrine and exacerbated a deep rift in the royal family.

Since the 1992 Memorandum of Advice to King Fahd, two strains of Wahhabi scholarship—entirely similar from an external perspective but directionally unique in context—had developed. They both held to absolute tawhid as al-Wahhab had but took differing stances on jihad: the first held jihad as a separate concept from tawhid and instead stressed taqarub or reconciliation between faiths, the second drew no distinction between jihad and tawhid and thought them both integral to the practice of true Islam. Within the royal family Crown Prince Abdullah endorsed the more mod-erate strain of clerics, although the death of Sheikh Baz dealt this group a serious blow, while Prince Nayef, the interior minister, a much more fundamentally religious man, endorsed the hard-line strain of Wahhabism. This ideological difference which began with the Crown Prince's ascension as regent, was exacerbated by the attacks of 2003 and then formalized by King Fahd's death in 2005, and exists to this day, dividing the royal family along the same lines as the clerics.

After the attacks, Nayef, who possessed a largely independent power base, began to crack down on Abdullah's reforms, especially women's rights, by strengthening the secret police force responsible for enforcing Islamic morality and sharia. While the struggle between Abdullah and Nayef prevents legitimate progress, a true existential challenge for the Kingdom will come with the next generation. For the entire history of the unified kingdom Ibn Saud and his sons have kept a stranglehold on political power, while elderly Wahhabi clerics have maintained religious control. However, as these individuals age into their 70s, a new generation is preparing to take over the reins of leadership. This generation is as polarized as it is diverse and sprawling. It is split between Western-educated royals who wish to bring the kingdom forward into politically and religiously moderated modernity, and vehemently anti-Western clerics who were schooled under the tutelage of the most extreme Islamic dissidents of the era and possess their own base of support among less moderate royals.

The future of the Kingdom is dependent on who takes the reins of power, and judging from past history whoever it may be will require the sanction of the established ulema for legitimacy and any attempt at unified or peaceful progress. Wahhabi Islam is extremist, and that's putting it mildly. The power and authority of the Saudi royal family has always been connected to the social power and influence of Wahhabi clerics - the same clerics who preach an Islam which is becoming increasingly problematic to Saudi Arabia's Western allies. Thus the problem facing the royal family is: how do they reign in the extremists without also undermining the stability of their rule?

Donna Abu-Nasr writes in the Guardian:

The kingdom today has a 21st century infrastructure but 18th century mores, particularly where the sexes are concerned. New, shiny cars fill Saudi streets. But women may not drive them, and may only get into a car with men who are relatives or they all risk jail for the crime of "mixing." ... Malls boast famous designers and tempting underwear. But the country's religious police prowl about to make sure not a hair is showing from beneath a veil, that men do not stare at women and that queues at food courts are segregated. A woman arriving by plane cannot leave the airport unless escorted by a male guardian.

While many Saudis feel stifled, they still turn to clerics for rulings on the minutest aspects of life. A woman caller to a TV program, "Edicts on Air," pleads for permission for her daughter to pluck her eyebrows bushy and hurting her marriage prospects. The on-air cleric is adamant: God made the eyebrows bushy, and bushy they must stay. ... At one point, according to al-Malki, [the Wahhabis] resisted the teaching of physics and chemistry. The Al Sauds overruled them on that, but they have been reluctant to challenge them on social ones, especially those pertaining to women.

It seems unlikely that the Wahhabi clerics will themselves liberalize any time soon - and that means that if Saudi society is going to progress, it will be in *spite* of the, not *with* or *because* of them. They will fight any sort of liberalization - and that means that the Saudi government will have to start making some hard choices. They may be better off risking the ire of the Wahhabi leaders and undermining some of their own authority with them. The benefit, though, may be to improve their authority among the general population - at least, among those who are interested in reforms.

9

The Rise of Terrorism

Using a Weberian perspective informed by Critical Theory, this chapter investigates the interaction of economic, cultural and political causes and potential outcomes of Islamic terrorism. Islam's decline vis-à-vis Christendom was constrained through three major internal moments: 1) limits to modernity, 2) religious conservativism, and 3) ressentiment of the West. Islamic societies responded proactively to the rise of the West through two strategies: 1) Westernization and 2) Islamic modernism, which have both been strongly resisted. In the 20th century, due to the internal suppression of secular political movements among other factors, puritanical fundamentalisms such as Wahhabism arose. Fundamentalisms in various religions explain reality by blaming social problems on the departure from religious morality and promise redemption via a return to an idealized community. In face of decline, colonization, and economic stagnation, ressentiment of the West became widespread in Islam.

Fundamentalisms interacting with ressentiment may turn militant, as in the case of Al Qaeda. A war on terrorism is not likely to end terrorism. To solve the problem of terrorism requires addressing its roots: internal constraints, dictatorships sponsored by the West and the under-development that results form neo-liberal globalization. We suggest terrorism will wane in the face of the evolution of modern Islamic public spheres that might challenge religious conservatism. In wake of 9/11, both moderate and radical religious movements are likely to remain a basis for mobilizing alternative identities to globalization. At the end of the 15th Century, Islamic societies stood at an economic, political and cultural apex. They were affluent and philosophically, scientifically, technologically, and administratively advanced. Mighty armies and trade networks had spread the hegemony of Islamic culture from the Atlantic coast through the southern Mediterranean and North Africa to the Middle East, Southeast Asia and parts of China. Challenges were repelled.

The Crusades affected a small part of the Islamic world. After the sacking of Baghdad by the Mongols (who were converted to Islam within one hundred years), politically and economically, Islam more than recovered. However, religious conservatism had become a major influence in Islamic culture and Europe had just begun its Renaissance, based in large part on the intellectual heritage of Islam. Christian Europe of the 15th Century was poor, ignorant, politically fragmented, and save the Italian city-states, less developed than Islamic society. Yet, between 1492, when Spanish imperialism moved to the New World, and 1588, when the Spanish Armada was defeated, the expanding commerce of Europe began a move from the Mediterranean to the Atlantic that would unleash the forces of capitalism. The decline of the Ottoman Empire would mark the end of Islamic hegemony.

While capitalist, industrial Europe joined with American capital become world hegemonic, the Islamic world became a number of peripheral and semi-peripheral areas. Today, with the events of 9/11, the development of conflicts between Western and Islamic societies between has been brought to the forefront of concern. There is no singular explanation for decline of Islamic hegemony, the failure of modernization efforts, and eventually the rise of (fundamentalist) Islamisms and terrorist movements. A complex interaction of economic, political and cultural factors needs to be studied. To frame this discussion, we draw on Weberian studies, the critical, dialectical traditions of the Frankfurt School and psychoanalytic insights. We employ a comparative historical analysis of ideal typical articulations of Christianity and Islam as world religions oriented to salvation.

There are, of course, vast differences within groups due to local traditions, classes, interactions with other cultures, history, etc. Yet, we will argue that contemporary terrorism needs to be understood in relation to certain broad social factors that have informed the decline of Islam since the 16th Century. One key factor is that just as the Reformation played a major role in the transformation of Christendom into modern Western Europe, the failure of Islam to have a Reformation would impose certain barriers to the embrace of rational modernity. Key political economic factors include Western domination and rise of dictatorial governments in Islamic states. Eventually, Islamic societies responded proactively to the rise of the West through two strategies that have yet to be fully realized in Islamic states: 1) Westernization and 2) Islamic Modernism. The economic decline, military defeat and colonization of Islam vis-à-vis Christendom/the Modern West served to constrain the modern cultural and political development of Islam through three major internal moments:

1. *Limits to modernity*: The nature of Islamic theology, ethics, culture and law limited the impact of foreign ideas and/or presented indigenous barriers to the emergence of the economic, political and cultural rationality, especially after the 16th century.
2. *Religious conservativism*: In face of various political or economic challenges, from the sacking of Baghdad in the 13th Century on up to the secular modernity of contemporary globalization that might change power and/or gender arrangements, there was a retreat to conservative forms of Islam like Wahhabism or other worldly Sufism that served to maintain tradition and resist social change. Wahhabism, a severely Puritanical

form of Islam, emerged as the Ottoman fell in decline. It was embraced by the House of Saud to legitimate themselves as the guardians of the holy cities of Mecca and Media (and was used, in part, to maintain a Saudi imperial claim on oil wealth in 20th century). More recently, in face of modernity, we have seen the growth of Islamisms and in some cases, dramatic religious terrorism.

3. *Ressentiment of the West*: Just as Nietzsche suggested that the marginalized Christian artisans of Rome saw themselves as morally superior to the rich, powerful and debauched, Romans, so too, do many Muslim voices see the secular West as morally degenerate compared to the "superior" morality and ethical practices of Islam that promise a return to a righteous society and glorious rewards in heaven.

Based on historical and current scholarship, this chapter discusses some of the general causes of Islamic terrorism and possible outcomes. Fundamentalist traditions sometimes turn militant. To understand the rise of Islamic terrorism, the questions we now address are threefold: 1) how do conservative religious political/moral goals become translated into acts of terror; 2) how are these acts justified, especially when they result in large numbers of deaths to non-combatants-often the elderly, women and children; and 3) what are the possibilities for elimination of the causes of religious terrorism and moving beyond terrorism?

Rise and Fall of Islam

In the 7th Century, the conflicts between Persia and Byzantium fostered a southerly movement of trade routes through the deserts of Arabia that were largely populated by warring nomadic tribes ever involved in vendetta and counter-vendetta. Particularistic tribal religions stood as barriers to the expansion of the urban, merchant classes and threatened the security of caravans. These conditions would dispose the emergence of a unifying religion that would extend across many lands, uniting the populations, and securing the general conditions for aggressive commerce and trade. The trading classes were aware of Judeo-Christian monotheism yet felt scorned and in turn excluded from its teachings, yet they were wanting of a monotheistic religion. Muhammad, an illiterate merchant articulated a divine message, attributed to archangel Gabriel.

As an emissary of Allah, he would become a charismatic, prophet. The Quran, the word of Allah, God, became the foundation of a new faith that provided a monotheistic salvation religion rooted in both Jewish and Christian traditions of prophesy, incorporating their ethics and many of their customs. Muhammad, as a prophet and skilled arbiter, found a ready audience among the growing classes of merchants, whose status disposed an "elective affinity" for a salvation religion that would establish an "imagined community" of people united by faith that provided members with valorized, sacralized identities and a God ordained ethical regulation of everyday conduct conducive to commerce. As Weber noted in the case of Protestantism, ethical standards between members of the religious "brother-hood" of a "world" religion, even if strangers, were an important basis for the conduct of business in large markets.

Salvation religions tend to be expansionist, seeking both to control how people behave in this world and to ensure entry into the next. In its formative period, Islam was typically spread by conquest or jihad, holy war. It is impor-tant to note that jihad, with variable meanings, would remain an essential element of Islam along with its five pillars of faith. The central meaning of greater jihad was the inner struggle to live a spiritual life according to Quran and Hadith (holy teachings). Military conflict was considered a lesser jihad. In political economic terms, the lesser jihad empowered the expansion and defense of the largest empire of its time. Soldiers justified imperial conquests as a religious duty. For Islam, soldiers who died in jihad, martyrs would gain automatic entrance to paradise.

For Islam, political control was more important than the conversion of the conquered. Indeed, compared to other religions, Islam was highly tolerant of Judaism and Christianity that the Prophet saw as preceding his work. In Islamic societies, the monotheistic religions were sometimes celebrated in same shrines. However, there was an active destruction of polytheistic folk religion and ways. There was dialectic of Islamic imperialism in which violence was used to eliminate tribal parochialism and create and enforce religious universalism. The tolerance of the major monotheisms facilitated cultural exchange and political stability. Another factor in the expansion of Islamic political control is that converts were from powerful families.

At the time of its origin in Mecca, the eschatological religion of Muhammad developed in pietistic urban conventicles that were likely to withdraw from the world: subsequently in Medina and in the evolution of early Islamic communities, the religion was transformed into a wide-spread Arabic, status oriented, and warrior religion. "Muhammad was both an ethical prophet and a charismatic politico-military leader. He overcame tribal particularism by surpassing its polytheism and ritualism with monotheism and a legal ethic, and by transforming feuding tribes into a national-Arabic movement of conquest... Mohamed was...not a marginalized prophet of doom, and certainly not a wandering charismatic preacher; instead, he was a religio-political leader who knew how to realize his intentions step by step, especially through the skillful use of time honored tribal practices of the creation and resolution of conflict...With the successful reception in Medina, the transformation of Islam from an eschatological religiosity into a political religion into a religion of national-Arabic warriors was inaugurated."

Early Islam as a religion of knightly warriors had little room for sin, humility, or vocational asceticism. But Muhammad was also a merchant and encouraged the expansion of trade. "Under Muhammad, Arabian society made a respectable leap forward in social complexity and political capacity" Islamic mercantilism grew, prospered and eventually supported centers of learning devoted to art, science, medicine etc. Weber emphasized that there was generally a relaxed relationship in Islam between faith and reason. While Islamic societies were tolerant of secular reason, more so that Christendom (initially), the Quran and Islamic law, sharia, defined morality in a traditional way that constrained political and economic behaviour.

That is, Islam gave license to philosophy, generally a pursuit of elites, and technical innovation, but not to moral life. In ethical terms, Islam, in most of its expressions, is a highly codified religion that is meant to oversee many aspects of everyday life, and whether and to what extent this was practiced is highly variable. Lawyers and administrators regulated traditional Islamic society, not a clergy. Jurism in Islam was not centrally litigated or legislated. It was engaged through interpretation and local decision. It was highly important that for Islamic societies, social rationality was closely tied to the foundations of specific religious categories, beliefs, and exercises in relation to everyday life, commerce, and governance. More specifically, the legal codes of the Hanafi School based in large part on what had been local traditions, would facilitate the rapid growth of Islamic commerce, but would eventually acquire a fixity that would act to prevent later generations from making revisions as conditions changed.

Islam Triumphant

Within 500 years, Islam had spread across vast tracts of North Africa, the Middle East, the Caucuses, India and parts of Asia from China to what is now Indonesia and Malaysia. As Islam initially spread, institutionalizing faith and laws, it established the conditions in which a new kind of society of merchants emerged. Economic trade was sponsored by religion in a number of ways. Supported by the flows of large populations making the Hajj (pilgrimage to Mecca), an extensive trade network helped sustain an Islamic world across many cultural boundaries. Arabic became the lingua franca for the realm. A banking network (with checking system/exchange) eventually formed. Islam was spread outside of the Arab world by trade by merchants, not by wars of conquest. The fairly universal (but flexible) Islamic law, sharia, also enabled the expansion of trade throughout the region.

However, Islamic societies continued the tradition of religious justification, if not mandate, for political/territorial expansion, as in the case of the imperialist armies of Ottoman Turks. It should be noted that as Islam grew, Christian soldiers tried to wrest the Holy land from the infidels. While they established some Crusader cities, Saladin ultimately cast them out the Holy Land. Ever since, there has been a degree of suspicion toward Christians. Notwithstanding, Islam became a far more tolerant religion than either Judaism or Christianity. Culturally, in contrast to the European Enlightenment, for Islam, there were no contradictions between the life of faith and the intellect, reason, and science. Given Muhammad's injunction to study knowledge from many cultures, including practical knowledge, Islamic societies regarded worldly and sacred knowledge as complementary; worldly knowledge was useful and desirable.

There was a drive in early Islamic societies to amass knowledge, starting with that of other civilizations (including Byzantine, Rome, Greece, Egypt, India, China and the ancient Middle East). The theology and philosophy of Islam was strongly influenced by Neoplatonism and eventually Aristotelian metaphysics. Once amassed, knowledge, technology, science, philosophy, ethics, etc., was critiqued and elaborated. Eventually new forms of knowledge were created, including social theory, which advances were unfortunately usually available only to small circles of elites. The Golden age Islamic scholars of Baghdad, Cordoba, Arabic Egypt, etc., were renaissance thinkers, working simultaneously in the fields of medicine, science, philosophy, and theology. Islamic scientists developed the scientific experimental method and refined Indian mathematics and Chinese material arts and developed innovations in many of sciences: astronomy, medicine, physics, etc. Muslim performed cataract surgery almost 1,000 years ago.

As the Golden age of Islam was nearing its end, the Medieval Catholicism sustained by dynastic rule, held relatively closed, narrow cosmological worldviews and showed religious intolerance-its "holy wars" were the pontifically blessed Crusades From about the time that Islam emerged, till the Renaissance, the Church maintained the hegemony of the landed classes. Its promises of salvation appealed to knightly warrior elites while its magical practices and dramatic rituals and practices appealed to the uneducated, agrarian feudal peasants. With the growth of trade, ironically an unintended consequence of Crusades, there came a growing merchant class of cosmopolitan traders centered in Italy yet found throughout the Mediterranean-the Venetian mini-empire covered a wide area.

This newly affluent class would attempt to articulate a distinct identity, valorizing difference from either the feudal aristocrats or peasantry. Their artists and intellectuals "discovered" their heritage in the Greco-Roman era. (Muslim scholars had preserved much of the legacy of Greco-Roman philosophy, arts and science.) This "rebirth" or Renaissance fostered new expressions in art, perspectivism, literature, vernacular, science, astronomy, and philosophy, e.g. the emergence of feudalism. Humanism, the philosophical expression of the Renaissance, was a reaction to clerical orthodoxy and its heliocentric cosmology. The intolerance of Christianity may have forestalled a more gradual transition to rational society, a more gradual secularization of ethics and/or more tolerance of other religions.

The Renaissance opened a cultural space for new ideas, and this would eventually extend to theological critiques. This began when Humanism influenced theologians such as Erasmus. With the growth and spread of the merchant classes, as well as a rising free peasantry, there emerged potential bearers of a critical theology- as was indeed evident with the teachings of Jan Huss whose "heresies" led to the stake. But in face of potential theological challenges, the Church became more rigid and dogmatic. But the growing merchant and free peasant classes would then be structurally disposed to alternatives to Roman Catholicism. The reaction of the Church to challenges was greater, intolerance and orthodoxy.

Eventually, Christian exclusivity from Holy Roman imperialism and exclusive religious claims and intolerance, including the extremes of the Inquisition such as the rejection of Galileo and Copernicus, led to the Reformation as a critique of its corruption and relative backwardness, rigidity, and theological conservatism of the Catholic Church. Whereas Huss had few supporters, between the changing class structure, and availability of paper (from China via the Muslims) and moveable type, Luther became one of the major figures of the Reformation. Protestantism would have independent consequences for the growth of commerce and science. It would encourage the eventual rise of the European hegemon. The bourgeoisie would foster and embrace the Enlightenment whose doctrines were influenced by the rational traditions and sciences of Islam, as well as being reactions to the exclusivity and rigidity of Christianity as an inflexible realm of faith that resisted the development of secular reason.

Retrenchment and Barriers to Modernity

Toynbee (1939-61), Spengler (1962) and other historians have suggested that civilizations grow, flourish, stagnate, fail to meet challenges, and eventually decline in face of other civilizations. Such analyses do not specify why this happens, nor do they explain the meaning of "challenge," save in military terms. We argue that the same factors that led to the rise of Islam, dialectically understood, thwarted the emergence of modernity. As Toynbee (1939-61) suggested, when cultures limit variability and diversity, they lose their capacity to adapt to changing circumstances. How can this be explained sociologically in terms of classes and ideologies, etc.? In the face of challenge and threat, typically from actual or imagined competing classes or ideologies and challenges at cultural, institutional and personal levels, groups become more rigid, dogmatic and intolerant.

We suggest that two moments of political economy be noted. Firstly, as we suggested, the same legal codes that had enabled Islam to flourish in its early eras, would thwart economic growth. Secondly, and perhaps due to the economic stagnation, there were military defeats and setbacks. In face of these challenges, Islam retreated to orthodoxy. Rokeach's (1960) now classical studies of dogmatism have shown how dogmatism, rigidity and absolute certainty are comforting positions in the face of challenge. In his studies of, he found that at the time of social or theological challenges, the Catholic Church retreated to more orthodox, dogmatic positions. We similarly suggest that in face of various assaults or challenges to Islam, from the sacking of Baghdad by the Mongols to the Inquisition and expulsion from Spain, and more recently the decline of the Ottoman Empire in the 19th Century, Islamic societies and leaders repeatedly embraced more conservative positions, which for reasons to be discussed below, became entrenched cultural formations.

When the central scholarly community of Baghdad was destroyed by the Mongol invasion, a center of liberal, diverse learning was lost. This happened again in the Iberian Peninsula. Cordoba had been one of the primary Islamic cultural/intellectual centers, where liberal forms of Islam thought and science were practiced and developed. With the consolidation of Aragon and Seville into a unified Spain, the rising Spanish merchant classes encouraged the Inquisition that cast out infidels. With the Inquisition, an ideological justification for purifying Christianity, competition with Muslim or Jewish merchants was eliminated. Progressive alternatives to Islamic orthodoxy were lost and a need for solidarity and a sustaining ideology was needed. This resulted in retrenchment and cultural conservatism. By the time the merchant classes of Christendom became ascendant, and as Venice became a major economic power in the Mediterranean, the cultures and political economies of Islamic society began to stagnate and ossify.

It might be recalled that in 1492, not only did Columbus reach the New World and begin to plunder its gold, but the Spanish Inquisition cast out the Muslims foreshadowing a gradual realignment of the world system as Christian Europe became a core and the Islamic world fell to peripheral and semi-peripheral status. Even within Islamic states, European and/or Jewish merchants and professionals began to play ever more important roles. While Islamic societies tried to incorporate some of the European scientific, technological and cultural innovations, social barriers proved too strong, the indigenous economies too weak, and the administrative apparatuses, too inefficient, though more benevolent than in Europe. There are a number of reasons why Christendom surpassed Islam. Given the nature of Sultanism and dynastic rule, patrimonial organization, a religious orientation rooted in a warrior ethic, and other factors outlined below, Islam presented formidable barriers to the economic modernization, qua the diffusion of instrumental rationality, individualism, the embrace of democratic institutions and rational, meritocractic bureaucratic administration.

We would suggest that seven factors limited the impact of foreign ideas and/or created indigenous barriers to the emergence of the economic, political and cultural rationality that enabled Christendom, and in turn, capitalist modernity qua secular nationhood, administrative rationality and a culture of critique and equality:

1. *Economic barriers and the law*: For Weber, the great jurists establishing the legal traditions of Islam were more "legal prophets" establishing substantive-theological

"stereotyped jurists law...that opposes secularization" than formal-juridical (rational) legal codes. Sacred law eliminates the space for predictable legal procedures. The economic practices dictated by Quranic law, Kadi justice and Hanafi codes thus precluded large-scale economic enterprises and capital accumulation. Firstly, Islamic merchant trading associations, whether or not familial, could not assume the legal form of a corporation with juridical rights independent of the owners. Second, Islamic succession and inheritance laws meant that when one of the associates died, the partnership was terminated and inheritance was divided in egalitarian ways as opposed to European laws that allowed limited inheritance, e.g., a single person could inherit a share of an enterprise that nevertheless survived the loss of a partner. Thus, a business could continue to grow and amass fortunes long after the death of a founder(s). Indeed many of the successful merchants of Italy were families such as the Medici's. But, Islamic codes kept business small, limited and ephemeral, no great merchant families emerged.

Third, proscriptions on either long-term investments or short-term usury meant that financing of economic enterprises was limited. Thus, while one could invest in a particular venture and be repaid from profits, and while there was an extensive network of banks that enabled check cashing across the Islamic world, there was not much incentive to investment banking. Hence, borrowing was not rationalized. While Islam developed an extensive banking system, it depended on personal relationships and thus never achieved either the rationality of the later Western banking nor the economies of scale that would take place in the West to finance factories, railroads etc. Commerce was regulated by Quranic laws that would limit the growth of a secular, commercial, sphere; Muslim merchants were unable to practice the kinds of economic rationality, e.g., double entry book keeping or joint stock corporations as the Italian merchants whose commerce flourished. Muslim merchants were unlikely to become bearers of a worldly ethic of practical action. Between the 12th and 15th Centuries, the diversity of occupations declined while military and bureaucratic occupations grew, Islamic economies then began to stagnate. The commercial-legal Hanafi codes that had once promoted expansion and regional trade would thwart economic growth at later periods and would need to be jettisoned, as has been done in Turkey, Malaysia or Indonesia or Egypt.

2. *Islam as a decentralized religion:* Islam, while a world religion, unlike Roman Christianity, was decentralized, without a singular supreme authority or centralized hierarchy. This enabled a number of competing learning centers and variations in local practices and precluded a Reformation as a form of resistance to Church control. As Islam remained compatible with both its merchant and warrior traditions, there did not emerge an oppositional class that would foster a public sphere, embrace a separation of Church and state and/or foster a systematic critique of religious dogma. Indeed, to this day, many, most Islamic states openly embrace sharia law while theological dissents (and many secular acts) are often met with fatwas, religious/legal decrees to maintain orthodoxy and censure threats to Islamic society. Without a Reformation, in spite of the advanced development of science, philosophy, technology and ethical-legal thought, an Enlightenment-based embrace of modernity and its secular institutions and politics was not forthcoming.

3. *A theology of determination*: It is important here to note that differences between the theology of predestination in Protestantism and pre-determination in Islam. The former is based on problematic salvation in the next world and the latter on the guarantee of Allah's will in this. Thus, the power of Allah to impact this world

disposed a fatalism that would stifle the attempt to control/dominate nature and other people inherent to capitalism in which salvation anxiety provided an "inner determination" that impelled economic action qua this worldly asceticism and a methodical orientation to everyday life in which each moment was part of a career. Thus guilt and turning inward were essential moments of Protestantism. Otherwise said, Islam did not generate that intense "salvation anxiety" that became a compulsive orientation to work seen as a morally based vocation, a sacralized career (beruf). Insofar as Islam fostered both a warrior ethic of paradise in heaven and a petty bourgeois orientation of booty on earth, there is an inherent avoidance of introspection. Save among elite scholars, there has been little tendency to locate causality from within. There is thus tendency to locate causality from without and deny culpability from within. This is often seen in psychotherapy as denial, the inability to see oneself responsible for ones actions, but rather to attribute ones misfortunes to others. Thus the relative underdevelopment of Islam today is typically blamed on the West, Jews, or both. This is not to ignore the many injustices of colonialism, underdevelopment, geo-politics and globalization.

4. *Political centralization.* It is also necessary to note that whereas ascetic Protestantism was a rational bourgeois religion from the start, Islam began as a religion of ruling stratum, Herrenreligion, and to a large extent, despite its formal egalitarianism, it disposes the acceptance of Caliphism, Sultanism and/or other forms of dynastic rule, and more often than not, legitimates suppression of democratization and pluralism. In this way, there is little difference between God ordained kings, presidents for life, and one party state. Both internal and external political forces exacerbated this trend. For example, following WWII, American policy in the Middle East, devoted to stopping communism, supported a number

of dictatorial governments that, no matter how heinous, corrupt or duplicitous, were well rewarded if they opposed communism. Budding progressive, secular movements in Muslim countries from socialism to nationalism were both resisted by indigenous power arrangements and thwarted from without by American policy-read oil interests.

5. *Close relations of church, dynasties and commerce:* There was a seamless relation between mosque, political dynasties and the merchant classes. Indeed many mullahs and imams either came from the merchant classes, as did Muhammad, or were themselves still actively engaged in commerce and trade. The merchant classes could not find themselves in conflict with the existing political arrangements in Islamic societies, partly due to the close regulation, sponsorship, and housing of markets by political and religious authorities. Thus, merchant classes would not become a powerful autonomous class as did the Europeans, nor would they stand in opposition to the ruling classes. Thus, Islamic societies did not have social conditions disposing an ideological critique of dynastic rule or religion. There were generally no sources of resistance that might lead to the emergence of a public sphere that might be a locus for counterhegemonic discourses of resistance, strategies of mobilization, and alternative visions.
6. *Conservatism and Limits to Diffusion:* In its maturity, in face of challenges and weakened by "internal" strife, Islamic societies turned to orthodoxy and resistance to change. Indeed, in sharp contrast to early Islamic societies, later societies actively maintained various barriers to external cultural influences. While this repro-duced Islamic cultures and preserved social arrangements, it created the conditions that resisted the incorporation of Western innovations from factories to nationalism, etc. The highly advanced Islamic pursuit of science and philosophy ceased to develop. "Independent inquiry virtually came to an

end, and science was for the most part reduced to a veneration of a corpus of approved knowledge." Further, Christendom was largely identified with a defeated Byzantium and a vague land of barbarians beyond. At the same time, there was a great deal of ethnocentrism in many parts of Europe against the "evil Turks", a generic, often derogatory term toward all Muslims. In addition to having little interest in the Infidel lands, Muslims feared to live or travel there. These fears were sustained by religious edicts against living with the infidels. Hence, the Renaissance, Reformation and Enlightenment were relatively unknown in early modern Islamic societies and the European innovations in technology, philosophy and commerce little impacted Islam.

7. *Individualism and pluralism:* Perhaps one of the most important moments of modernity was the rise of the autonomous, self-interested individual with the capacities to adapt to new situations. For Weber individualism emerged with Protestantism when the believer faced his/her God by him/herself. Some suggest it began earlier when the Church institutionalized confession. Still others suggest that with the rise of bourgeois commerce and the emergence of childhood, individualism was evident in the Renaissance and valorized by humanism. The importance of the individual in the West can clearly be seen in contrast to the value of the community (umma) in Islam. One of the central factors that hindered the spread of modernity in Islam has been the intolerance of individualism, the absence of a commitment to individual rights and personal freedom which serves to limit change and innovation. Consider how many academics are silenced, jailed or murdered in Muslim countries compared to the West where radical critiques are typically ignored and relegated to obscure journals, book chapters and sociology classes.

Notwithstanding the defeat of Byzantine and rise of the Ottoman Turks who would eventually assume control over much of the Arabic world, Islamic societies began a long and gradual decline relative to ascendant Christendom. Islamic cultures, as we noted, had a number of inherent qualities that limited its capacity to modernize in the Western sense. The nature of Islamic theology, ethics, culture and law limited the impact of foreign ideas and/or the emergence of the economic, political and cultural rationality. Rather, shorn of its centers of liberal thought and toleration for pluralism, without an autonomous "public sphere" there was a retreat to more conservative forms of Islam. Henceforth, in face of challenges, Islam often embraced orthodoxies such as Wahhabism or other worldly Sufism that served to maintain tradition/resist social change. The barriers to changes, the retreats to conservative theologies, together with ressentiment to the West limited the flows of people and information with the morally inferior infidel cultures and the adaptation of their technologies and secular-rational forms of governance and organization. Societies that would embrace "Westernization" would prosper.

Defeat and Domination

By the 17th Century, European military and economic powers from Russia to Portugal began to encroach upon Islamic hegemony. With the defeats in Vienna and Buda, Ottoman rule began to contract. By the 18th Century, European merchants often traveled to Muslim countries. Within Islamic states, European and/or Jewish merchants and professionals had begun to play ever more important roles in commercial life. But, rarely did Muslims come to Europe. At the end of WWI, the Ottoman Empire, after a long decline, fell by virtue of its alliance with the defeated Axis powers. This was presaged by earlier defeats, such as by the expanding, modernizing Russia using more advanced naval artillery. But the end of the 19th C., following the Tanzimat reforms, Mustafa Kemal Ataturk, led a secular, nationalist revolution in which Turkey embraced Western modernism and established secular law-backed by its military which has often intervened against traditionalist elements.

The Europeans (British, French) colonized most of the Islamic Middle East. While modernity included many major social changes, neither the Europeans nor their sponsored intermediaries attempted to empower the Islamic people and encourage pluralistic democratic governance. Indeed, colonialism sustained both economic and political underdevelopment. Local authorities, dynastic or military, in turn gained wealth-sustaining autocracy. The transformation of the once powerful, majestic Islamic word into fragmented, colonial, neo-colonial, or peripheral states with autocratic governments having little popular support, had a number of adverse effects, not the least of which was to foster the kinds of humiliations, powerlessness and dependencies that foster ressentiment, envy and rage. Today, between rapid population growth, an obscene inequality generated by neo-liberal globalization and autocratic governments, there has been a general economic stagnation. In turn, the poor, unemployed and often even the more educated feel thwarted and/or humiliated. They often find compensatory solace and comfort in fundamentalist mosques where they embrace politicized, purified versions of Islam.

Many Muslims, finding means to transform the present blocked, turn to the "glorious past" to reclaim a glorious future, embracing a powerful cultural meaning system within vulnerable Islamic societies that explain social problems on the basis of lack of religious fidelity and valorizes the universal Islamic community, umma, granting dignity and recognition. Islamic societies such as Egypt, Syria or Iran with some commercial development (many cars, televisions, cell phones, skyscrapers, and the embrace of some Western technologies) remain highly traditional as seen in autocratic governments, unequal treatment of women, harsh penal systems and deplorable records on human rights. On the other hand, Lebanon was, and is again becoming, a very educated, sophisticated, urbane society, in part due to having been a trading country since the Phoenicians and in recent times, a "modern" banking center. Many Lebanese are actually Christians, not subject to the economic barriers of traditional Islam.

Responses to the West Westernization, Modernism, Fundamentalism

As European power expanded in the 19th Century, there were attempts by Islamic societies to modernize. The introduction of newspapers and the telegraph by Europeans in the 19th Century made widely evident the "backwardness" of the "Oriental". Other. two major strategies were developed to proactively respond to Western power and its expanding hegemony. First, leaders and intellectuals advocated westernization and secularization as the surest way to compete with Europe. This vein won out in terms of political power. As the west carved up the Islamic world into various states, indigenous leaders led the secularization of some Islamic societies, notably Turkey, promoting western education, law, science, etc. Much like the Japanese Restorationists, modernity was backed by the military. Second, a relatively small circle of intellectuals advocated an Islamic Modernism, arguing that Western methods and key institutions, legislatures, modern administrations, banks, could be revised along the lines of Islamic law. This movement was neither able to influence either the Westward leaning, secular political elites of the day nor the conservative Islamic religious authorities. These ideas did not reach the uneducated masses. Hence, Islamic development generally became polarized between Westernizing and conservative extremes.

Theorizing in the early 20th Century, Weber was personally troubled and theoretically concerned with the negative side of modernity, its rationalization of the world that dehumanized the person and reduced everything to what could be quantified. Economic striving, detached from a religious ethic, had become an empty striving for shallow materialism. A new industrial elite was emerging. A century after Weber wrote about the moral nullity of Western civilization, mass mediated consumerism, privatized hedonism devoid of meaning, has proliferated everywhere. The globalization of capital, secularization, and rapid social and cultural changes, together with population movements, has fostered both anomie and the attenuation of social ties. In face of changes, crises and challenges, one of the typical responses has been the embrace of dogmatic, orthodox positions. In a similar way, countries with economic challenges often embrace authoritarian governments, if not fascism. Fundamentalism and terrorism are both reactions to and moments of resistance to the dominating aspects of modernity and the shallowness of secularism. And, as discussed in Part III below, ressentiment mediated through radical fundamentalism can become part of the impetus for religious terrorism.

Nature of Fundamentalism

One of the most important religious social transformations of the last century has been the gradual rise of fundamentalism, the embrace of anti-modern religious orthodoxies. Why has there been a rise of fundamentalisms? Jurgensmeyer (2001) notes that religious fundamentalism across various religious cultures is on the rise globally for three common reasons: first, radical conservative religious movements reject the liberal values of secular institutions and blame society's decline on the loss of religious inspiration; second, these radical religious movements refuse to accept boundaries of secular society which keeps religion a private observance and not the public sphere; and third, these conservative movements are seeking to restore religion as central to social life. As noted above, in the face of challenges, groups may become more dogmatic and intolerant. We have suggested that in response to challenges, ranging from the sacking of Baghdad to the expulsion from Spain to the decline of the Ottoman Empire, that Islamic leaders have repeatedly embraced more conservative positions.

This created conservative traditions as the basis for a conservative response to Western secular encroachments. This, however, is a general global cultural phenomenon in response to rapid social change, uncertainty, attenuation of social ties, challenges to ingrained value precepts, etc. Fundamentalisms generally require unquestioning acceptance of transcendent religious precepts, a strict adherence to compulsory rituals and a subjugation of the self to higher powers. Fundamentalism may be defined as a conservative religious reaction to secular society that typically includes the following characteristics: Exclusive truth claims are typically based on a sacred text. It often has Manichean truth claims in which non-believers are constructed as immoral and an apocalyptic view of the world. Fundamentalism seeks to restore a glorious past from which people had strayed. Fundamentalism makes exclusive truth claims grounded in canonical religious, spiritual texts and seeks to recreate an idealized religious community while paradoxically embracing modern means: mass media, bureaucratic institutions, and destructive technologies in militancy. Christian, Jewish, Hindu, and Islamic fundamentalisms more or less follow this pattern. Thus, fundamentalisms resist the usually hedonistic, secular, materialistic values of modernity. At the same time, fundamentalists are modernists in that they use elements of tradition in combination with modern methods-advanced technology, institutional forms, and instrumental rationality-to transform the political order.

Radical religious movements often position themselves to act in the public sphere as moral agents. From the viewpoint of religious radicals, it is not so much that religion has become political as much as politics has become religious. The reasons for this deep antagonism are not merely political. Secular modernity and its valorization of Reason has made an assault on religious values and worldviews that erode the impact and power of religious institutions leading to a general crisis in religious belief. As secular society is suffering a crisis of morality and meaning, there is a space for religious critiques of secular modernity and transcendental alternatives. The West, celebrating the secular materialism of modernity, spread through a political economic imperialism and mass mediated consumerism has created spaces for radical religious movements, both in the developed and developing countries.

Islamisms

Islamic fundamentalisms arose in various Islamic states. For example, Wahabbism was embraced in Saudi Arabia, as the Ottoman Empire declined in the later 18th, early 19th Century. As Western power grew and the division of the Islamic world proceeded, Western interests encouraged the suppression of progressive movements in the Middle East such as socialism or even nationalism. For example, the US has strongly supported the (oil rich) House of Saud, where Islam has turned increasingly conservative and militant in resistance. Islamic fundamentalism is a response many factors, central among which are the domination by the West, the relative poverty and underdevelopment of the Muslim world, and the lack of political outlets to express discontents. In the 20th Century, Westernization did not yield its promised results. Modernity failed Islamic states, for a variety of reasons mentioned above, especially the conservatism of its religion, the underdevelopment inherent in colonialism and foreign sponsoring of local elites, the lack of education of the populace, and, the conservatism of religious leaders.

Islamic states generally secured the wealth and power of the elites and sustained oppressive secular governments rather than seek expansions of democracy and human rights. With the failure of modernity to bring its promised benefits, conservative Islamic brotherhoods and movements, originally organized to address social justice issues attempted to reinvigorate, reform and reestablish Islam as the basis for revitalized Islamic states. As westernizing strategies in Islamic states failed and/or were suppressed in the 20th Century, conservative religious responses grew more pronounced, generating various Islamisms, Islamic fundamentalist movements. Note that in many developing nations, secular thought and autonomous institutions, especially democratically elected legislative bodies and executive are not very well formed or advanced. Religious ways of life and social-political institutions hold more public power, especially in Islamic countries. Hence, there is a strong link between religious belief and resistance to Western hegemony among radical religious movements in the Islamic world.

The rigid claims and orthodoxy of fundamentalism generally prevents a group from self-examination and critical reflection. This is not likely to change as long as the educational processes in the developing world remain tied to traditional religious institutions. Studying the Quran and/or Islamic studies does not much prepare the student for science, industry, commerce or critical thought. Conservative Islamic movements have pursued three main ends in Islamic society: reformism, revivalism, and radical defense. The main interest of these movements is to reestablish the moral and political virtues of traditional Islamic society. Islamism is modeled on the attempt to recapture Muhammad's early role of rebel in Mecca in criticizing moral corruption and need for lifestyle and political economic reforms grounded in religious mores.

For revivalists, just as Muhammad challenged false gods and immoral ways instead of a righteous life, Islamism is seen as a path to justice and equality against the Western ways of corruption and worship of its false gods. Islamist ideological analysis offers these reasons for the decline of Islam: 1) Islamic society declined due to the departure from the practice of religious values and dictates; 2) This decay made possible the Western intrusion; and, 3) The solution is to revitalize and return to Islam by a) reintroducing the

Shariah, Islamic law, while purging most Western cultural influences, but not science and technology and b) re-politicizing Islam, along lines of Muhammad's role as administrator and law giver in Medina.

The rise of Islamic fundamentalism was the result of many factors beginning with general factors that have also fostered the growth of Christian fundamentalism, Orthodox Judaism and even Hindu fundamentalism. But further, in Islamic societies, the barriers to modernity have joined together with economic underdevelopment, traditional education, and the suppression of political dissent to dispose fundamentalism. Further, various Islamic institutions have provided cheap alternatives to public education, in which young boys learn strict conservative forms of Islam, as for example the madrassas of Pakistan funded by Saudi Arabia. Islamism has often been directly reproduced through strictly enforced civic codes in which "moral police" vigorously patrol the borders of virtue as in Saudi Arabia, Kuwait, Iran and the former Taliban controlled Afghanistan.

There have been wide variations in the extent to which Muslim societies have embraced Islamisms, and within particular societies, there have been wide disparities in the appeal of Islamisms. For example, Afghanistan, under the Taliban, was an extreme, even by fundamentalist standards. But so too was (is) Afghanistan, one of the poorest, least educated societies in the world. In contrast, Pakistan was (is) not a fundamentalist country. After General Zia took power, he tried to impose fundamentalism from the top down. It had few adherents, not more than about five percent of the people, primarily among tribal groups-looked down upon in Pakistani society. The Saudis financed madrassas that were accepted by subsequent governments in order to divert scarce funds to nuclear weapons programs, in response to India.

Islamic fundamentalism was accepted by elements within Pakistani Security (the ISI) who used these schools to provide "volunteers" to fight against India in Kashmir as well as train US-financed mujahadeen that would fight a proxy war against Russia. In Algeria, a prolonged conflict between urban, Western modernists and rural fundamentalists has cost perhaps 200,000 lives. Although fundamentalism has been widely embraced in the Muslim world, and it often promotes hatred of infidels, the vast majority of fundamentalists do not become terrorists, and not all terrorists in Islamic societies are "holy warriors". Nevertheless, the world wide rise of fundamentalism, with its Manichean division of the world into those who are good and those who are evil, with it assertions of patriarchy and promises of redemption, creates an atmosphere in which terrorism can thrive.

Religion and Ressentiment

Marx understood religion dialectically. Religion was an expression of the real pain and suffering engendered by the political economy, as well as an opiate that made that suffering tolerable bearable by providing compensations. Religion, as a hegemonic ideology, sustains domination by providing quite genuine social and emotional gratifications, creating a realm of hope outside the political economy. As Durkheim noted, collective rituals evoke the efflorescence of powerful emotions that celebrate and reinforce social solidarity. So too did Freud (1989) argue that religion, while an illusion resting on powerful unconscious longings for a benevolent father figure, could nevertheless evoke powerful feelings, "oceanic feelings" of unity with the universe recapitulating a blissful symbiosis with the mother. While religion may well assuage domination and yet sustain it with compensatory emotional experiences from either the group or the unconscious, as Weber would note, religion, providing a theodicy of the distributions of fortune articulated by virtuosos, nevertheless took particulars forms with theologies that had an "elective affinity" with the status positions of its followers. Thus religious values and doctrines, guiding both everyday conduct and eschatological ends, provided its followers with affective gratifications and indeed hope.

Weber was highly influenced by Nietzsche, who called Christianity a "slave religion" in which there had been a transvaluation of the ethical. For Nietzsche, the dominated classes of Rome embraced Christianity, a slave "mentality" with its values of mercy, justice, forgiveness and compassion. Slaves would ask for their master's mercy and justice rather than plan the overthrow of their masters. Christianity represented a "transvaluation of the ethical," the values of strong and powerful, the expressions of will, bravery, conquest or indeed cruelty that had been considered "good" were redefined as "bad," indeed "sinful". Christianity defined "goodness" from the standpoint of the weak, the powerless, and the alienated. Christianity traded docility and subordination for strength and power. But the renunciation of the "will to power," the subordination of the Dionysian for the Apollonian came at a cost, sickness of the soul and the contraction of the self to the banality of the pitiful masses.

In articulating a critical theory of religion, located in the Frankfurt School tradition of immanent critique Siebert (2001), emphasized the contradictions between the promises of religion, often utopian, and the actual conditions of people's lives. In order to understand the relation of religion to material factors in the development of religious terrorism, we need consider the important role of ressentiment as first articulated by Nietzsche to note the allure and response of Christianity as a religion of subalterns:

With the emergence of Christianity we have the successful slave-revolt in morality with its accompanying new set of values and virtues, and its underlying ascetic ideal. The slave revolt in morality begins when ressentiment itself becomes creative and gives birth to values: the ressentiment of natures that are denied the true reaction that of deeds, esteemed, desired and possessed by the noble. It is the rejection of external goods such as honor and prestige, political power and influence, wealth, physical strength and beauty; and as well a disparagement of those virtues, especially courage and pride, characteristic of the GrecoRoman nobleman... The goods and virtues associated with the despised nobility themselves come to be hated as evil. In the place of the negatively apprehended values, traits and devices found expedient for sheer survival of the weak are elevated to the status of goods and virtues. Thus, the weakness of the oppressed is transformed into virtue and the original power and strength of the noble is now considered evil and sinful.

In other words, when superiors possess certain desirable actualities of power, wealth and dignity, as well as possibilities of freedom are and denied to subordinates, they will come to loath what they cannot have, materially, politically or morally and instead will embrace denial and asceticism that become valorized. But this ressentiment, as a repressed form of envy/ hatred of the other, becomes turned on the self as a sickness, as self-hatred that consumes. As Nietzsche put it,

Ressentiment: Everything hurts. Being sick in itself is a kind of ressentiment. The defensive and offensive instinct in man becomes soft-one does not know how to have done with anything-one does not know how to thrust back-everything hurts-men and things come importunately close-events strike too deep-the memory is a festering wound.

For the Christian subalterns of Rome, with the transvaluation of the ethical, their kingdom of God would be the next life-where the vile Romans were consigned to hell. As Greenfeld (1992) has argued, the ressentiment of the bourgeoisie toward dynastic rule impelled the rise of the Nation State that would empower people as citizens with dignity based on membership in an "imagined community". Similarly, religious terrorists may see terrorism as hope, as the only means to overcome their despised secular oppressors, find agency and even secure dignity in a "purified" state. Following Nietzsche, we suggest that dominated groups, lacking public means for the realization of will qua agency and empowerment, denied recognition and dignity, facing humiliations, experience ressentiment that in turn disposes the embrace of religious fundamentalism a vision of hope in attaining a "better world", often of restoring a lost "Golden Age" in which the "redeemed" faithful regain a lost sense of agency and dignity. For Nietzsche, the only way to overcome ressentiment was to give up the desire for vengeance-but the hatred to other typically makes that impossible for all but the "ubermench."

To bring meaning to the world and control human passions, all societies develop frameworks of meaning and understanding to explain the nature of the world, prescribe ethical regulations of everyday life and explain injustice and promise redemption. Religions typically provide a theodicy that explains the contradictions between the promises of God and worldly injustice. Further, these theodicies typically provide a course of amelioration from the abnegation of the world. "For Horkhiemer, religion or theodicy was the expression of the longing for the Infinite: for perfect justice. This perfect justice could never be realized in the secular history. Even if a better world would take the place of the present social disorder...the past misery would not be made good and the predicament and plight in the surrounding nature would not be superceded".

As Islam became culturally stagnant in face of a growing Christendom, Christian Europe became economically, politically and militarily vastly superior to what had been a far more advanced culture. One cultural consequence was the development of a long-standing ressentiment against the upstarts, whose crusaders were cast out of the Holy Land, defeated in Constantinople, who would eventually colonize and or control much of the land that had been under Muslim rule. Until the 19th C., Islamic societies mostly ignored the West. Following the end of colonial domination, despite the many Western educated leaders and intellectuals, none of the Muslim states were able to throw off the shackles of history, again fostering ressentiment to the West and attribution of blame almost verging on the paranoid. For example, many Muslims in places like Egypt accept the Protocols of the Elders of Zion and blame underdevelopment on Israel, the US or whomever.

This became even more pronounced following colonization and partitioning of the Islamic world by Europe and the failure of post-colonial Muslim societies to achieve widespread economic growth. Following WWII, there were vast changes throughout the world that impacted Islamic states. This began with the increasing importance of oil and the alliances between dynastic rule in the Gulf States and Western capital. In addition to Western economic domination, autocratic governments, whether secular (Syria, Iraq, Egypt) or theocratic (Iran, Sudan), the suppression of personal freedom and dissent has also maintained political barriers to economic growth then came the founding of Israel as an alien, secular, Zionist state. The ressentiment toward modern infidels was evident in 1937 when the Grand Mufti of Jerusalem rejected the Peel commission suggesting partitioning Palestine and granting a "homeland" to Western Jews. In 1947, the UN partitioned Palestine and Israel, leading to that war, as well as wars in 1967 and 1973 that ended in humiliating defeats in which a small, secular power triumphed over the armies of far larger, more populous countries.

There were of course other events such as the seizure of the Suez Canal and the CIA engineered overthrow of Mossadeq and installation of Shah Palevi in Iran that showed the political weakness of Islamic states. Western manufactured goods became more common, as well as Western companies providing these goods, attesting to the economic backwardness of their economies. The conditions of modernity have fostered greater and greater ressentiment. One of the consequences of globalization has been the annihilation of time and space. Islamic cultures have been increasing exposed to the secular values of the West, especially its shallow materialism, individualism and instru-mental rationality that have challenged many traditional beliefs of orthodox Islam. The diffusion (and appeal) of the popular culture of the West, with its narcissistic hedonism and sexual freedom, among the educated classes, especially youth, has been an affront to the culturally dominant conservative traditions of Islam. Further, the growth of satellite television and/or VCRs and media representations of the West have highlighted the value differences between Islam and the West. Large numbers Muslims, have access to mass media (many have the internet).

Many Muslims receive reports from family members that are part of the migrations and student sojourns to Europe and the US. Muslims witness how they are represented as subalterns in the West. "Orientalism" constructs the Muslim (and Islamic culture) as denigrated other. S/he is seen as lazy, dirty (despite Islam's almost fanatical concerns with cleanliness), ignorant, treacherous, duplicitous, corrupt, violent and/or barbaric. Muslims everywhere see how blatantly their societies are materially poor compared to the West. They are well aware of the power of the US and the many injustices it fosters. They find that their religious values are challenged and in response, they are more likely to defend their values, even as they often know it is hard to defend certain laws and practices, e.g., slavery, the treatment of women and autocracy. This disposes the embrace of fundamentalism that valorizes and sacralizes their culture that is denigrated by others. Nevertheless, fundamentalism, while rarely violent, may become used as its justification.

Varieties of Terrorism

Radical conservative religious movements have become linked to terrorism in places as diverse as the Middle East, Ireland, Japan, and the U.S. It is necessary to examine terrorism before further exploring the link between radical religion and the embrace of violence. It is difficult to define terrorism. One person's terrorist is another's freedom fighter. There are various types of egregious political violence that are sometimes conflated. Official documents on terrorism rarely define the term or differentiate it from other forms of violent political action, e.g., guerilla movements, ethno-nationalist conflicts or progressive movements that take direct action. Nations often brand opposition/resistance/demonstrations as "terrorist" to demonize and discredit those who might dissent Ahmad (1998) offered a typology of five varieties of terrorism: state terrorism, religious terrorism, criminal terrorism, pathological terrorism, and secular oppositional, or political, terrorism. There are different motives for these.

Some highly visible exprcssions of terrorism can be thought of as spectacles of violence, media events staged to dramatize an issue by gaining the attention of the world. Terrorism acts as both a symbolic message and supposed means of social change aiming at political transformation. The terrorist act dramatically "advertises" the grievance to a larger community that may support their goals. Further, the "pain and suffering" inflicted is believed, at least by the terrorists, to avenge a prior injustice and/or attain the organization's goal. Some terrorists seek to destabilize a regime through low intensity warfare that is often entwined with foreign policy of states, whether explicit or implicit. The types of terrorism can overlap. While terrorists are not typically members of official State organizations, the line between state terrorism and oppositional terrorism gets blurred at times as imperialistic States or state agencies (e.g., KGB, CIA, MI6 or ISA) often support terrorists to attain geo-political goals.

For example, Ahmad notes that the United States has sponsored various types of terrorism and terrorist agents: the contras in Nicaragua, paramilitary death squads in El Salvador, and the Mujahadeen in Afghanistan. While a combination of factors such as hatred against oppressors, poverty and blocked opportunities may breed the conditions for terrorism, terrorist organizations nevertheless require resources provided by rich States, e.g., Iran's support of Hezbollah or rich individuals such as Bin Laden's support of Al Qaeda. The focus of Western political and corporate media discourse is on the types of terrorism against its States and/ or its globalized political economy. Oppositional and religious terrorism are generally far less destructive than egregious state sponsored violence; 9/11 wanes pale compared to the 500,000 Huks slaughtered by Sukarno, 200,000 Guatemalans killed by US trained/financed death squads or the 20,000 Argentines who "disappeared".

The spread of terrorism today is facilitated by technologies of media, communication (cell, phones Internet), and advanced means of lethal mass violence. It is increasingly possible, perhaps inevitable, that radical terrorists may gain or develop weapons of mass destruction, whether biological, chemical or even nuclear. Oppositional terrorism, our focus, whether based on secular or religious political struggle, can be understood then as the actions taken by members of quasi-military organizations, more or less unified by a Manichean ideology of good friend and evil foe where there are not innocents. They attack noncombatants, military or civilian, and/or the infrastructures of a "dominating power" in order to attain a certain political or cultural goals or conditions.

Religious Terrorism

Political economic goals and values have long been cloaked with religious justifications and cosmological goals. For example, at various historical moments, the Holy Land gave rise to three different monotheistic faiths that have often killed each other, in God's name. Indeed, the Holy War tradition of God ordained combat that became jihad in Islam or Crusades for Christians originated in Judaism when God bid Joshua do battle against the Canaanites who ordered the soldiers to smite every last man, woman and child. Almost every ethical code tries to establish controls on the impulse life and thus proscribes the taking of life. Religions often preach mercy, kindness, charity and love of neighborbecause as

Freud (1930) said our natural inclination is to do otherwise. This is clear in the Abrahamic tradition where "though shall not kill" was carved in stone, yet in the name of God, nation or worthy cause, there are a number of justifi-cations to kill. Consider the many injunctions to smite the criminal, the enemy or the one who violates a religious code.

There are religious justifications to smite gays, harlots, adulterers etc. Nefarious others who (would) do harm to the group, challenge its social hierarchies and/or violate its moral order must face "just punishment," lex talianis. As Durkheim noted, traditional societies, with mechanical solidarity, demand the most severe punishments. When religious fundamentalism becomes militant, what has been described as "clerical fascism", and embraces the use of force, it's exclusive truth claims, eschatology, and intolerance of sacrilegious Others often demands their death. Religious terrorism thus justifies and rationalizes inflicting death upon enemy infidels, unholy others from within or without. The development of religious terrorism is complex, historical legacies become intertwined with conservative reactions to modernity and political economy in such ways that ressentiment, mediated through cultural understandings and insults, political/social movements, and characterological factors, sustained by certain individuals, organizations, networks and/or states, are manifested recurring terrorist actions. The willingness to engage modern technology, including modern weapons, creates the conditions for catastrophic religious terrorism.

Ressentiment and Religious Terrorism in Islam

Today, as a deviant "Other" to the hegemonic West, Muslims often experience humiliation and contempt, deprivations of dignity and recognition. Political economic domination, political centralization, capital's repression of secular lines of democratic resistance, liberal or socialist, absence of a modernizing ideology, together with cultural isolation and denigration have been major factors that have given rise to ressentiment vis-à-vis the West, Islamic fundamentalism, and the rise of religious terrorism. In almost every Muslim country there are a number of anti-Western organizations that would and do embrace terrorist means. For example, Al Qaeda, grounded in both Wahhabist philosophy and adamant militant resistance to the West, is situated throughout the Islamic world. This combination of ultra-conservative worldviews promoting self-sacrifice and militant resistance disposes religious warriors to become terrorist-martyrs, as was seen in 9/11.

While terrorism can be cloaked in the teachings of any religion, there are certain unique aspects of Islamic terrorism rooted in its own history and culture. Foremost is the articulation of ressentiment-based claims of moral superiority in face of the material advantages and secular morals of the West. Thus certain aspects of Islamic traditions, lesser jihad, martyrdom and the primacy of sharia, are drawn upon to legitimate terrorist activities as Islam traditions of tolerance, equality and respect for difference are ignored. Islam ressentiment is rooted in one of the basic polarities of our age, the dialectical conflict between modernity and tradition in the modern age, between religion and the secular. Just as the Catholic Church long resisted modernity (read: class interested culture of the rational bourgeoisie), so too has Islam resisted modernity on a number of levels, e.g., intolerance to any questions of either theological leadership or political leadership that rests on religious claims.

Secular, democratic governance is not only feared by indigenous elites who would be quickly replaced, but the repression of modernist elements such as pluralism and intellectual/political dissent is often used by certain authoritarian secular leaders to justify the repressive nature of their regimes, claiming to the world that the alternatives might be fundamentalists. Laquer (2001) has suggested that the basis for the increased Islamic terrorism has been the failure of western ideologies such as secular nationalism to take hold, leaving an intellectual and political vacuum in which the only alternative forthcoming has been Islamism and terrorism-neither of which can ameliorate the lives of those who would embrace their doctrines. In militant Islamisms, the moral superiority of Islam is framed in conservative theological terms and is expressed through political resistance articulated through terrorism, legitimated as a jihad, a holy war, against the secular West.

However, for the US, Europe and Israel, the bombings of buildings, hotels, malls, discos, embassies, etc., in Lebanon, Kenya, Tanzania, Saudi Arabia etc, the Palestinian intifada, the bombings of the WTC, the attack on the Cole and above all, 9/11, have been seen as acts of terrorists. While oppositional and religious terrorism has been used as a political instrument to attain certain goals for a long time and has often been cloaked in religious justifications, the legacies of Islam give its expressions of terrorism a distinctive hue. Specially, its early legacies of warrior-based jihad now inform contemporary articulations of holy war or "sacred terror" that renders holy warriors mujahadeen. But however brave and fearless these warriors may be, direct military attacks on the vastly more technologically advanced Western militaries is unthinkable. Thus, by the logic of holy war, in which all infidels are regarded as "enemy", there are no innocents. Attacks on civilian targets, including women, children and elderly are seen as morally justified by radical conservative religious militarists. But as many would note, if America were to completely disengage itself from the Islamic world, if Israel ceased to exist, the conditions of the one billion Muslims would not only not improve, but would actually deteriorate.

Social Psychology of Terrorism

Structural conditions and/or collective sentiments do not "impel" action per se. To understand oppositional terrorism, sacred or secular, we argue that subordination and ressentiment to superordinates is necessary, as are religious (political) justifications of violent means to attain moral or political ends. But these are not sufficient to lead actors to the passionate intensity of terrorism; powerful emotions are needed to realize value rational goals. What must happen for people to savagely kill "innocent" civilians or indeed, martyr themselves to do so? We thus need to consider the relationships of ressentiment to the social psychology of identity and desire that dispose terrorism. This is not to reduce the social and political to the psychological, but rather argue for the importance of psychosocial mediation using multiple levels of analysis, a critical interdisciplinary stance first articulated by the Frankfurt School that stood in the shadows of Marx, Nietzsche, Weber and Freud.

As Nietzsche noted, under conditions of domination and ressentiment to the dominator, the will is turned upon the self, the person seeks revenge and this leads to a sickness. In Freudian terms, when the outward expression of aggression is blocked, it turns upon the self as a self hatred that joins with the external forces to sustain and reproduce domination by thwarting and stifling the person, leaving him/her angry, depressed and/or symptomatic or otherwise incapable of resisting domination. The work of Fromm (1941) remains a source of insight to explain how social conditions intersect with character to dispose an ideological stance that is more or less congruent with behaviour, or more accurately, ideologies are embraced if they legitimate certain actions/ provide self enhancing feelings such as pride or dignity. Fromm and later Adorno (1950) thus argued that some character types were typical of certain cultures or class locations, e.g., the authoritarian character, rule bound conformists, disposed to dominate subordinates and defer to superiors, showed certain characterological tendencies, especially in response to weakened social ties and structurally based powerlessness.

Fromm argued that with the attenuation of social ties and greater powerlessness of the petty bourgeois classes at the time of the Reformation and again with the post WWI conditions of German, there were three responses what he called "mechanisms of escape", social forms of defense mechanism. These were submission to those deemed powerful, projection of aggression to those "outsiders" responsible for one's malaise and legitimate aggression to those seen as responsible for ones misery. In other words, under stress, there was an "escape from freedom". For Fromm, the elective affinity of class-character was a crucial factor in understanding the appeal of Luther and the rise of Protestantism, and later, the appeals of Hitler and embrace of Fascism. Afary (2001) in her biographies of two Iranian women, Zahra Rahnavard and Marziyeh Dabbagh, who "paradoxically" embraced Ayatollah Khomeini's fundamentalism (patriarchy), suggested that Fromm's insights remain a useful paradigm linking history and the individual. More specifically, authoritarian personalities, intolerant of freedom and individualism, found gratification in 1) submission to rule bound doctrines and the 2) exercise of power over others.

If we look at the death, pain and human suffering that results from terrorist acts whether shooting pro-choice doctors, planting bombs in cars, school buses or mailboxes or crowded public places, gunning down people in streets, crashing planes into buildings, or even the potential use of weapons of mass destruction, our first reaction is that the people who plan human slaughter and/or commit such deeds must be cold, heartless killers or deranged, maddened individuals. Most research suggests otherwise. Psychological profiles of terrorists have revealed that in general, they are fairly typical of the groups from which they come, and these groups are especially prone sensitive to the consequences of domination. Indeed, terrorist organizations do not want unstable, psychotic individuals who may be unpredictable. Terrorists may be more assertive and outgoing, but there is little evidence of striking psychopathology or irrational hatreds.

We suggest that the motives for terrorism are little different than the factors that dispose fundamentalism in general. Rather, these motives become more intense due to such factors as social location, age, and most often, a prolonged period of humiliation followed by socialization into a fundamentalist or terrorist organization, e.g., fundamentalist mosques, madrassas, Al Qaeda camps, Hamas camps, etc., where "total institutions" foster particular (intolerant) world views, and squelch alternatives or critical interrogation. What is being suggested is that terrorists are people who desire what most people want, but the conditions in which terrorists live foster limited options, their social ties to larger community attenuated, self realization and fulfillment become blocked by structural conditions and the emotions these conditions generate. Between the humiliations of denigration, powerlessness in face of domination and hopelessness for the expected future, terrorism becomes a means to a goal that ameliorates ressentiment through revenge.

We are not "blaming the victim". As Nietzsche suggested and Fanon (1961) demonstrated, in face of colonization and domination, the cultures and identities of the colonized were denigrated and deemed inferior compared to the more affluent and powerful colonizer. This of course leads to ressentiment and rage, but the subaltern's rage is often turned inward, upon the self. The violence done to the culture of the colonized, the "wretched of the earth" fostered self-hatred and self-destructive behaviour such as crime, addiction or interpersonal violence Terrorism serves to redirect this rage to the oppressor and thus empowers the person, to restore his/her dignity and honor-qualities highly valued in Islamic societies. Violence to the colonizer is not only cathartic, but becomes viewed as the means to overcome political, economic or cultural domination. Projecting ressentiment outwards, a small number of radical fundamentalists, typically young, unattached, underemployed males, turn militant and turn to terrorism.

As Weber notes, rational action can either be oriented to instrumental rationality (zweckrational) or to realize values (wertrational). But, Weber maintained a Kantian trifurcation of Reason, Emotion and Will. Nietzsche understood the unity of agency and desire. That is people may practice certain actions, self-denial, or rational means to attain certain functional or ideological ends that, at the same time, secure powerful affective gratifications. We suggest that just as psychopathology is often the extreme of normalcy, terror is one of the most extreme expressions of political, economic or cultural frustrations. Just as religion and/or nationalism may generate positive consequences, terrorism represents the other side of this dialectic. We start by assuming that a person's identity, his/her narrative of selfhood, is based on his/her membership in an identity granting community of meaning. This can range frorn the clique of the "popular kids" of an American middle school, to a Nation-State, or even a universal community of faith, the umma, for Muslims. One of the consequences of modernity in general has been to erode traditional collective identities and provide the person with greater freedom and choice. As traditional communities and identities are first eroded and then denigrated, modernity does not provide compensatory alternatives.

Identity and Desire

Identity, as conscious scripts and narratives of selfhood, "self-identity" for Giddens (1991), is a mediating linkage between the individual, dynamically understood, and the larger society. One's identity is not simply a set of identifications, but is a reflexive, conscious locus of subjectivity, as it moves through the flow of social time and space seeking affective gratifications in the enactment of the routines of everyday life. But this is also the site where frustrations, humiliations or insults are experienced. Otherwise said, people seek emotional gratifications or the avoidance of frustrations. This is not a simple hedonism in that people will suffer great deprivations to sustain their identities. The may even give their lives People: 1) seek membership and attachments in identity granting communities of meaning that provide social bonds and attachments; 2) strive for recognition and dignity granting statuses; 3) exercise agency in striving to overcome powerlessness; and 4) given a universal fear of death, seek a value system that provides explanations for pain, suffering and injustice, remedies and/or promises of amelioration, even if in the next life.

1. *Community*: For most of human history, between the powerful bonds of an infant's attachments to caretakers, to family/clan work groups, to the periodic solidarity rituals of large groups, people are social creature with needs to be part of a community. For Freud, group life depended on "aim-inhibited cathexes". Later psychoanalysts like Bowlby and Winnocott, have seen early bonding as the foundation of healthy development. Similarly, sociologists have long argued that collective rituals like religion, national celebrations etc, or interpersonal rituals serve to sustain community, solidarity and engagement.

   At the same time, capitalism, under girded by Protestantism, served to attenuate social ties and connections. With globalization, this tendency became universalized and has even impacted peripheral societies including most Muslim societies. Given our Western (Protestant) traditions of individualism, it is easy to slight the importance of community in traditional societies, and in the case of Islam, the community of faith (the umma) is sacralized. Between the political-economic impacts of globalization, and the mass consumerism that individualizes people as consumers (even if commodified, pseudo-individualism) social ties are attenuated, if not rent asunder. This social fragmentation is often resisted. In this way, fundamentalism can be seen as a way of resisting, rekindling and affirming those bonds. Terrorism, would act as a penultimate expression, the terrorist might even perish to sustain his/her community, and if s/he died, the funeral would fortify and re-affirm the bonds of community.

2. *Recognition*: Following Hegel's understanding of the master-slave struggle for recognition as the basis for self-consciousness, a number of psychoanalysts and scholars have noted the importance of recognition as the basis of self esteem; some consider the pursuit of self esteem, "honorific status" much more powerful a motive than sexuality. And indeed far more men have died for the sake of honor in combat than for the love a woman. Following observations by Sennett and Cobb (1972) echoed by Honneth (1995), and Taylor (1998), struggles for recognition/dignity may be seen as central to both the person and his/her groups.

   Conversely, shame and humiliation, assaults on honor and selfhood foster rage to assuage the insult. The failure to acknowledge unconscious shame, leads to destructive conflicts and violence Scheff (1994) For Fanon, the only way to overcome colonization and the denigration of the self was through violence. We would say that his analysis applies to the neo-colonialism of the globalized political economy as well, although the oppressor is more difficult to identity. Terrorism serves as a violent response to the violent conditions that deny recognition, honor and dignity.

3. *Agency*: A long line of philosophical critique, as articulated by Spinoza, Kant, Hegel and, Marx suggested that active self-constitution, striving for realization and creating reality is an inherent human tendency. With Nietzsche, philosophy moved from epistemology to psychology. Will, now framed as agency, became a central quality of investigation. For Marx, alienation the consequence of wage labor, externalized production. Commodity production stood as an external power, thwarting his/her agency, his/her humanity and self-hood. The humanly constructed systems of domination refluxed back upon the person to render him/her powerless. To understand humans as willful is to see people as active agents, who strive to make their everyday lives

meaningful and to attain certain long-term goals and values.

Powerlessness, the denial of agency is generally an extremely potent motive for individuals and groups. To be powerless is often humiliating and shame can be a powerful motive that fosters attempts to gain empowerment, to overcome domination. Indeed from slaves cutting of limbs to escape the chains of servitude, to masses enthralled with the empowering promises of a dictator, people seek empowerment. As Nietzsche suggested, to accept domination, to assent to slavery, leads to the sickness of a revenge denied. So too does fundamentalism dialectically foster subordination to power by establishing "micro-spheres" of empowerment that provide illusory realms of power. But at the same time, fundamentalism can shade into terrorism and provide realms of actual power-indeed what can give a person more power than the power to take the lives of others-the very power of God.

4. *Meaning*: People have a fundamental need to make their lives meaningful, they need frameworks of meaning that provides anxiety reducing significance to ones life, ethical codes of regulation, a theodicy of the distributions of fortune, and above all, they need to assuage the painful reality of the inevitability of death. For most of human history, religion has provided people with meaning and direction for their lives, and in many cases, hope for some kind of immortality. But again following Weber, the "disenchantment of the world" eroded the sacred and the realms of transcendent meanings.

   As religion waned in the West, nationalism emerged as a "modern" political framework in which "invented communities" of meaning granted identities, recognition and above all, meaning. But insofar as nationalism was a secular, Western framework dependent on an autonomous public sphere, it has generally held little sway in the Muslim world. As globalization began to erode the basis of nationalism, a highly fragmented mass mediated popular culture of privatized hedonism became widely diffused. But participation in cultures of consumption of modernity is beyond the means for the vast majority of Muslims. At the same time, Western materialism and narcissism is offensive to Islamic values. Fundamentalism offers an alternative, a repudiation of secular Western ideologies that is easily available. Much like early Christianity provided compensatory ressentiment, so too does fundamentalism provide a palliative alternative to secular Western, meaning systems based on hedonistic indulgence.

Character and Reactions to Domination

When domination is imposed from without and internalized at the level of character, when recognition, dignity and agency are frustrated or denied, when selfhood is humiliated and enfeebled, the person both reproduces the structural conditions of subalterity and thwarts resistance at the price of the person's actualization and fulfillment. As noted, with the waning of Islam, the rise of the Christian hegemon, and finally, colonization (or neo-colonization through local intermediary autocrats), fostered ressentiment and the desire for revenge. But that revenge would consume and destroy the self. Moving from Nietzsche to Freud, ressentiment based on domination, denigration, shame and humiliation of being inferior to a powerful Other, can be interpreted in terms of insults to character and dignity, and frustrations/denials of desires for community, agency, recognition and meaning. This is typically handled in at least three intertwined ways:

1. *Denial*: Denial and external blame are typical ways of handling the shame and humiliation that might come from seeing oneself as culpable or inadequate vis-à-vis the Other. For example, the person fired had a horrible boss; the flunking student had unfair teachers. On a social level, this tendency to project one's shortcomings

on other has long been studied in terms of scapegoating, prejudice, etc. In medieval times, ill fortune was blamed on witches, and many innocent women died. Perhaps nowhere was this as clear as Hitler's blaming the Jews and Jewish conspiracies for all of Germany's problems.

In terms of the issue at hand, we can see that denial, blame and projection are typical forms of explanation in Islamic societies. Poverty, illiteracy and scientific backwardness is due to either the infidels of the West, pro-Western leaders like King Hussein or Anwar Sadat, or an Israeli conspiracy. For example, when the WTC was attacked, a common story that appeared in Al Ahram (government newspaper), widely believed in Egypt and Saudi Arabia blamed Mossad. The story claimed that 3,000 Jews were told to stay home from work at WTC. Arabs were said to lack the capability for such an operation. It was almost 6 months later that the Saudis finally acknowledged that 15 of the 19 men were Saudi nationals, and even then most Muslims did not believe other Muslims did it.

Such an accounts keep a people from either looking within themselves or questioning their own leaders. Indeed, certain leaders typically blame others for general misfortune and not only deflect self-criticism, but mobilize people to hate and condemn an outside party and in the process, secure their own power and legitimacy. As most people know, or should know, conspiracy theories of history, while quite useless as explanations, are often quite useful for a leader or group to avoid self examination and/or avoid changes that might undermine power. Leaders have long found that scapegoating, casting blame on someone else can mobilize support for a regime. To paraphrase Sartre, if the Israelis didn't exit, Muslim states would need to invent them.

2. *Profound distrust:* The limited economic opportunities on the one hand due to both internal and external

factors, and the denial of recognition and dignity and the other, have colluded to foster structurally based blocked opportunities that in turn engender anger and rage and a sense of revenge to redress the humiliation. But insofar as much of anger is to the self, and it is denied, not acknowledged, it becomes expressed toward an external object. In psychoanalytic terms, there is a "splitting" a disavowal of dissatisfaction of what is within and its attribution to that which is without is intensely distrusted and hated. In a similar vein, to loosely borrow from Melanie Klein, one of the most archaic forms of agency can be seen in projection/aggression seen in envy.

More specifically, given the helpless and dependency of infancy, there is frustration and in turn anger and resentment that are projected to the "bad object" that is both needed and yet is hated and must be destroyed. While for Klien this "paranoid position" is an inevitable part of infancy that is transcended, in later life, certain social conditions reawaken the primitive rage and destructive fantasies of early childhood. Scheler had noted that ressentiment is based on envy, but we are suggesting that this envy has powerful unconscious underpinnings. Following her insights, psychoanalysts like Kernberg or Kohut have theorized that narcissistic insults, primarily the lack of recognition of the self and/or failures to achieve dignity and esteem elicit narcissistic rage toward denigrated objects.

Thus, a number of scholars, from Wilhelm Reich to the more recent work of Scheff (1994), seem to suggest that a combination of humiliation and powerlessness can foster intense, irrational forms of hate, rage and indeed a willingness to die. But, to whom must that rage be expressed? In the case of Islam, distrust and rage to the West have become mediated through selective interpretations of Islam that denigrate the infidel. As such, there is a profound distrust of the Western infidel and intense reactions to those who might seem to advance Western interests or ideas. Sadat was assassinated and Rushdie was condemned in a fatwa.

3. *Rage, terror and death*: These factors, given both very real and attributed injustices, foster intense anger and rage that would destroy the enemy Other. As Freud argued, there were two fundamental drives, Eros, the sexual impulse (libido) that would bind people through love, sexual or aim inhibited, and Thanatos, the Death Instinct (aggression) that would destroy and tear down. Freud's formulation should be seen as a poetic metaphor rather than an essentialist psychology. But following Freud's cultural psychology, Fromm (1967) argued that the domination of the subject, led to impairments of self love, the thwarting of self constitution and realization that leads to the embrace of nihilism and necrophilia, the love of death and destruction whether of self or other.

   This attenuated attachments and capacities to love others, and becomes a constraint upon agency that can only be overcome through violence. Perhaps we might also note Theweleit's (1989) study of the Freikorps, the veterans of WWI, petty bourgeois men without jobs or job prospects who disdained women and erotic love; they sought only war, death and destruction. To die in combat was preferable to living in peace. In sum, some who suffer from various forms of domination, social constraints or limitations on agency, may find community, meaning and identities in battle, death and devastation that provide compensatory forms of dignity and agency.

   Insofar as both Islam and Christianity condemn suicide, there have instead emerged cults and rituals that celebrate, valorize and imitate death. Salvation religions that promise a better life in this world, offer a ready escape from domination and hopelessness in this life, death. Consider only the passion plays of medieval Christianity, or the various flagellant parades among Catholics and Muslims. Islam, as a warrior religion celebrated the martyred warrior hero who died in holy combat. While Islam forbids both suicide and killing innocent civilians, some fundamentalist clerics have interpreted the Quran in ways that legitimate "sacred terrorism" through suicide missions such as shootings and/or bombings directed at civilians.

In sum, given decline, domination, political economic distress, together with cultural insults, humiliations, degradations and despair, anger, rage and hatred is generated and channeled through the available means of resistance. This kind of rage can be mobilized through secular political channels, e.g., various extremist groups turn to life destroying terrorism, Bader Meinhof, Red Brigades on the left or the Contras on the right. But so too can terrorism become religiously interpreted to be God's will.

Terrorism and Identity

Young men in particular social/cultural locations are especially prone to certain social and political stresses and influences that foster their identities. The lower middle classes of Islam tend to be religiously observant, fearful of modernity, a resentful of their condition. The rage of the unemployed, subjugated and humiliated, is much the same whether in the ghettoes of America, the marginalized lower middles classes of rural America or the souks of the Middle East. Young men, without alternative sources of agency and respect, turn to compensatory identities of hate and violence preached in cults of death. The difference between the gangbanger, right wing militiaman and terrorist is a function of socialization, institutional support and a justifying ideology.

In many Muslim societies, men and women do not date, have sex, nor can they marry unless and until they have jobs and/or means of livelihood. But most Muslim countries are showing demographic explosions and even with modest economic growth, there are not enough jobs for the growing numbers of youth and declining per capita incomes for most.

Without jobs or prospects, many unemployed or underemployed young men have nothing to do and nowhere to go. Yet they are welcomed into the mosques or madrassas where they learn a theology of anger that disposes terrorism. This is often the case in refugee camps. Palestinian camps such as Balata and Jenin are notorious spawning grounds for terrorists. The situation of these dispossessed men stands in sharp contrast with media constructed hegemonic global masculinities; the suited, forceful western businessmen and politicians express a dominant, celebrated masculine identity.

In most Muslim societies, the institutionalization of patriarchy has disposed a machismo demeanor, yet subaltern masculinities are insulted, humiliated. For young men without work and socialized into traditional Islam, ressentiment is not only a hateful envy in response to political-economic domination, but is also directed to racial/cultural subjugation and humiliation, this "emasculation" disposed hate and violence. According to Kimmel (2000), through disenfranchisement, the loss of status and employment, and emasculation in contrast to the empowerment of women in western societies, lower-middle-class men "may continue to feel a seething resentment against women, whom they perceive as stealing their rightful place at the head of the table, and against the governments that displace them." A central complaint by fundamentalists against the West is the brazen, immoral behaviour of Western women.

Note in this context that the Taliban regime attempted to restore masculinity and empower men, requiring the beard as the marker of masculinity, and to re-feminize and control women by exclusion from jobs, education etc. Most Islamic terrorists, including the 9/11 terrorists, are men under the age of 25, caught in the tension between exclusion from modernity and the inability to realize traditional roles. The violence of terrorism, even if as a martyr, restores the sense of self. In some cases, even members of the more educated classes embrace terrorist causes. As was noted in the press, the 15 Saudis of 9/11 were not uneducated teenagers of poverty and refugee camps but of the educated classes. Most had come from a rapidly changing region, one of the poorest in a now stagnating, declining Saudi Arabia. Even when living or studying in Europe, or because of it, exposed to prejudice and denigration as Europe's Other, they gravitated to fundamentalist mosques that provided them as sense of community and valorized identities. Islamism provided them with a solution to society's problems, pride in their heritage, and affirmed personhood/manhood. But, along with that came hatred to the infidel so great they became sacred warriors facing death and martyrdom.

The absolute certainty of Allah's rewards in the next life made earthly sacrifice a component of recognition and dignity that is often wanting in this world. Europe is a relatively closed society, in relation especially to immigrants. Law enforcement officials have found extensive active terrorist networks in Europe, but not in America, for good reason. In this regard, Hundley (2002) notes, "Europe — with its burgeoning population of Muslim immigrants and relatively limited opportunities for them to gain access to the social and economic mainstream — has become a factory for turning frustrated men into religious fundamentalists and political fanatics." We might add that the general ethnic monocultural prejudice and racism of European societies is a remnant of the same type of exclusivity that led to the Reformation and the secular Enlightenment. In face of economic retrenchment, Europe shows little welcome for "foreign" immigrants and worker.

From what has been said, in face of ressentiment, emasculation and subalterity, becoming a terrorist gives compensations, a valorized identity, a sense of dignity, purpose, meaning, and hope, especially when conditions are hopeless. Consider by analogy, the Jews who fought the Nazis in the Warsaw ghetto. Notwithstanding the futility of their efforts, they nevertheless held out against the

Wehrmacht longer than did the Polish army. While many died, they did so with a sense of agency and dignity that will long be remembered. We suggest that the motives of the Warsaw Jews, secular or sacred, are not so different than the Islamic terrorists of today, secular or sacred.

More specifically, if we consider articulations of desire, 1) Membership in a terrorist organization, from the time of schooling and/or recruitment, to training camps to the planning/execution of missions, places one in a highly valued publicly esteemed, cohesive community. 2) Resting upon the legacy of the esteemed warrior, the terrorist finds recognition and dignity in his acts (on some occasions her acts). Some gain pride in this life (seculars), those who go on to the next (holy warriors), are remembered and esteemed by friends and family. 3) Powerlessness, being without agency to shape one's own destiny, leads to an intense anger and hatred-that is turned upon the self. But as a terrorist, by turning passivity into activity, empowerment and agency are realized, however destructive and inhumane may be the consequences. 4) Finally, given the historical legacies/current realities that engendered ressentiment, in face of the rapid social changes of the modern world and attendant anomie, exposed to the empty materialism of the West with its "disenchantment of the world", terrorism, sacred or secular, provides a framework of values and meaning that saves one from insignificance, finitude and even the fear of death.

Islamic cultures provided their followers with various major identities or narratives of self such as the merchant, the warrior and the scientist-scholar. Weber emphasized the warrior tradition for a number of reasons, not the least of which is that in most cultures, warriors are more likely to be heroes than merchants or professors. This phenomenon long antedates Islam, let alone the modern culture industry. Identity formations, and the actions and routines they enact, may provide affective gratifications. But, under the conditions of social fragmentation, humiliation, domination, and meaninglessness, there is often frustration and regression. A readily available identity for a Muslim male is the warrior engaged in lesser jihad against infidels. In many ways, terrorism can be understood as a way of redeeming the self and returning the society to the time of its "Golden Age," a moment of both religious virtues and culture, free of external domination, where various gratifications can be found.

Globalization and the Dialectics of Terrorism

Following Weber, to end our historical and analytical discussions, we would like to consider some trends and possibilities since 9/11. We suggest two potentials in the confrontation between the West and militarized fundamentalism. First, military and police networks may become highly intertwined and form a *de facto* global police force. We predict that the "War on Terror" is likely to lead to the gradual decline of large scale terrorist organizations, but will not eliminate terrorist acts in the context of guerrilla warfare in isolated locales nor potentially catastrophic terrorist acts of mass destruction by individuals and small groups. The military technologies of advanced capitalism dispose a potential for imperialist wars, and in turn, destructive terrorism as resistance, whether organized or random. Given the emergence of the Islamic Brotherhood of Egypt in the 1930s, the growth of Islamic fundamentalism in the past few decades, and the proliferation of religious terrorisms such as Hamas, Hezbollah, Abu Sayyif and of course the globalized terror network of Al Qaeda, it might well seem as if there is an emerging "clash of civilizations" and a protracted conflict between Christendom and Islam.

We reject this thesis for many reasons. The Islamic states vary greatly in their traditions and interests. "Civilizations" include a number of classes and groups there are often very much in conflict, for example, the bazaari vs. intellectuals, westernizers vs. traditionalists, etc. The most deadly conflicts in recent times have been within and/or between Muslim countries: Iran-Kuwait, Iran-Iraq, Turkey-Kurds, or the civil war in Algeria. Moreover, national and regional politics today are very much caught up within various moments of, economic, political and cultural globalization. This, however, is not to deny that Islamisms and the Right wing in the West often frame Islamic-Western conflicts in terms of a "clash of civilizations" whose rhetoric aggravates conflicts and legitimizes military mobilizations. On the other hand, to counter the various adverse consequences of neo-liberal globalization, increasingly powerful global civil social institutions and global governance are emerging to create mechanisms that regulate the global economy and control the forces of militarization to foster peace, justice and equality. The project of modernity, with its emancipatory promises and rationalized institutions creates the possibilities for global democracy. Progressive movements, ironically, are often resisted by secular elites, who might lose power, as well as religious fundamentalists.

Responding to Terrorism

To understand the root causes and possible outcomes of terrorism, it must be kept in mind (dialectically speaking) that terrorist movements, especially in the developing world, are not only resisting the undemocratic, exploitative face of globalization but are reacting to the long standing grievances and injustices based in the hundreds of years of political economic domination by European powers of other societies and their own workers. Religious movements as movements formed at the interaction of cultural and national independence are rooted deep in the psyche and history of dominated peoples. The roots of fundamentalism and hence terrorism are very deep. The ways the contradictions of modernity in a global age may play out is very complicated. There are progressive and reactionary ways to address the issues underlying the drastic consequences of globalization. The potentials of resistance are complicated by the flexible responses of global capitalism. Hence, the solutions to the injustices of global capitalism, if any, will probably be global in scope. The Al Qaeda network is one such global if reactionary response that indicates the necessity of attending to the root causes of the inequality and political domination that disposes the embrace terrorism.

In face of stagnant or declining fortunes, many young Muslims have turned to fundamentalism and a small minority move on to terrorism. For the poor and less educated, and/or often educated in fundamentalist schools and madrassas, there are few job prospects that will allow them to fully participate in their own societies, e.g., to marry, have families and homes. Such men find community and solace in fundamentalist mosques where they can find dignity in religious virtue and devotion. Given the proximity to comparatively affluent Europe with its relatively open borders, many people go there to find jobs. And as we have seen, this includes many of the educated and more skilled those have trouble getting jobs either in their own stagnant societies and go to study or work in Western Europe. But with ten percent unemployed, but the still relatively "homogeneous" European nations regard them interlopers with disdain and contempt. Unemployed or underemployed given their credentials, such men too gravitate to fundamentalist mosques. In both cases, we see the spawning grounds of those might become terrorists. The former take up guns and/or bombs and go on terrorist missions.

The later learn to make bombs, design and execute plots, and send the former on suicide missions. These factors, individually or collectively may bode ill for the future. As we have seen these conditions and attitudes create an atmosphere that condones terrorism as well as generates likely recruits. Islamic countries that are poor, undeveloped, and prone to seemingly ever more religious fundamentalism thus engender people willing to use terrorism on a mass scale. 9/11 may be a preview to the use of weapons of mass destruction against civilian targets. The Al Qaeda network may well have cells in over 60 countries around the globe ranging from Somalia to Malaysia, alliances with a number of local terrorist organizations and perhaps the support of "rogue" states like Iran or Iraq. Such a network of cells, mosques and social welfare agencies spanning perhaps 60 countries cannot be easily or quickly dismantled. And with its careful planning, logistics and autonomous nature of its cells, that may well include well-armed sleeper cells. There may well be more dramatic incidents of terrorist activities. We do expect that to happen.

On the other hand, there have been a number of recent developments that counter these developments and may well reduce terrorism. Kepel (2002) argued (before 9/11) that Islamism was becoming politically and morally bankrupt; jihad had exhausted itself and was in a state of retrenchment following repudiation of its excesses and the failure of theocracies (Iran, Taliban) to improve the living conditions for the masses. Indeed, in a decade or two, historians may look back at 9/11 as the heyday of Islamic terrorism. One unintended consequence of 9/11 has been to mobilize a concerted, worldwide effort against terrorism. While this was perhaps spearheaded by the American retaliation against the Taliban, this effort was indeed underway long before 9/11. The highly unpopular Taliban were quickly overthrown in Afghanistan and the Al Qaeda network and training camps were seriously degraded and are unlikely to be reconstituted.

It seems as if a great deal of intelligence was found in notebooks, computers and records of Al Qaeda and the Taliban that listed many terrorists and disclosed many plans leading to a number of arrests and confiscations of explosives, etc. in places like Malaysia and Singapore. Since that time, all over the world we have seen growing cooperation of intelligence agencies that have become far more diligent and aggressive in surveillance and arrest of terrorists. The day of this writing, Italian police stopped a plot to poison the water of Rome. There have also been hundreds of other arrests of terrorists linked to Al Queda in Germany, Belgium, Spain, France, England, Turkey, Malaysia, Indonesia and the Philippines, etc. A number of governments that have in the past supported terrorism and anti-Americanism have made major changes in direction, often beginning before 9/11.

Perhaps most important has been Pakistan where President Musharraf was paid several billion dollars for withdrawing support from the Taliban who were strongly supported by his own ISI (Pakistan's military intelligence). He then provided a great deal of logistical and intelligence support for the United States military campaign. He closed a number of fundamentalist mosques, changed the curricula of the madrassas and reduced the influence of the ISI. Yemen, site of the Cole bombing, was relatively uncooperative in investigating the crime. But since 9/11, Yemen has embarked on an anti-terrorism campaign, replete with American military advisors so too has Sudan, once home to Bin Laden, moved toward the US. In 1999, the Emir of Bahrain, Sheik Hamad bin Isa al-Khalifa, assumed the throne. He immediately opened the jails, released all political prisoners and allowed the return of political exiles.

More recently, he declared himself king, but with plans to create a constitutional monarchy with democratic elections in which both men and women can run for office and/or vote. The Saudis, who have indeed contributed to the problem of terrorism, are now facing problems of their own. Some Princes have been raising questions about the need for changes. They are suggesting that more should students study banking, science, engineering and business administration. While millions of foreign workers have been sent home to give Saudis jobs, there have been voices for gradual changes of Saudi laws and practices. They have offered Israel recognition if it withdrew to it's 1967 borders. (Ending the Israeli-Palestinian conflict would end one major irritant to many Muslims.) They have become more cooperative with US intelligence after 9/11. There have been louder calls for women's rights and even demonstrations.

Teenagers and young people have found more and more creative ways to use cell phones and the Internet to plan rendezvous, out of the sight of the moral police. Using state military and police networks to control terrorism yields a mixed outcome. With the increase in police and military expenditures and loss of civil liberties there is also is the attempt to recreate a safe world. We question the merit long term of a militarized response. Note the cases of Vietnam, Ireland, Bosnia, and Palestine: violent suppression often leads to violent resistance rather than the intended outcomes. The "War on Terror" will probably lead to a decline in wide spread terrorist organizations but not to the end of terrorism or resistance to imperialism.

Globalization as both Oppressive and Liberating

Neo-liberal globalization, fostering greater and greater inequalities, has created vast wealth, most of which has gone to elites. While global capital has provided few job-generating investments in the Islamic countries, Transnational Corporations have nevertheless found/created large markets for their products and have developed various "exotic" sites for tourists. The mass media display an outside world of plenty while rich tourists from that world's display their wealth. At the same time, Western media celebrates a secular, hedonist mass culture that is morally offensive to traditional Islamic values ranging from autocracy to patriarchy. Insofar as globalization has infiltrated many of these countries, clerics and political leaders deplore, resist and condemn the self indulgent, erotic hedonism and quite rightly fear that it will corrupt their culture and their cultural power may erode. In part due to the factors noted, Muslim countries have not been incorporated into the new worlds of commerce.

Even a "wealthy" country like oil rich Saudi Arabia has seen its revenues stagnate and its population explode leading to a decline in per capita income from $22,000 to $8,000. Across the Islamic world there are population explosions, unemployment, underemployment and mismatched skills, e.g., many college students graduate with degrees in Islamic studies-with no job prospects rather than science, technology or business administration. There is a generally unfavorable view of the US and its policies based on its hyperpower political-economic status, the geo-politics of oil, its support of tyrants, its uncritical support for Israeli treatment (occupation) of the Palestinians, and the materialistic culture. Many believe that the US is run by the Jews, if not by a Zionist conspiracy. A recent Gallup survey of over 9,000 residents of Pakistan, Iran, Indonesia, Turkey, Lebanon, Morocco, Kuwait, Jordan and Saudi Arabia found that more than half had unfavorable view of the US. While some that resentment is a displacement from dissatisfaction with local leaders, the fact remains that most people have a negative view of the US, not entirely undeserved.

Marx celebrated capitalist modernity as liberating; it rent asunder the personal ties of fealty and ended the idiocy of rural life that sustained the domination by kings, lords and bishops. Capitalism would create the seeds of a socialist society. In much the same way, globalization has liberating effects. It sows seeds of modernity that, if they sprout and flourish, can act in the Muslim world, much like the Reformation in Christendom, initiating a transformed religion that can both lead Islam into the modern world, and at the same time, recapture its own now often forgotten legacies of tolerance, justice, philosophy, and science.

In this light, what are some of positive outcomes and developments since 9/11? At them most recent meeting of the pro-business World Economic Forum in New York, in the shadow of 9/11, such issues and critiques of alternative globalization movements were given attention by the elites of global capital. In contrast to previous WEF meetings, business, political and cultural leaders debated alternative globalization critiques of neo-liberalism. At the same time, at the pro-union/social movement 2nd World Social Forum in Porto Alegro, Brazil, 50,000 participants, including representatives from around the globe, formulated structural strategies for democratic globalization. We suggest that the events of 9/11 might contribute to the growth of a global civil society and new political structures to administer and enforce international law. Certain global trends interact with the response to terrorism. First, 9/11 and the "War on Terror" highlight the growing importance and power of regional and global political bodies and pacts such as the UN, EU, G-8, and NATO.

While there are tensions within and amongst such bodies as well as protest movements against them and while the U.S. has often acted unilaterally, the U.N. and European states were involved in the initial legitimation of the "War on Terror" and have been very involved in the postwar organization of the government Afghanistan and in the peace keeping missions. Secondly, the gradual institutionalization of progressive treaties such as the International Criminal Court may well offer caution to even leaders of the industrial nations, who might sponsor terrorist organizations or engage in state terrorist acts. Third, with the growing pressure of net mediated global justice movements, such as the World Social Forum which produced statements strongly criticizing U.S. policy in Afghanistan and the War on Terror, we can see the beginnings of a transformation towards a global civil society to complement and challenge the U.N. and push for regulation and democratization of the global political economy.

In the light of such and other developments in reaction to globalization, we see possibilities for a struggle between neoliberal and social democratic forces ultimately yielding a more democratic global society. To accommodate critiques and challenges and still sustain profits, there may be a return to neo-Keynsian economics at a global level. This would seem to call for a global, social democratic welfare network state to moderate the domination of some states over others (constrain imperialism), alleviate poverty (moderate capitalism) and modernize education (modernize traditions). The growing calls for debt relief and increasing challenges to IMF/World Bank neo-liberalism should be noted. While various dystopian and utopian scenarios are possible, with a wide range of options in between, we suggest that although there may be risks of further terrorist attacks, the shock of 9/11, followed by the intervention in Afghanistan, War or Terrorism and the increased recognition of the global scope of governance and militarization, in the long run will encourage the world to embrace more global governance serving not only the elites, but all of humanity.

In other words, 9/11 and subsequent developments may be a watershed, political and cultural moments, that will lead to greater awareness of the adverse consequences of globalization that dispose globalized terror. Various alternative globalization movements, progressive NGOs, and now even some of the elites of globalization are suggesting ameliorative actions and strategies. To understand the spread fundamentalism, in this case Islamic fundamentalism, as a search for religious certainty and purity rooted in an imagined past, and violent terrorism as a rare but visible political means to restore that past, we must look at the historical roots of the phenomena. Military conquest and trade networks spread the hegemony of Islamic culture, and it's shariah based codes for life, law and society, from the Atlantic coasts of Iberia through to western China. The growing affluence of the Islamic world fostered great centers of advanced learning and culture. Within 500 years, Islamic civilization reached a level previously comparable only to India or China.

Although Islam engendered a very advanced civilization, and indeed enabled the Renaissance in the West, the values and conditions that made the rise of the Islam possible, together with various challenges and defeats from other societies, led to an erosion of its dynamism, to stagnation, dogmatism, and a turning inward and a waning of its hegemony. Lewis (2002) and others have asked, "What went wrong?" In contrast to Islam, ascendant Protestant Christianity, freeing the person from the shackles of feudalism, with its rationalization of its economy, administration and legal systems, and a rejection of abnegation of the world, together with its subjective moment, "salvation anxiety", impelling an "inner determinant" for instrumental action, disposed the rise and proliferation of rational capitalism. This eventually led to the European subjugation of Islam and the reduction of Islamic societies to peripheral status, and in turn, ressentiment to the wealthy and powerful West. Within 500 years of the Reformation, Christendom, now including the US, achieved global hegemony and unprecedented economic, technological and military might. Following WWII, global hegemony was dominated by America.

In face of modernity and political economic domination, the many assaults on traditional values and identities, and the homogenizing tendencies of globalization, in spite of the liberalization of beliefs and pluralism, there has been a worldwide embrace of fundamentalism. For Islamic fundamentalists, the secular governance, toleration, individualism and personal freedom (sexuality) of the West are abhorrent. Its materialistic culture is seen as shallow and godless, its toleration for democracy, human rights, gender equality and sexual freedom are heresies alien to Islamic traditions. Its mass mediated popular culture is an apostasy. Hence, in face of economic, political and cultural challenges and ressentiment, for societies where the diffusion of globali-zation has been limited, as has been the case in many Muslim countries, there was a broad impetus for religious renewal. Islamic societies, at the time of their Golden Age, practiced toleration, justice, pluralism and equality. But that past has also included internal factors that have acted as limits to the growth of modernity. Between fundamentalism and ressentiment, that has been violence against memory that stems from the need for revenge.

The "invented" past of fundamentalism that would place the blame for social ills on ethical lapses and reclaim a glorious theocratic future, provides compensatory identities and affective gratifications to its followers by paradoxically preaching dogmatism, intolerance, hatred, blame and violence, all of which sustain poverty and despair. For a marginal few in particular social locations of age, class and gender, there is an elective affinity for terrorism and the celebration of Death. Ressentiment meets the death instinct and joins with the ideology of a Holy war through resistance to external oppression that leads to unspeakable, violent acts. Religious terrorism is a dark moment of the collective soul, grounded in hate. It is a rigidly defensive ideology of retribution that reproduces the very conditions it would seek to ameliorate. The options for Islamic societies are vexing. Secular westernization at the state level has been undone and/or resisted from within by Islamist reactions and by neo-colonial forces from without. In most Islamic states, efforts to elaborate Islamic modernisms, the pursuit of tolerance, compassion, and understanding, in syntheses of Islamic culture and modernity have either been suppressed or lacking a ready public. Yet there are traditions within Islam of metaphorical interpretations of the Quran, of free speech and diversities of interpretation.

In recent years there has developed a cottage industry of Islamic scholarship examining the texts and the actual historical roots of the Quran and its evolution in early Islam. What must be noted is that most of this scholarship is located in Western universities; in most Muslim countries, questions that the Quran is anything other than the actual word of God, revealed by Gabriel, are typically met with fatwas and violence. The transformations of Islamic fundamentalism, with its conservatism and literalism that would silence the clerical fascists that preach hate and destruction, that would recapture the vibrant heterodoxy and toleration of its Golden Age, made relevant to our global age, can only come from within Islam. In the West and in the more pluralistic and materially advanced Islamic states such as Lebanon or Turkey, hard compromises and creative syntheses are being worked out between modernization and tradition. Kepel (2002) has argued that we are on the cusp of a new, post-Islamist age in which the traditions of Islam become reconciled with the democratic and pluralistic side of globally based modernity.

It remains to be seen if the emancipatory, liberalizing forces of globalization will temper the adverse consequences of its neo-liberal forms that have unconsciously colluded with the reactionary elements within Islamic societies that prefer stability to democracy while many people suffer. The adverse moments of modernity, American geo-political interests and its mass mediated consumer culture are found everywhere in world in which time and space have been compressed. Throughout the world we have seen fundamentalism growing as a response to pains of globalized modernity. The unique culture, histories and legacies of Islamic societies have led to dislocations, humiliations and ressentiments that have been expressed in Islamisms, ethno-religious conflicts and terrorism that give voice to an oppressive modernity. Perhaps more important than ideological debates over the nature of Islamic history is the future of reform in Islam. Kepel (2002) suggested that Islamist terrorism does not, nor can it produce its intended goals and has become consumed with a fantasy of a world-wide triumph of radical Islam.

Dreams of world domination generally lead to many deaths before they exit from the stage of world history. We are left with the dilemmas and solutions of Marx and Weber. To remedy the injustices of global capital, we must create global solutions through political solidarity across ever more permeable boundaries. To reform the nullity of modern civilization, now freed of any transcendental meaning and based on a frantic pursuit of profit gained through heartless, technical reason, we must base education and understanding on a critical, value-based reason, tolerant of a plurality of differences. The growing numbers of educated Muslim women suggest a gradual tempering of patriarchy, toleration for the individual and voices for justice.

The development of the positive possibilities of modernity, social justice, equality, democracy, and pluralism, are needed to balance or, hopefully, to transform oppression. In a global age, to survive terrorism with growing access to technologies of ever more lethal destruction, part of the solution requires that we allow public spaces for the social sources of forgiveness and kindness that reside in most moderate and progressive religious traditions, which also serve as bases for mobilizing alternative globalizations. Notwithstanding the media images of bloody bodies, masked gunmen, falling towers, suicide bombers and fanatical clerics, Islam societies have long traditions of toleration, pluralism, and hospitality to the Other. There are voices within Islamic societies that would reclaim these traditions, as well as progressive forces from without that would join with them in ushering in a new era.

Bibliography

Armstrong, Karen. *Islam: A Short History.* New York: Modern Library, revised ed., 2002.

Ali, Syed Ameer. *The Spirit of Islam: A History of the Evolution and Ideals of Islam,* with *a Life of the Prophet.* London: Chatto & Windus, 1978.

Bloom, Jonathan and Sheila Blair. *Islam: A Thousand Years of Faith and Power.* New Haven, CT: Yale University Press, 2002.

Booth, E. *Aristotelian Aporetic Ontology in Islamic and Christian Thinkers.* Cambridge, 1983.

Bowker, John. *What Muslims Believe.* Oxford, UK: Onewworld, 1999.

Burrell, D. *Freedom and Creation in Three Traditions.* Notre Dame, 1993.

Burrell, D. *Knowing the Unknowable God: Ibn Sina, Maimonides, Aquinas* (Notre Dame: 1986).

Cook, Michael. *The Koran: A Very Short Introduction.* Oxford, UK: Oxford University Press, 2000.

Corbin, H. *History of Islamic Philosophy,* trans. L. Sherrard. London, 1993.

Craig, E. (ed.), *Routledge Encyclopedia of Philosophy.* London, 1998.

Davidson, H.A. *Proofs for Eternity, Creation and the Existence of God in Medieval Islamic and Jewish Philosophy.* Oxford, 1987.

Elias, Jamal J. *Islam.* Upper Saddle River, NJ: Prentice Hall, 1999.

Fakhry, M. *A History of Islamic Philosophy* , 2nd ed. New York, 1983.

Gibb, Hamilton A.R. and J.H. Kramers, eds. *Shorter Encyclopedia of Islam.* Leiden: E.J. Brill, 1997 (reprint ed.).

Hodgson, Marshall G.S. *The Venture of Islam,* 3 Vols. Chicago, IL: University of Chicago Press, 1974.

Keller, Nuh Ha Mim, trans. *Al-Nawawi's Manual of Islam.* Cambridge, UK: The Islamic Texts Society, 1996.

Leaman, O. *An Introduction to Classical Islamic Philosophy.* Cambridge, 2002.

Marmura , M.E. (ed.), *Islamic Theology and Philosophy.* Albany, 1984.

Nasr, Seyyed Hossein. *The Heart of Islam: Enduring Values for Humanity.* San Francisco, CA, Harper San Francisco, 2002.

Newby, Gordon D. *A Concise Encyclopedia of Islam.* Oxford, UK, Oneworld, 2002.

Peters, F.E. *A Reader on Classical Islam.* Princeton, NJ: Princeton University Press, 1994.

Qadir , C.A. *Philosophy and Science in the Islamic World.* London, 1990.

Renard, John, ed. *Windows on the House of Islam: Muslim Sources on Spirituality.* Berkeley, CA: University of California Press, 1998.

Renard, John. *Seven Doors to Islam: Spirituality and the Religious Life of Muslims.* Berkeley, CA: University of California Press, 1996.

Ruthven, Malise. *Islam in the World.* New York: Oxford University Press, 2nd ed., 2000.

Schimmel, Annemarie. *Islam: An Introduction.* Albany, NY: State University of New York Press, 1992.

P

R

S

T

U

W

Schuon, Frithjof. *Islam and the Perennial Philosophy.* London: World of Islam Festival Publ. Co., 1976.

Sharif, M.M. *A History of Muslim Philosophy,* 2 vols. (Wiesbaden: 1963-6).

Stern, S.M. *Medieval Arabic and Hebrew Thought* , ed. F. Zimmermann, London, 1983.

Stern, S.M., Hourani, H. and Brown, V. (eds.), *Islamic Philosophy and the Classical Tradition.* Oxford, 1972.

Waines, David. *An Introduction to Islam.* Cambridge, UK: Cambridge University Press, 1995.

Watt, M.W. Islamic Philosophy and Theology. Edinburgh, 1962, revised ed. 1985.

Watt, William Montgomery. *The Formative Period of Islamic Thought.* Oxford, UK: Oneworld,1998.

Watt, William Montgomery. *What is Islam?* London: Longman, 1970.

Williams, John Alden, ed. *The Word of Islam.* Austin, TX: University of Texas Press, 1994.

Wolfson, H.A. *Studies in the History of Philosophy and Religion* , ed. I. Twersky, G.H. Williams, in 2 vols. Cambridge, MA, 1973, 1977.

Wolfson, H.A. *The Philosophy of the Kalam.* Cambridge, MA, 1976.

Ziai, H. "Islamic Philosophy," in *The Oxford Companion to Philosophy,* ed. T. Honderich. Oxford , 1955.

[illegible], *[illegible] Philosophy [illegible]*, MA, 1976.

[illegible], *[illegible] Philosophy [illegible]*
Philosophy, ed. T. Fishacre, Oxford, 1985.

Index